INSIDE INDIAN POLICE

INSIDE INDIAN POLICE

Joginder Singh

Foreword by
A.M. Ahmadi

GYAN PUBLISHING HOUSE
New Delhi - 110002

INSIDE INDIAN POLICE

ISBN : 81-212-0727-4

Published in 2009 in India by
Gyan Publishing House
5, Ansari Road
New Delhi 110 002
Phones : 3282060, 3261060 Fax : 3285914
E-mail : gyanbook@del2.vsnl.net.in
Visit Our Web Site At http:\\www.gyanbooks.com

Laser Typesetting: Grow Computers, Delhi

Printed at Chawla Offset Printers, Delhi 110 052

CONTENTS

Foreword

The author, Mr. Joginder Singh, a retired police officer, has endeavoured to trace the history of policing in India from the ancient, medieval to modern times. Policing, as we all know, is a very complex and difficult task, more so in a democratic society wedded to the rule of law. The task is all the more difficult in a pluralistic society where the police is, in times of disturbances, required to walk on razor's edge. The author has, while highlighting the difficult paradoxical role of the police to be responsive to public demands for service and protection on the one hand and at the same time, on occasions, to use force against those disturbing public order, made some useful suggestions based on his vast experience to improve the functioning of the police force and its image as a disciplined (uniformed) force. There can be no doubt that there is an urgent need to raise the level of public confidence in the police force, which at present is unfortunately low, to encourage public participation to aid the police in crime detection.

The author has dwelt on the deficiencies of crime investigation in the country and has referred to political interference as a factor affecting the quality of investigation. Unfortunately police force in India can not be described as essentially professional and totally apolitical. Although understandably the police try and project themselves as apolitical and responsive to the Constitution and laws, in reality the public perceives them as susceptible to political pressures of the powers that be. If those in the seat of power wield disciplinary power, power of promotion and transfer, how can one blame police officers who succumb to their pressures? After all an average police officer is not sufficiently insulated by the system or the support of his superiors to withstand such pressures. This is not the occasion to dwell at length on reform in the system but I can say that if the power to punish and/or transfer is placed in hands of an apolitical body which functions under a set of guidelines, it will provide the required insulation against political interference and will boost up the confidence and image of the police in public esteem. Secondly, what is urgently required is to separate the investigation wing from the enforcement wing so that it may be possible to impart intensive and extensive training in scientific investigation to this small group of officers.

We have not paid sufficient attention to the vital aspect of training. Postings in Police Training Academies are generally viewed as punishment postings undermining the image of the individual trainer. In India the police force still functions in the colonial mode and we have failed to transform it to democratic policing culture to conform to human rights culture. Civility in the behaviourial pattern is missing. The Colonial rulers wanted a police force that would brutally suppress any violence, which would pose a challenge to their rule, and hence they recruited lowly educated rough and tough ones in the constabulary. Must we continue to do so? We must raise the level of education for entry into the police force at all levels, raise their salaries, improve their working conditions and train them to link the exercise of their discretionary power to confirm to human rights, individual dignity and democratic values. Only then will the Indian police force present a friendly humane face to the public.

I have checked the temptation to write about several other aspects which bear on the extant criminal justice system and its failure to deliver the goods but in the present environment of POTO and MACOCA I can not help mentioning that harsh draconian laws have always resulted in a low conviction rate. The police are always happy to be armed with extra-ordinary powers; power is enjoyable only in its abuse for otherwise it is a burdensome duty. Experience of the working of the infamous TADA has manifested its abuse. Extraordinary powers afford tempting opportunities for corruption and result in sloppy investigations. Beat the suspect red in the face, secure his confession and the case is solved. Naturally the conviction ratio falls.

In India, the suspect is first arrested and the investigation is carried out thereafter. In other advanced countries the police normally shadow the suspect, keep a close watch on his movements and close in on him only after they are reasonably sure that the suspect is the offender. In India, since the suspect is arrested first and the investigation is carried on thereafter, the police investigate with a mindset that the suspect is the offender and therefore often the real culprit goes scot-free. The police is not willing to admit its mistake of having arrested and detained for long a wrong person and therefore there is a tendency to book him and allow the Court to do the rest. It is high time this methodology is changed.

The book gives a comprehensive idea of the development of the police force in India. It will prove useful to students, trainees as well as the members of the police force in general. The author deserves to be congratulated for some candid remarks and suggestions for reforms. I am sure the book will have good circulation.

A. M. Ahmadi
Former Chief Justice of India

Dated : January 12, 2002

PREFACE

Assigned as the protectors of law and order, no other executive wing of the Government, has come in for as much criticism as the police force. Its high visibility, is the main factor, responsible for the focus on it. Despite the fact that the colonial rulers, gave us the present police system, its inadequacies and shortcomings had been the subject matter of intensive debates, even during the British rule. The debates had shown dissatisfaction with the police functioning. Suggestions had been given from time to time for improving the police. Individuals, societies and organisations have to respond to the need for change and adaptation, depending upon the requirements of a particular age and time. There can be no finality to any situation and procedure. The organisations will perish if they do not adjust and adapt to the changed conditions.

The citizen wants quick and ready justice at his doorstep and is not interested in legal niceties of the present system based on western ideas. The poor man can neither understand it, nor put his faith in its infallibility. What succour is there to a litigant, when his case lingers on, indefinitely for years? The number of old cases pending decisions in courts, is going up year after year. This state of affairs only benefits those who have money or power. People fail to understand why hardened criminals responsible for heinous crimes, are so easily let off, on bail, only to victimise them, further. This increases the burden on police. Because of the intricate system of appeals and revisions, they rarely get convicted or jailed. How can the society, then protect itself, from thc nuisance of anti-social elements, without either taking the law into its own hands, or helping the police to use brutal methods?

The law of the land distrusts the police to its own disadvantage. It has placed so many restrictions on them, that a policeman finds himself, in the dock, when he puts up an accused in court for trial. To avoid this trauma, in course of time, short-cuts have been evolved, in police methodology. The use of third degree, is one of them, to extract a confession or recovery of stolen property. In fact, the entire administrative system, is directly or indirectly responsible for this state of things.... The concept of the police as the strong arm of the administration, charged with the duty of keeping a political party in power, is not contemplated in the laws. But it has become so in practice in some places. The police protection to the common-man even against oppression and illegalities of the Government is available, under the laws and the Constitution. Its political and bureaucratic control needs to be relaxed to allow police, to work in a free atmosphere in accordance with the dictates of the law. This is the only way for them to win respect of the people and get their co-operation in tackling law and order and crime. The nearness of the police to the people they serve, is the only genuine guarantee against strong-arm methods and their brutality. The entire police concept of a people's police, gets distorted when the police start acting as the private army of a select set of people, operating at their behest and in their interest.

This book outlines police developments from the earliest times, including the appointment of the two police commissions by the British Indian Government. It traces the efforts at reforms in free India. There is hardly a State, which did not appoint a Police Commission or Committee to suggest reforms. Police Commissions and Committees set up by Uttar Pradesh, Madhya Pradesh, Punjab, Delhi, Bihar, Tamil Nadu, Assam, Kerala, West

Bengal and National Police Commission have examined the police working threadbare. I have examined extensively, what each had to say. I have not said anywhere what is the best method for overcoming any problem. That part has been left to the reformers, to select the best and go ahead for giving a better police to the country. The police, as it exists in India, is the creation of the British. It is based on the recommendations of 1860 Police Commission Report and the 1861 Police Act. The laws on which the country's criminal justice system rests, the Indian Penal Code, the Criminal Procedure Code, and the Indian Evidence Act were enacted during the British rule.

It were the British who introduced the concept saying, let nine guilty persons escape rather than one innocent person be punished. The benefit of doubts were given to the accused and the individuals and not to the State. In fact Sir John Malcolm, Governor of Bombay observed in 1830:

> "The task of seizing the most notorious criminal is easy compared to that of proving their guilt, according to the principles and the forms of our courts of justice. There is seldom that full evidence and the consequence is that they require annual discharge of well known plunderers to recommence their career of guilt and to take ample vengeance on those whom they suspect of having aided in their apprehension. If our laws are not modified to meet this great evil, it can alone be mitigated by the change in the Executive Branch of the Police, in those provinces that are inhibited or subject to the inroads of predatory tribes."

Each chapter contains some suggestions for reforms, either by the author or by several Committees and Commissions. It is difficult to say which reform or change will deliver the goods and in how much time. The reform suggested, mainly consists of suggestions for removing bottlenecks in the system, removing abuses, and for improving the cooperation of the people. About the objective of this work, as for anybody else proposing reforms, I share the views of the Police Commission of 1902-03, which observed that they

> "Are not sanguine enough to believe that their proposals even if fully adopted will result in the immediate removal of all causes of complaint. These reforms can in any case be only gradually introduced; and years must pass before their full effects are realised. Inferior men have to be got rid of in all ranks, and evil traditions have to be broken in the force. The attitude of the people towards the police, and public opinion in regard to the uprighteousness and corruption have to be raised. All this must be before the objects aimed at can be satisfactorily achieved."

I have made extensive use of the reports of several Police Commissions and Committees set up by various State and Central Governments in the country. In free India, more Police Committee and Commissions have been set up by the various State Governments, than by all the Governments in the past. Regarding the implementation of report, the speed of progress, will even put a snail to shame. As the State Governments set up these commissions and committees, their reports present almost the same picture of the police and police functioning everywhere. The remedies suggested vary. Each section contains the existing position, the efforts at reform and the reforms suggested either by the author or some Committee or Commission. I have not ventured anywhere to say as to what is the best remedy for any particular situation or problem. A very important feature of this work is the views and ideas of the senior officers on various aspects of the police interviewed by me. They refused to be quoted by name, though they said they had no objections to their views being quoted.

In this work of mine I have quoted only a few representative views out of the hundred of discussions I had with various people in different walks of life, including the senior police officers and administrative officers. It may be said that any one set of reforms will not be universally acceptable or desirable all over the country as the problems vary from place to place. This work is an effort to put at one place all the reforms, which have been suggested for bettering the police in the country. In other words, it contains at one place, what best has been thought and said about police by all the Police Commissions and Committees since 1860. My own experience, achievements, and frustrations of working in the police department, as member of the Indian Police Service from 1-6-1961 to 31-10-1997, naturally are at the back of the work.

I would like to thank Gyan Publishing House for publishing this book in such a short time. I also thank my numerous friends and well wishers who have encouraged and supported me. I hope this book inspires readers to remember that 'ask not what the nation can do for you; ask what you can do for the nation' can be applied for the citizens of a country who have to work together towards its progress. Efforts should continue towards reforms no matter what barriers come on the way. This is the only path to progress for a better future for the generations to come.

September, 2001

Joginder Singh
IPS (Retd.)
Former Director, CBI

D-1/59, Bharti Nagar
New Delhi-110003
Ph.: 4652921

INTRODUCTION

Commenting on the change, in the administration of free India, a former Director of National Police Academy, which trains the Indian Police Service entrants and senior officers, said:

> "Regrettably, even after the country gained its independence... and we adopted a democratic framework of Government, with the most laudable concepts of Freedom, Liberty, Equality, and Justice, enshrined into the Constitution, pretty little has happened to indicate a change in the administrative approach towards the citizen. The ideals written in the Constitution are almost a dead letter for the man in the street, who has not perceived any change for the better, of those charged with the enforcement of the law... Infact ...the country has been slipping backwards, slowly, but perceptibly, both ethically and morally. This process has been most marked, as the stalwarts of freedom struggle days are passing from the scene one by one, and are being replaced by mediocres of the self-seeking variety. It must be admitted that the leadership has miserably failed to show the way. The political environment, created by them, has on the other hand, been mainly responsible, for the blatant violation of the Rule of Law, so glaringly visible today.
>
> It can be argued that a well disciplined and idealistic police force, could have set the pace for others, by its own lawful and correct behaviour as happened in the nineteenth century in Great Britain. But this was too

much to expect from a much maligned, misused, abused, and colonial police which the country got in legacy, at the time of transfer of power when the British left. The need of the hour is to reshape and reorient the old police, so as to fit into the new concept of a democratic and free society, which the country aims at creating. But this was not to be. In the rat race for power, no one thought of the reform of the police. They were left to their own fate, starved, undermanned, without adequate resources and ill trained to meet the challenges of the new situation. Not only that, over the years, the police has been badly politicised and misused for partisan ends. The people should not expect too much, from such a badly neglected police force, and not endlessly blame them, when they fail to measure upto their expectations. The present situation is not conducive, to any better performance by the police. Unless the present indifference, to the police reform is shaken off, their working conditions improved perceptibly and they are unshackled from their political stranglehold, no improvement is possible. Mere rhetoric and platitudes cannot produce results... It goes without saying and contradiction that the present social scene in the country, particularly in the Northern States, is poignant with violence of different varieties. With so much violence around, and this does not exclude even our political, religious, and social leaders, the police, which are, but a small section of the same society, cannot be any different. It would be a travesty of justice, to expect policemen to be angels, in such an atmosphere, and to hold them responsible for all that is happening in the country. Police are violent, because the society permits it and even wants the Police, to suppress violence with equal violence.

The people can also not be blamed, as they have no other choice. The judicial system has completely failed to help in curbing crime, which is getting more and more accompanied with violence. The system has failed to respond to the social requirements. It has formed a citadel of its own which is impregnable for the common man. The system has not shed its elitism. It is too sophisticated and complicated, to benefit an ordinary citizen. It is also extremely dilatory, for people to put their faith into it... The failure of the judiciary, to play its part, in the control of crime and criminals has put too much pressure on the police to suppress crime and maintain peace by hook or by crook. Even the most ethical and ardent supporters of human dignity would not hesitate, to cajole the police to use extra-judicial measures, when they themselves are in trouble. They would have no compunction, if the police used violence, to help them out against an adversary or a suspect. This has been more than evidenced by the happenings of Bhagalpur in Bihar, or the numerous fake encounters staged by the police to liquidate suspected dacoits and marauders. Undoubtedly, this is done with the support of the public and their connivance, as they are obviously sick of their nefarious activities"

Reform is required not only in the police, but in all sectors connected with the prevention, detection, and prosecution of the crime and the judicial system. One without the others would not serve the required purposes. For an efficient criminal justice system, it is essential that not only the police should be very efficient, the prosecution branch should be well officered, with dedicated officials. The system of judicial administration should also be streamlined by suitably increasing the number of courts, and also changing the laws to bring them on a par with the changing social scene and society.

An efficient police without an equally efficient prosecution agency and a responsive judicial system would never be able to meet the challenges of a changing society. It is no use finding fault with the judiciary because in the existing system of laws, violent characters and known criminals get away. The judiciary is required to go by the evidence placed before it. It acts more like an umpire. It is not its job to hunt for the real criminal. It is unlike the French system where the Investigating Magistrate also acts in the interest of the justice to find out the truth, When we find fault with the judiciary, it will be fair only to say that judiciary is hamshackled by the Rules of the Game under which it is required to provide justice. Many judicial luminaries, including the law ministers, former chief justices of the Supreme Court, Prime Ministers, and even the President have remarked about the urgent need for judicial reforms. Justice D. A Desai, former chairman, Law Commission remarked that "there was an urgent need for restructuring the present judicial system. Under the existing situation, one cannot hope to get justice in his life time", he said adding that "the rule of law has become the rule of class". ...A basic structural change in the mode, method and forum for resolution of disputes is absolutely necessary before the system is engulfed by its own debris. The Law Commission has recommended numerous reforms in the system. The process of law changes is so laborious having numerous agencies involved in the process, that it has been no changed situation. Each one of the officials, processing any legal changes has a veto power. The result is that in spite of over five decades of independence and even the Prime Minister talking about the urgency to change the judicial system; it has had no effect. Legal system has remained static.

Certain vital matters have remained pending pretty long, like the recommendation for 'One Appeal' only to clear the backlog. The need for considering the question of 'one appeal' only arose from the vastly prevalent tendency to go on questioning the decisions of Courts till the last court of appeal, that is the Supreme Court of

India. In this process, the only beneficiaries are those with the money and capacity to engage expensive lawyers to fight their cases till the end. This way they expect to prolong the proceedings till a decision in their favour is taken, till such time, money flows like water to pay the hefty fees of the lawyers. In this process, a very big casualty is justice and judicial time. Otherwise the same time could have been spent in disposing off new cases. A change is needed not only in the Police but also in all the branches of the entire criminal system of the country. The one problem, which the reformers have faced, is that they have looked for the reform in a particular segment and have been inhibited by their background, their past and present professional inclinations. Thus, if a Reforms Commission is predominated by the policemen, any reforms recommended by it, have consciously or unconsciously taken up the narrow departmental views, and seen the things only from the policemen's point of view. Similarly, if a body headed by the ex-Judicial Officer has proposed any reforms, it is only with the views of the judiciary. In the bargain, the sufferer is the State interest and the justice to the aggrieved party. The sole beneficiary in such cases is the accused and not the victim.

The abstract concept, that let nine guilty persons escape, rather than one innocent be punished, does not cut much ice with the person, who has lost property or limb; who has seen a dear and near one killed and who also has the misfortune to see the known accused let off on technical grounds. A question for consideration is, whether we should still give the benefit of doubt to the accused of the State. Immediately interlinked to this is the question about the safeguards for prevention of abuse of authority by the Executive and the Police. The question is: how far the should police be trusted and the executive relied on giving justice to the citizen? Does the past record give any confidence in this regard? Is it necessary to stick to the past or should a new beginning be made of trust and confidence in the police of free India?

A gratifying feature of the administration of the criminal justice system has been that even from the earliest times efforts have been directed for making the administration responsive to the public needs. In 1840s, Mr Dampier who had been appointed as a Superintendent of Police in Bengal had observed:

> "The best security... for the correct and safe administration of justice, is in doing all that gives reasonable hope to success towards employing an honest police for the instituting of enquiries, and collecting evidence in regard to the crimes committed. It cannot be too often or too earnestly impressed upon the Government that it is not only the pay of the Darogha of a Thana that should be made sufficient for respectability. The Moharrirs and Jamadars, who must be daily employed (as in this case) with independent powers, are excessively underpaid... It cannot be a matter of surprise that parties so paid and exercising such great authority, under very little practical check, should be found to be open to temptation, and to lend themselves... to the gratification of private malice."

The Second Police Commission (1902-1903) also commented on the unsatisfactory state of policing in the country and the indifference of the people towards the police in the following words:

> "One of the strongest proofs that the Commission has received of the corruption of the police is the testimony of respectable parents, teachers and other gentlemen, to the difficulty experienced by a young-man in accepting one of the direct appointments of the Sub-Inspector and Inspector which are now sometimes offered. He finds himself a member of a corrupt service; he is surrounded by influences that forbid

his acting uprightly. In more than one province, the Commission has had before them, teachers who said, that they could not encourage good lads to go into the police service, and parents, who confessed that they had to remove their sons from appointments in it so as to keep them straight. The evidence in most provinces is that the canker of corruption affects the force in greater or less degree from constables to inspector." ...

Neither does the Commission forget that much may be said in excuse for the misconduct of the police. The excuse lies in the generally indifferent attitude of the people in respect of crime, in the encouragement of corruption, by the readiness with which the people offer illegal gratification's, and in the low pay and poor prospects of the Police Service. But honourable exceptions and mitigating circumstances cannot efface the general impression created by the evidence recorded. There can be no doubt that the police force throughout the country is in a most unsatisfactory condition, that abuses are common everywhere, that this involves great injury to the people and discredit to the government, and that radical reforms are urgently necessary. These efforts will cost much, because the department has hitherto been starved, but they must be effected."

Obviously not much appears to have been done between the period which elapsed when the above observations were made by the Police Commission of 1902-03 and now. The first Police Commission of free India observed:

"Functioning under the constraints and handicaps of an outmoded system, the police performance has undoubtedly fallen short of public expectation. The present culture of the police system appears as a continuation of what was obtained under the British regime when the police functioned ruthlessly as an agent for sustaining the Government in power. In public estimates, the police appear as an agency more to implement and enforce the objectives of the Government in power as distinct from enforcing laws as such as an independent and impartial agency. The dividing line between the objectives of the Government in power as such on one side, and the interests and expectations of the ruling political party as such on the other side gets blurred in actual practice, and the image of the police as an impartial law enforcement agency suffers in consequence. In the situation the police find it difficult to play their lawful role and make their performance acceptable to the people at large. In the perception of the people, the egregious features of the police are politically oriented partisan performance of duties, brutality, corruption, and inefficiency, degrees of which vary from place to place and person to person. The basic and fundamental problem regarding the police today is now to make the function as an efficient and impartial law enforcement agency fully motivated and guided by the objectives of service to the public at large, upholding the constitutional rights and liberty of the people...What the Police Commission said in 1903 appears more or less equally applicable to the conditions obtaining in the police force today."

A former Cabinet Secretary felt that neglect of the training of the policemen was the main reason for the present state of affairs. He felt that atleast one-fourth of the police should always be under training to acquaint them with the latest thinking and the techniques of policing. Ideally the figure for the training of the policemen should be one-third. He also felt that the absence of the political interference would go a long way in improving the situation. Though the USA was a democracy like India, there was no political interference in the police functioning there.

A former Chief Secretary felt that for maintaining the police efficiency, it was essential to maintain the hierarchy and unless the political parties and the party in power accepts this basic premise, no improvement will be possible. There are no easy solutions to the bettering of police image in India, but continuous efforts by the department can go a long way in this regard. He also said that regarding the recommendations of the Chief Minister's Conference in 1979 to cut out political interference, nothing has been done. A former Director General of Police said that: "The present state can be described as a Mughal Rule, wherein the father was killed by the son for the sake of position. The only difference is that here in the place of the father, the position of the senior is sought to be pulled down by the juniors through the extraneous factors and influences." The senior police officers try to further their interests by taking the help of politicians and juniors copy them. As we need a looking glass to have a look at ourselves, so as a department, we need an outside agency to look into the working of the Police Department. At present there is no evaluation of the working of the Police Department. An agency of the legislature on the lines of the Committee on Public Sector undertakings, perhaps could be set up to review the working of the department. The Committee could confine itself to the working of the Department like the investigation of cases, pendency and disposal of court cases and it should not be concerned with the transfers and postings.

A former Chief Minister of a State said that:

"I can take a bet that if there is no political interference, the police can handle any situation. The police should have no fear while doing its duty. Because if fear is there, the police would not be able to do its best in redressing the grievances of the people. The police should have the assurance that there would be no interference in its work. When I was the Chief Minister,

I had totally stopped political interference in the police transfers and postings and had accordingly told the members of my party— and they fully co-operated— though initially it was difficult for them not to interfere. I had also told them that I was willing to transfer two Tehsildars, but not a single Sub-Inspector at their request. The morale of the police and the army should be kept very high. Because otherwise you endanger the internal and external security... It is because of the morale of the police, that not even ten thousand policemen can keep law and order in a city like Bangalore with a population of over 80 lakhs. In the interest of the country and the State, police matters should not ordinarily be discussed in the Assembly, but at some other suitable forum. As the police deals with the life and liberty of the people, it should be ensured that they are not starved of the basic needs of vehicles. Delay in the late arrival at any place of rioting and conflict can mean more serious damage and loss of life and property. The police officers bringing pressure on the Government for furthering their interests also should be dealt with firmly for misconduct and punished accordingly. But when the police officers do a good job, they should be appreciated. Both the police and the people should have the fear of the law."

A former Commissioner of Police said: "He had not allowed the interference in the administration but in the bargain he had incurred the hostility of his own bosses, who were more than keen to oblige any and every interfering politician." Another former Commissioner of Police and a Director General said that "If the officials explained the reasons to the politicians as to why a particular thing could not be done, it will be appreciated, as politicians were after all human beings. He said that firm and fair dealings with the subordinates always yielded excellent results.

In a businessman's opinion, the policemen are treated, as the scum of society. We seem to be following a policy, which considers a position high or low according to salary offered and the hardness of job at hand. Thus, the person, who work the hardest, like the stone cutter, the bus drivers, the policemen standing in the sun get, the lowest salary. Far from educating their children in good schools, the wages given are not even fit for minimum levels of subsistence. If the Government were to give atleast a decent wage, most of the corruption will go away, or atleast be considerably reduced. The workload on the police department, is too much. Considering the huge population, the strength of the police is too little. The general behaviour of the police, is one of unmitigated rudeness. As the police deal only with the criminals and the scum of society, so their general behaviour, with the public, is the same as with the criminals. The police should be strong like the army; strong and disciplined so that internal peace is maintained in the country. The political interference, should be completely stopped. Ninety-five per cent recruitment to the police is being done at the instance of the highly placed politicians. I have seen criminals being recruited as sub-inspectors. This could only happen under political interference and pressure. The minimum qualification, even of a constable should be atleast 12 pass, and the recruitment should be done only on merit. I have seen policemen who cannot write even a word, occupying important positions in the department. Regarding curbing corruption, it is essential to give overriding powers to the vigilance department so that the corrupt cannot get away. Delay in the disposal leads to the corruption and ways and means should be found to cut it out. Procedures of the Government are very complicated and they need to be simplified.

An officer in charge of the Police Station in a big city said that Section 25 of the Indian Evidence Act (which states that no confession made before a police officer will be admissible in a court of law) should be amended as people are not willing to come forward and give evidence. It is anomalous that confessions made even to senior officers are not admissible. Fortunately, now, there is talk among government circles for amending CrPC, in order to correct the situation. The training of the constables and head constables does not include investigation training. Their training needs to be modified separately so as to include an element of investigation. There is a need to fix duties so that continuity is possible. The public expects too much from the police.

Odd jobs like removing the trees from the road, blocking the traffic, are required to be done by the police. Sometimes the stinking dead bodies are to be handled by the police and the investigating officers and the police constables are reduced to the position of scavengers. The jobs which are degrading and damaging to the police dignity and which are not part of police functioning should be done by the other concerned departments and the departmental superiors should not insist the same to be done by the police subordinates. The characters of the police is such that even in true cases the people change their stance, leading to the wastage of time of the courts and the police.

A constable said that though they lead very hard lives and are exposed to the risk, at all times, their avenues of promotion are practically nil. More than 85 per cent of the constabulary join as constables and retire as constables and there are no refresher courses or training for them and even if they wish to improve their qualifications and seek better avenues, they are not encouraged. Many a time the good work done, by a constable is shown, as the work done by the senior officers. At least the officer class are provided some facilities, but there are none for the other ranks. Moreover, the maximum pressure for police duties is on the constabulary and it is they who get kiiled or injured in riots, but recognition is not given by the public or the department to their services all the time. The facilities given to the constables, are almost the same as are given to any class IV employees of the Government and the senior officers of the department also consider them the underlings however educated a constable may be. Their services utilised only on routine jobs of sentry or at the best of Station Writers. To utilise the full potential and to impart training, it is essential that some constables at least are given simple cases for investigation and inquiries.

A Professor of the Indian Institute of Public Administration said that: "Any worthwhile study of the police cannot be considered in isolation of the other institutions of the society. At present most of the police reforms are targetted from the internal efficiency point of view only. The police efficiency should be determined by its relations with the courts and other institutions of society. At present there is too much emphasis on the internal working of the police, to the neglect of various other factors. Everybody writes on the role of police constables, and head constables and sub-inspectors and inspectors and other ranks, but when it comes to giving the facilities, nobody is helpful. For instance, the entire planning machinery is dependent on the village level worker, but he is not given even the basic facilities like house, training, or office.

The problems of the country are reduced to the problems of bureaucracy, within five square kilometres of Parliament Street in New Delhi. The top bureaucracy within five sq. kms. of Parliament Street does not hesitate in proliferating their posts, instead of providing facilities to the grassroot level where they are most required. The top bureaucracy does not create posts only because there is work, but because so and so has put in umpteen years of service and hence he must be promoted to the next higher rank, and so 'a square peg is fitted in a round hole'. Training is very important in all walks of life, but the same without the facilities and promotional avenues does not serve the desired purpose. The department does not respect its junior-most functionaries like: constables, and the village level workers. It is only the senior bureaucrats who are capitalising for getting promotions and they are neither concerned nor interested, in what is happening in the field.

An experienced sub-inspector said that a lot of police time is wasted in miscellaneous duties with which the police has no immediate or distant concern or connection. In nature of the complaints registered with the police vary, from the entry of a goat into a house, to checking driving license and railway tickets, railway passes, identity cards of the college students, Central Government Services Health Scheme cards and the individuals identity cards for entry into their offices. The police have to deal with the reports of unclaimed dead bodies or missing articles from the bank lockers. Thus, the police manpower is wasted in areas not required or essential for actual police work.

Summing up the reforms suggested in this book mainly consist of suggestions for removing bottlenecks in the system, removing abuses, and for improving the cooperation of the people.

1

POLICE IN ANCIENT AND MEDIEVAL TIMES

The subject of police arouses a lot of interest for an average Indian. In the perception of an average citizen, the police are neither a great or even an ordinary success in the matter of prevention and detection of crime. They are also not capable of maintaining law and order, at the time of serious trouble and clashes. Numerous communal riots are fresh examples imprinted in the minds of its citizens. The police as an institution has been there in ancient and medieval India. The modern time police have been put on firm footing by the British. The *Ramayana* mentions about policemen, spies, and guards.

The policing arrangements have also been described in Kautilya's *Arthashastra*. *Arthashastra* also details the duties of the ruler. It lays down that ruler should keep a watch and engage spies for guarding the kingdom's borders. At the time of writing of *Arthashastra,* the responsibility of preventing thefts and other crimes was entrusted to the village Headman. It was his responsibility to recover the stolen property, or make good the loss, from his own pocket. The criminal law was stringent and the disposal of the cases was prompt. The law was weighted in favour of the State. There was a little scope for the accused to escape. During Chandragupta Maurya's period covered by *Arthashastra,* the country was very well governed. According to the Chinese visitor, Megasthenese, the people were law abiding and crime was very rare.

System of Administration in Chandragupta Maurya's Period

Manu Smriti details information about the ruler's duties and the arrangements to be made for recovering the stolen property. The king was expected, to restore the stolen property to its owner. He was also to make arrangements, for appointing suitable officers for dealing with the thieves. He also had to post spies. The thieves not only had to make good the loss of stolen property, but also undergo punishment. The cardinal principle was the responsibility of the village headman, either on his own, or assisted by the village council. The State continued to be responsible for making good the loss of stolen property. Fahein, a Chinese Buddhist was in India for nearly six years. He mentions about the prevailing conditions during the reign of Chandragupta Vikramaditya, as peaceful and free from serious crime. Anybody in that regime, could travel, from one end of the empire, without any fear of molestation, injury or theft.

During the above period, all the officials were paid adequate emoluments in cash. However, in some cases, the payment was made, by way of assigning land, or villages. This was the beginning of feudalism. Wherever the land or the villages were assigned to any person, generally the revenue, police and administrative functions, were also transferred to him. The criminal offences were dealt with harshly and this indirectly helped to control the crime.

System of Administration in Mughal Period

When the Mughals took over the rule, their main objective was to sustain their empire and authority. They introduced only those changes, which suited their objectives. They made all higher appointments hereditary. The Provinces were put under the Subedars or Governors. Subedars were responsible for the administration, including the system of criminal justice and keeping peace and order in his jurisdiction. Under the Subedars, were Faujdars incharge of Sarkars or roughly the present Districts. Their responsibility was the suppression of crime and rebellion, keeping peace and providing protection to the law-abiding citizens. In actual practice, the Zamindar or the grantee of the land of the villages, was made responsible for peace and security of the area under his charge. The Faujdar acted as a check on them. Every area under the charge of a Faujdar was divided into Thanas and Chowkies; each placed under the charge of Thanedar. The Thanedars were paid by the Zamindars, though the Faujdar appointed them. Roughly each Faujdar had 500 to 1500 Sepoys under his charge, depending on the size of the district or Sarkar. The Mughals were urban people. They did not care much about the rural people. They left them to their own fate, to be governed by their feudal lords or Zamindars. The Chaukidars, or village watchmen, employed by the village community, were expected to maintain peace and provide security. As the Faujdars had large areas to supervise, they did not have any effective check or control on the village police or the people living there.

In big urban centres, the chief of city police was called Kotwal. The duties of Kotwal included the arrest of thieves and criminals and guarding the life and property of the citizens. According to *Ain-I-Akbari* the Kotwal was to maintain a record of the houses and inhabitants. The Kotwals were to appoint spies and keep a record of happenings. The description in *Ain-I-Akbari* reads: "When any theft, fire, or other misfortune may happen, the neighbours shall render immediate assistance; especially the public informers, who failing to attend on such occasions, unless unavoidably prevented, shall be held responsible for the omission. A certain number of persons in each district shall be appointed to patrol by night and several streets and environs of the several cities, towns, villages, etc, taking care that no strangers infest them and specially exerting themselves to discover, pursue and apprehend robbers, thieves, pick-pockets, etc. If any articles are stolen or plundered, the police must restore the articles, produce the criminal or failing to do so, become responsible for the equivalent. In these transactions integrity and probity are indispensable requisites."

The Mughals also had a vast network of spies, who would report orally or in writing to the Daroghas of the *chowkies.* It was a kind of police establishment. The Quazis dispensed the justice according to the Muslim laws and Quazi-ul-Qazat was the name given to the chief justice. Mufti, a kind of expert in interpreting the law, assisted him. The criminal or Faujdari courts or Adalats were presided over by the local landlord who was called Zamindar. The Mughals did not approve of bribe taking. They issued strict orders against corrupt practices. Notwithstanding, the orders of the rulers, against bribe taking, the officials like Quazis and Kotwals and other revenue officials, were more often than not, corrupt. The main reason for this was the nominal salaries paid to them from the State Exchequer. Moreover, the people then as now, were not very keen to complain against the officials.

Shivaji also adopted the Mughal system of administration, except that he modified, basing it on Hindu traditions and giving Sanskrit names in place of Persian names. He also abolished the hereditary officials and in their place appointed officials who could be transferred from one place to another. Shivaji had a good system of spies and intelligence collection. They kept him posted, with whatever was happening in his kingdom, including the lapses of the employees under the administration. By and large, the villages were left to themselves. The village administration was made the responsibility of the village Headman. The village headman was made responsible for all the offences occurring in his jurisdiction. It was his responsibility to recover the stolen property in his area, or make good the loss. In the cities, the duties of police and the magistrate were combined in the Kotwal. The police performance according to Eliphinstone was good on the whole. Murder and robberies committed with violence were very rare.

The criminal administration was vested in the revenue officials. There was no equivalent of Criminal Procedure Code and the Evidence Act or the Indian Penal Code. Manu's laws, customs and traditions of the country governed the methods of investigation and punishment. Exemplary punishments were awarded to the offenders. It struck terror in the minds of the potential offenders. The Mughal system of administration was improved by the Marathas to suit the local needs and genius. Later on, during Nana Farnavis' time's detective inspectors, independent of Revenue officials the Mamlatdars were appointed. According to the English writer, Eliphinstone, "The country was free from crimes".

System of Administration under East India Company

The Mughal system of justice and police administration collapsed with the decline of Mughal empire and the take over by the East India Company after their victory in the Battle of Plassey on 23rd June, 1757. People found themselves living in utter chaos and lawlessness. After Plassey victory the Company assumed the rights of Talukdari and Zamindari, granted to them by Nawab Mir Jaffar. The Company took over Orissa, Bihar, and Bengal. It established its military and political hegemony over the areas. The Company's rule was a free for all for its employees, who indulged in bribery, corruption, and plunder. The tottering Mughal Empire, received a further death blow when the Mughal Emperor gave away the Dewani of Bengal, Bihar and Orissa. Mughals also gifted the Districts of Burdwan, Midnapore and Chittagong and 24 Parganas in perpetuity to the East India Company. This way, the civil and military power as well as the resources of the country, were passed over to the British.

The East India Company's interest was only to collect as much money as possible and trading. It did not bother about the people, or the law and order, which continued to deteriorate. Lord Clive, as the Governor General introduced the system, in which all the power was vested in the Company. However all the responsibility lay on the Nawab.

The Revenue administration was entrusted to Naib Divans, who were based at Patna and Murshidabad. They were responsible for the collection of land revenue as well as policing and criminal administration as Naib Nazim. For policing, the Zamindars were expected to maintain the staff including Thanedars for the law and order duties and for maintaining peace in their charge, as well as dealing with crimes and criminals. There was hardly any supervision over their work. Their payments were not regular. This way, the situation continued to deteriorate. It led to chaos in the country.

The East India Company's main interest was the collection of revenue. The fall of revenue, forced it, to improve the policing in the country. It is only in peaceful conditions, that it is possible for people to earn, their livelihood well and pay their taxes.

The Governor, Verelst started the institution of European supervisors in August 1769. They were placed incharge of districts. Their duties included the maximum collection of revenue for the Company. They were told to stop oppression of the poor by the Daroghas, Kotwals and other functionaries, maintained for the protection of the people. They were asked to reform the system and the functionaries of the policing system. The British got fed up with the police functionaries. They abolished the institutions of Faujdars except in the Districts of Dacca and Hooghly in December 1770. As there was no adequate force available and the Supervisors did not have enough powers, this system did not make any difference. Warren Hastings came to India as Governor of Bengal on 13th August, 1772. He renamed the Supervisors as Collectors and gave them all the responsibility for the collection of revenue. Hastings said: "New Government of the Company consists of a confused heap of undigested materials as wild as the chaos itself. The powers of the Government are undefined, the collection of revenue, the provision of the investment, the administration of justice (if it exists at all), the care of the police are all huddled together, being exercised by the same hands, though most frequently the latter two offices are totally neglected. Added to the difficulties attendant on the arrangements, we have them all to separate; and bring into order at once."

Hastings' Reforms

Hastings reorganised the judicial system with the Collector at the district level as the head of Faujdari Adalat and the Presidency Court Sadar Nizamat under the Governor and Council. In the meantime, the problem of dacoity had become worse. The Committee of Circuit pointed it out in their letter of August 15, 1772 and said;

> "The dacoits of the Bengal are not, like the robbers of England, individuals driven to such desperate courses by sudden want; they are robbers by profession; and even by birth; they are formed into regular communities and their families subsist on the spoils which they bring home to them."

The Governor of Bengal issued the 35th Regulation, which makes an interesting reading as under:

> "That whereas the peace of this country hath, for some years past been greatly disturbed by the bands of dacoits, who not only infest the roads, but often plunder whole villages, burning the houses, and murdering the inhabitants, and whereas these banded outlaws have hitherto found means to elude every

attempt, which the vigilance of the Government hath put in force, for detecting and bringing such atrocious criminals to justice, by the secrecy of their haunts and the wild state of the districts which are most subjected to their incursions; it becomes the indispensable duty of the Government to try the most rigorous means, since experience has proved every lenient and ordinary remedy to be ineffectual." It was ordered that "a dacoit on being found guilty should be carried to the village to which he belonged and be there executed, for a terror and example to others; and for further prevention of such abominable practices, that the village of which he is an inhabitant shall be fined; according to the enormity of the crime; and inhabitants according to his substance; and that the family of the criminal shall become the slaves of the State, and be disposed off, for the general benefit and convenience of the people, according to the discretion of the Government."

Notwithstanding the severe provisions made in the regulations, there was no appreciable improvement in the situation in the absence of adequate machinery to enforce the same. Hastings declared: "A rigid observance of the letter of the law is a blessing in a well regulated State; but in a Government as loose as Bengal is, and must be for some years to come, an extraordinary and exemplary coercion, must be employed to eradicate those evils which the law cannot reach". He also observed that the "country was infested with multitude of dacoits, who had been guilty of the most daring and alarming excesses." Hastings proposed that Faujdars should be appointed for providing protection to the people as well as detection of robbers. He also ordered maintenance of centralised intelligence in the Presidency, on the basis of the information sent by the Faujdars. Hastings' idea was to extend the system of Faujdars and authorise the Zamindars to exercise the Faujdar's jurisdiction. They were also to be responsible, for all the offences committed in their jurisdiction.

Hastings was charged with bringing the country's government 'to such a state of weakness and insignificance, as not even to carry the appearance of a government either to its own subjects or foreigners.' Hastings replied to this criticism, saying 'all the acts of policy' could not conceal the power by which these provinces were ruled and neither 'all the acts of sophistry avail, to transfer the responsibility of them to the Nawab, when it could be visible, as the light, of the sun, that they originated from their own Government, and that the Nawab was a mere pageant, without so much as a shadow of authority.'

Considering the situation that new regulations did not produce desired results, Warren Hastings issued a Proclamation on 29th June, 1782 which declared, 'whereas the peace of the Province has been greatly disturbed through the negligence or connivance of the Zamindars, it is hereby ordered and proclaimed that all Zamindars, Chowdhris, Talukdars and other proprieters of land, do conformably to the original and fundamental tenure on which they all hold their Zamindaries or other portions of landed portions of landed property, take effectual care that no robberies, burglaries or murder be committed within their District and that they do their utmost to bring the offenders to justice; that they do erect Thanas in such places, as shall be pointed out to them by the Magistrates, and be answerable for the good behaviour of the Thanedars and other officials appointed thereto, and for their punctual obedience, of all orders issued to them from the Magistrate; and it is hereby declared that if any robbery be committed, the Zamindar to whose District, the robber appertains or in whose District the robbery was committed, according to the circumstances of the case shall be made to refund the amount. But if any Zamindar shall either commit or connive at any murder or robbery or other breach of the peace, and it shall be proved against him, he shall be punished with death, or if any Zamindar shall refuse, or neglect to obey any orders issued under the authority of the Government, he shall be punished as the nature of the case and the degree of the crime shall require'.

Though it had been brought home to the government that Zamindars would not be able to discharge the responsibilities of policing for various reasons, Hastings chose to substitute effective policing by brave and high sounding proclamation as quoted above. The Thanedars were appointed and removed by the Zamindars and were paid no salaries, but were given some land. The Zamindars appointed Thanedars on considerations other than merit. Many Thanedars got mixed up, with the criminal elements to enrich themselves. The system led to conflict between the Magistrates and the Zamindars, as the former were keen to stop the harassment of the poor and ensure protection of the Company's interests. Though the Magistrates, were keen to take over the control of the rural police, the government was not keen. It would have meant incurring regular expenditure, on the maintenance of the police. In this way, the reform of the Indian Police was foundered on the consideration and need of saving to the government of the day more than two centuries ago.

After the exit of Hastings in February 1785, the Council empowered the Magistrates to try cases of assault and some other petty cases. This was the beginning of the system of combining judicial and executive powers. Sir John Shore a member of the Executive Council observed 'people accustomed to a despotic authority should look to one master. It is impossible to draw a line between the revenue and the judicial departments in such a manner as to prevent their clashing; and in this case, either the revenue must suffer or the administration of justice must be suspended; the present regulations define the object of two jurisdictions with clearness and precision; yet they continually clash in practice; complaints are so blended that it is often impossible to determine to which tribunal they belong. It may be possible, in the course of time, to induce the natives to pay their rents with regularity, and without compulsion, but this is not the case at present. If any force is offered, a complaint is made in a court of justice and whether true or false, a temporary protection is given to the complainant, who is released, from the demands upon him; to realise them afterwards is no easy matter.'

When Cornwallis came to India in 1786 he found, abundant evidence of frauds, peculation, and corruption. He also saw that murders, dacoities and other serious crimes were daily committed with impunity. There was a general feeling that life and property were not adequately protected. Cornwallis enhanced the powers of the Collectors. He authorised them to take action against the Zamindars suspected of conniving with the criminals. As most of the Collectors were engaged in private commerce and trade themselves, this hardly improved the position. Cornwallis noted that almost all the Collectors were deeply engaged in commerce in the names of either a friend or a relation. They had become the most dangerous enemies of the Company's interests, and the greatest oppressors of the manufacturers. As the Daroghas and the lower officials continued to be corrupt, so the collusion between Zamindars, criminals, and Daroghas continued, and thus the crime was still out of control.

According to one of the Collectors, the continuance, if not the increase in crime, was due to corruption prevalent in the Criminal Courts, because of paltry sums paid to the principal officer's as salary. The criminals believed that they could always procure their release, by spending a part of the plunder. "The Burdwan Magistrate declared that the Zamindars who had come under his personal observation, were the sources of all robberies and outrages, and that the Faujdari proceedings furnished repeated instances, where Thanedars had either kept dacoits in their employ, or received from them, large considerations of all recoveries, for granting them protection and screening them, from justice. The reason was that all orders for the seizure of dacoits issued by the Magistrates had to be executed by the Thanedars and it depends on them whether they shall be executed or not. He added that the most strenuous endeavours of the Magistrates were too frequently counteracted and defeated by these men".

Another Magistrate said that "the Mofussil was, almost every where, unprotected, that murder, burglary, robbery, etc, were frequently committed and all the vigilance and activity of a Magistrate was insufficient in the existing system to prevent their perpetration, that all he could do was, on receiving intelligence of any outrage, has to send a party in pursuit of the offenders and that the success of the search, was often precarious and that frequent escape hardened the wretches, to such a degree, that they soon became capable of the most daring and desperate attempts."

Cornwallis said in a letter that "the best rules and regulations that can be framed will be totally nugatory and useless, unless it is decided and fixed principle, that liberal salaries, shall be annexed to every office of trust and responsibility, at all the Presidencies; that all perquisites shall be abolished, and that most rigorous checks, shall be established for the purposes of checking the activities, of the employees of the company, particularly for ensuring that they did not amass fortunes, at the cost of the company. The system that has been so fatally pursued in this country, of granting trifling salaries to men employed in high trust, and who are surrounded with greater temptations, and of leaving them to look for their subsistence and future hope of retirement, to perquisites and unavowed emoluments, is as cruelly destructive of the morals of individuals, as it is ruinous to the interests of the company."

Cornwallis' Regulation on Police

Cornwallis also noted that "the professional and systematic marauding which from the earliest times had existed in this country." He issued orders on 7th December, 1792 for establishing a uniform system of police in the country. The Regulation declared

> 'the establishment of an efficient police throughout the country, whereby offenders may be deprived of all hopes of eluding the pursuit of the officers of the justice; being as essential towards deterring people from committing crimes, as the speed and impartial trial of the offenders, when apprehended and the clause in the engagements of the landholders and farmers of land, by which they are bound to keep peace, and in the event of any robbery being committed in their respective estates and farms, to produce both the robbers and the property plundered, having not only being found nugatory, but in numerous instances proves the means of multiplying robberies and other disorders from the collusion which has subsisted between the perpetrators of them and the police officers entertained by the land holders and the farmers of the land in virtue of the clauses mentioned above. The Governor General in Council, with a view to afford that protection to the persons and property of the people, which is so essential to their happiness, and to the public welfare, has been pleased to pass the following regulations, which are to supersede the existing rules repugnant thereto.'

The police of the country was placed under the exclusive charge of the officers of the government appointed for the specific purpose. The landholders and farmers were ordered to discharge their police establishment. They were told that it would no longer be their responsibility. They were relieved of their responsibility of robberies committed within their jurisdiction except in the event of connivance, receipt of stolen property or neglect to assist the government officers in preventing their escape or apprehending them. In all such cases, they were to be compelled to make good the value of the property stolen or plundered. The Magistrate was to divide his districts into convenient police jurisdiction. The district was to be under a Darogha with an establishment of officers. The Daroghas were directed to arrest forthwith persons accused of murder, robbery, house breaking, theft or other heinous crimes and to send them under safe custody to the Magistrate within 24 hours of arrest. The Daroghas were to be selected and appointed by the Magistrate. They could, however, be dismissed only on proof of misconduct subject to the satisfaction of the Governor in Council. Daroghas were authorised to apprehend, without written orders, the persons found in the act of committing breach of peace, or against whom a general hue and cry shall have been raised, or who shall be detected with stolen goods, in their possession, and notorious dacoits, or robbers, harbouring within the jurisdiction and vagrants and suspected persons of various description, who may be lurking about, in his jurisdiction "without any ostensible means of subsistence, or who cannot give a satisfactory account of himself."

In the village police system comprising of village watchman and Paiks were all placed under the orders of Daroghas. The watchmen were made responsible for the arrest of murderers, robbers, and thieves. They were also required, to give information, about vagrants and suspected criminals to the Daroghas. The Magistrates and police officials, were given the authority, to apprehend criminals, in other's jurisdiction also, while pursuing them. The Daroghas were permitted, to receive 10 per cent commission, on the recovery of all stolen and plundered property. Salaries were fixed for all police ranks. The salary of the Darogha was fixed at Rs 35 per month.

Cornwallis had hoped, that new regulations, would bring about a considerable improvement, in policing in the country. Collectors were more interested in the collection of land revenue, as a part of their salary consisted of commission, on land revenue. This interest resulted, in their neglecting the police duties. Cornwallis introduced a number of reforms. He tried to bring order to the chaos, as well as the lawlessness prevailing at that time. He issued instruction for a well-defined system of administration, with a clear hierarchy and controlling officers. He was the first person to introduce, full time and reasonably well paid, police officials in the country. He divested the Zamindars of the responsibility of policing and started paying the police officials from the government funds.

Sir John Shore who was also the Governor General of India wrote in a letter in December 1784 to William Bensley: "I am happy to reflect that his plans are fairly and usefully administered. He advanced wisely and with confidence. The judicial system proceeds well. People, who reason from former practice and experience only, rather than from principles, have objected to his arrangements; but the principles are just, and although the practices are not familiar to the natives, they have accommodated themselves to it. Two objections of importance only occur to the arrangements, the additional business imposed upon the Supreme Authority, and the difficulty of finding a sufficient number of able officers for the execution of them upon the whole I am satisfied that His Lordship's plan was solid, wise and has proved beneficial to the country. The people in general, enjoy a security of property, which they never possessed and the regularity of system has superseded the exercise of discretion authority."

The Governor General issued Regulation II in 1795. According to it, the village Zamindars and his farmers on getting permanent settlement were made responsible, for the maintenance of peace, and not to harbour thieves and robbers and other criminals. They were also made responsible and answerable for the stolen property, and in the event of its not being recoverable, had to make good the loss. Some suggestions were given, in making the punishment specific, thus removing the uncertainties of previous laws. Some other suggestions included, conferring the powers of Munsiff, and increasing the number of Thanas. It was also suggested that Magistrates should be authorised to try all criminal cases. It was because the system prevailing at that time led to delay. For this reason many complainants preferred to put up with the thefts and robberies, than complain to the police, as it involved vexatious delays in the rendering of justice and trouble, loss of time and expenses for attending criminal proceedings.

The most vital defect at that time was the inadequacy of the police force. Mr E Strachey, 3rd Judge of Calcutta Circuit submitted a number of reports on the subject and said that the existing wretched, mechanical inefficient system of police, provided no protection to persons or property, and that no civilised country ever had so bad a police. He also said that dacoits had with great success, established a respect for their order, by speedy, certain and severe punishments, and by judicious arrangements for removing obstacles and facilitating the execution of their plans. The dacoits knew, how to preserve their power. He also pointed out, that many dacoities were either concealed, or minimised due to the oppression, or extortion of Darogha or the vengeance of the dacoits. He further added that making the criminal law severe was no solution, as then further stricter proof was required, which was not forthcoming either due to the fear of the dacoits or the laxity of the Daroghas. This led to more acquittals. He pleaded that Zamindars should be punished and the Daroghas dismissed as soon as dacoity is committed. (Letter to Nizamut Adalat dated 9-10-1808 East India Judicial Selection Vol. II 1830 page 81).

Lord Minto came as Governor General of India in 1807. Apart from other reforms introduced by him, he issued Regulation No 10 which provided for the first time, for the appointment of Superintendent of Police for the Divisions of Calcutta, Dacca and Murshidabad. The preamble to the Regulation said: "By concentrating information obtainable from different parts of the country, in a particular office at the Presidency, a successful plan of operation might be devised and executed, when the efforts of the local police officers, would be unavailing. Information and measures, conducive to the discovery and seizure of the gangs, of dacoits, which still continued to infest many of the Zilas in the Province of Bengal, may especially be promoted by the appointment of the Superintendent of Police." The Superintendent of Police also held the office of Magistrate. He was also appointed the Justice of Peace of Calcutta and authorised to correspond directly with the Governor General of India.

Wellesley's Reforms

Wellesley, after becoming the Governor-General was keen to know the position of policing in the country. He issued a number of questionnaires, for formulating a plan, for the improvement of the police in India. The questions included:-

Is the present system of police, well calculated to ensure the apprehension of offenders? Are the Police establishments, in the division, subject to your jurisdiction, adequate to do the duties required of them? Are you, of the opinion, that number of crime committed annually in your jurisdiction has increased, or diminished, since the year 1793; and to what cause, you to ascribe the increase or diminution? What crimes of enormity, are most prevalent, in the district, under your authority? What is the cause of such crimes? What are the means, you would recommend, to be adopted for their suppression? What is your opinion, of the expediency of granting to Zamindars, farmers, and other persons of character, in your Division, Commission, empowering them, to act as Justice of Peace? Do you think, that such a measure would contribute, to the suppression of crime, and to facilitate, the apprehension of offenders? By what rules, would you regulate, the extent of jurisdiction of such persons? Would you confine it, to the estates or farms, of the persons, to whom the Commission, might be granted, or otherwise? Are there any rules and regulations, which you would recommend to be adopted, as being calculated in your opinion, for the suppression of the crimes in general? In your opinion, what has been the effect of Regulation, which declares, persons convicted of the crimes of perjury, liable to be marked, on the forehead? What has been the operation, of the punishment of transportation, introduced by the British Government? Are you of the opinion that the Mohammedan criminal law, with the alteration of that laws, made by the British Government is administered, with too much leniency, or too much severity and what do you suppose to be consequence, produced by the operation of the spirit, in which the criminal law is administered (Jud. Letter to Court 317.1801) The Interrogations issued numbered 40.

An analysis of the replies received showed that though, the system was an improvement, on the past and several gangs of criminals and dacoits had been apprehended, yet the police had not been able to bring about much improvement, due to the inadequate strength, as well as the inadequate number of the Magistrate's courts.

Lord Bentinck's Efforts for Reforming Police

Lord Bentinck the next Governor General of India he set up a police committee on 19th July 1804, to enquire into the present and former state of the police, in several provinces under the Presidency of (Madras). Colonel Munro, in his report, to the Police Committee, stated despite his best efforts, he had been unable to discover, whether there was any general police system in India in ancient times. He also said, that police system had been perverted, from its original purposes, during the times of disorder. A large proportion of the Taliars are themselves thieves. All the Kwaligars are either themselves robbers or employ them. Many of them are murderers. They now are afraid to act openly. Still, there is no doubt that many of them still secretly follow their former practices. Many Potails and Curnums also, harbour thieves, so that no traveller can pass through the ceded districts, without being robbed. Anybody, who does not employ either his own servants or those of the village to watch at night is liable to be robbed. Even this precaution, is very often, ineffectual.

Many offenders are taken, but great numbers also escape, due to connivance, which must be expected among the Kwaligars and the Taliars who are themselves thieves. The inhabitants often back out from giving information, from the fear of assassination, which was formerly very common. Where crimes, have long, been encouraged by the weakness of the government, by the sale of pardons, and by the connivance, whenever persons of rank were concerned, no improvement can be looked for, but from the operation of time and the certainty of punishment. (Col. Munro's Report 10-4-106 East India Journal Selection Vol. II 1820 page 214-33). He was of the view, that government should be vigorous, in maintaining order and ensuring the security of the people. The Zamindars harbouring thieves and criminals, should be punished.

Proposals of the Subsequent Police Committees

The Police Committee, after taking into consideration, the views received , recommend that Darogha, should be appointed, by the Magistrate on the recommendations, of the Zamindars. He should be paid from the public treasury. The Committee was not in favour, of excluding the Zamindars from police administration, as this would make them, hostile to the administration. The Committee found the Judicial system to be defective in two material points: (1) the way the superintendence of police was being implemented and (2) the way the criminal justice was dispensed. The Committee suggested, that immediate superintendence of police should be entrusted to the Collectors. The Committee added, that Collectors should only be authorised to commit the offenders, for trial before the appointed courts. The Committee also said in the end that "it would be observed that while they have avoided a system of espionage, which could not be maintained without incurring an enormous expenditure, and is not less characteristic of a government unpossessed of the affections of its subjects, then it is calculated to excite and disseminate distrust and disaffection, they have endeavoured to divest the Zamindars of any real power, which could be misused, but to leave to them their natural rank in the Indian society".

Their object was to weaken the influence of the Zamindars over the minds of their tenantry. It was to be done, by attaching to the Zamindars, with a distinct responsibility, and drawing them into immediate communication, with the Magistrate, whereas earlier they were accustomed to regard themselves as all powerful in their province. The plan professed, in fact, to unite all description of people, in preserving the peace and to make government avail their services. It did not envisage setting up of a distinct set of men, whose employment would be promotive of jealousy and distrust, and subject the government to a very great expense and the people to much vexation. The Committee took into account the mutiny of the Indian troops in Vellore in June 1805. It observed the recent unfortunate events marked in the strongest manner, the necessity of, infusing into the system, activity and vigour, qualities which can only be excited and maintained by the example, as well as by the authority of the Superintendent. It is almost needless to remark, that such an example cannot be expected from a Judge, whose whole time ought to be dedicated to the business of the civil court. Those events had impressed, more deeply, on the mind of the Committee, the expediency of placing, the Superintendence of the police, where it has hitherto vested, in the hands of the Collector, both as a measure of policy and of economy. They recommended, that authority, for the adoption, of this measure, should be obtained from the supreme government.

Lord Bentinck in a letter on 29.6.1814 said, that the heads of the villages, were the most proper persons, for police officers, as having the greatest influence. They would be pleased with the consequence, they would derive from it. They were the only persons, acquainted with every transaction. They have the power, in consequence, to prevent robbery and intrigue. Without their aid , there could be no efficient police. However, Madras Government did not accept the proposals of the Police Committee. Even the proposals, of the subsequent Police Committee in 1813, were not acted or accepted by the Presidency Government of Madras. The main reason, for the casual interest, by the Government of Madras in police was the financial stringency and economy, as it is even now.

2

CREATION OF THE POLICE FORCE IN MODERN INDIA

Report of The British Parliament Select Committee on Police

The Charter of the East India Company was due for renewal in 1813. Before renewing it, the British Parliament appointed a Select Committee to look into the management of the affairs of India by the Company. The Committee looked into all the aspects of the East India Company. Regarding the establishment, of an efficient police force in Bengal, the Committee observed, that the efforts had been least successful. The measures taken, had not been successful in controlling the dacoities and robberies. The reason for not controlling dacoities and robberies, was the lack of evidence, required for convicting the criminals. It commented on the facilities made available for the criminals to escape legally, and the scanty provisions made by the system, for suppressing gang robbery. The Committee admitted that it was lack of finances, which was the cause of uncontrolled crime. The Court of Directors, on the other hand, felt that expenditure had been rising in India. They appointed a Committee, to look into the affairs of the country. The Committee studied the position in the country by obtaining the records. It also recorded the evidence of the officials who had earlier served in India. Some of the questions asked were: (1) What is your judgement concerning the system of police established by the British Government? (2) Can it be rendered more perfect and efficient? (3) Do you think that it would be practicable and expedient to resort to any of the modes practised by the native government for maintaining the peace and order in the country'? (*East India Journal* 1820).

After getting the report, the Court communicated its observations: "It is the strongest possible, recommendation of the Taliary police, that it secures the aid and co-operation of the people at large, in the support and furtherance of its operations, because it is pursued, in a mode, which adapts itself, to their customs and usage's, and to that scheme of internal polity, by which, society among them, has been held together, from the earliest ages. We are firmly persuaded, that any system which has been or may be resorted to, for the general management of the police of the country, which is not built on that foundation, must be radically defective in its construction, and inadequate to accomplish its intended purposes. It can never be affected by the feeble operation of a few Daroghas and peons, stationed through an extensive tract of country, wanting in local influence and connection with people, insufficiently remunerated, to induce respectable men, to accept the office, placed beyond the sight and control, of the Magistrate, and surrounded with various temptations to betray their trust. The Zamindari system of policing has had a fair trial under the Bengal Government. The Magistrate had no other agency, to depend upon, for the maintenance of the public peace and order, than that of Daroghas and peons. The consequence has been that open and daring robberies, and every other kind of individual outrage, have prevailed to an extent which has rendered the persons and property of the inhabitants utterly insecure."

The Court of Directors, did not agree to the raising, of the salaries of the Daroghas and other ranks. They directed the village police be restored taking into consideration the usage's in the country. They also directed that the village police be placed under the control of the Magistrate. They also felt that the proper establishments of the village police in Madras will not only lead to efficiency, but also lead to the reduction in the police force as well as reduction in the expenditure which was maintained at a heavy expense. They also said, that superintendence and the control, of the police of the Zillas, be transferred to the Collector who it was said could effectively command the village police, and regulate and control, their conduct and proceeding. The Directors wanted the duties of the Daroghas to be transferred to the Tehsildars, so as to completely effect that union of the two departments, and that this arrangement was considered the best under the circumstances.

Police Structuring in Bengal

The Court felt that resumption of land at the time of permanent settlement, the Paiks and Pausubans were reduced to a position of poverty. It led them to commit thefts and other criminal activities. They felt that many abuses had crept into the police establishments. They felt, that proper course would have been, to reform the police establishments instead of disbanding them. They were referring to the abolition of the Nawab's police officers and Faujdars in 1770 by Hastings. The Court also felt that old police institutions should have been placed under proper control and incorporated into the reformed set up and that the institutions of village police, were indispensable for an efficient police. It was utterly impossible for any other means of gaining any, but the most imperfect knowledge, of the commission of crimes and misdemeanours. There was no other way of obtaining the support and co-operation of the great body of the community in aid of the police. Injurious consequences have arisen, to the peace of the country and the personal security of the inhabitants from the resumption of the lands appropriated for the maintenance of the village police. "We cannot look for a permanent continuance of the present improved order of things, unless we see the establishment, of those measures of prevention, which can alone be adequately and steadily secured by the general restoration, of the old system of village police."

They directed the Bengal Government, for taking necessary action. They advised, that measures be taken, for the gradual establishment throughout the country, of an efficient village police, which should be properly maintained and provided. They ordered, that it should be placed under the orders and control of the Company's Magistrates. It should be subject to such rules and regulations, as might be found, best calculated, to answer the purpose of such an arrangement and as may at the same time have reference to the former practice of the country. The court said: "We are decidedly of the opinion that the principles, of endowing the office, with land, should be steadily kept in view in all practicable cases, as being in itself, the most respectable and most permanent kind of provision. We have little doubt, that a proper course of enquiry, would in innumerable cases and instances, bring to light irregular and surreptitious assumption of territorial allotments which properly belong to the village police. These should be resumed and applied to their original uses, care being taken in the exercise of this power, not to interfere with the just rights of any party. Where the permanent settlement, has taken place and the produce of the police lands were excluded from the assets on which Jummah was calculated and fixed with the Zamindars, alienation's of this latter description, would also on general principles, be justly liable to be restored to their former purposes, and where this was not to be the case, an arrangement should be made, with the landholders for obtaining from the allotments of land for the police officers."

Regarding the contributions for the village police in the form of either cash or crop form, the court felt, that it would be extremely necessary to ascertain, whether they are not already subject to such payments, though clandestinely diverted, into an improper and unauthorised channel. Regarding the payments, to the village police, the court suggested that this should be done in accordance with the previous customs, and in consultation with the villagers and the old records. The court also directed that apart from transferring the superintendence of police to the Collector, and where Tehsildars still retained their agency, every practicable view of the subject should be employed between the Collector as Magistrate and the village police.

Thus, another officer, Tehsildar was inducted as supervisory officer over the Darogha. As the Daroghas were indulging in great abuses of their office, it was felt that vigilance exercised by the senior officer of the rank of Collector and Tehsildars, would go a long way in curbing the evils. This unquestionably, depended upon, the vigilance with which, the conduct of Darogha was looked after, and the vigour and energy, with which it was directed and controlled. The court said: "We are well persuaded, that Collectors will have it much more in their power effectually, to superintend the Daroghas in the execution of their trusts, than it is competent for a Zilla Judge to do." The pressure of work on the Judges and Magistrates had continued to increase. This naturally required more staff. Of course, all the time there was a complaint of chronic shortage due to the consideration of economy. A number of provisions were made, for enlisting the co-operation and assistance, of the landholders and Zamindars. The court also felt, that the general character and qualifications, of the Police officers, were such as to hardly inspire confidence in the respectable sections of the community and dispose them to co-operate with the police. (Judicial letter to Bengal dated 11-4-1836).

The court said, in a letter to Bengal Government: "We desire you will remind the Superintendent of the primary object of his appointment, as described in Regulation 8 of 1810. We expect him, to be vigilant and active, for the apprehensions of robbers, and to proceed himself, to those districts, which appear to require his presence. It is not enough for him, to deliberate on the reasons, assigned by the Magistrate, for the increase of crimes, giving his opinion, as to the sufficiency of their excuses and professing his inability to explain year after year. It is highly fit, that he should at the end of the year, report his opinion in the general causes, which may be supposed to have occasioned, an increase of the crime; but we attach more importance to his immediate personal exertion, and to the zeal, which he may infuse into the local officers. The Acting Superintendent complains that in most districts, the Judge and the Magistrate, have no leisure to perform all their duties. Under no circumstances can pressure of business be a sufficient excuse, for any Magistrate, who suffers dacoity to prevail in his district. It may be a sufficient reason for his neglect, of the least urgent, of his duties, but can be none, for his neglect of the most important. Your closest attention, is required to the manner, in which the Magistrates and the Daroghas, exercise their authority. The very simple powers, of coercion, vested in them may, if injudiciously applied, be productive, of great mischief. In endeavouring to suppress crimes, and to apprehend offenders, measures harassing to a community should be carefully avoided, lest the police become a burden to the people". (Judicial letter to Bengal on 20-10-1824).

According to the Minutes of Evidence, Select Committee, 1832 (1853) Volume 4 Appendix No 5; Page 630 the revenue in Bengal was computed to be over 11.5 crores of rupees and the expenditure on the judicial and police amounted 67 lakhs of rupees, and this proportion worked out to be less than 6 per cent of the annual revenue 1824-1825. Bengal Government introduced a number of changes. The Regulation No 1 effective from

1st March, 1829, provided for the appointment of Revenue Commissioner. The Revenue Commissioner was also given the job of superintendence of the police.

Abolishing of Post of Superintendent of Police and Appointment of Revenue Commissioners as Police Supervisers

The preamble to the Regulation No 1 said: "The system in operation, for superintending the Magistracy and the police, and for controlling and directing the executive revenue officers, has been found to be defective. The judges of circuit, do not possess sufficient powers, nor have they the opportunities of acquiring sufficient local knowledge, to enable them, to adequately control the police, or protect people. The great extent of country, under each of the Boards of Revenue, has similarly operated, to impede them, in the execution of the duties, which belong to them, as the general guardians of the fiscal interests, of the state and as the confidential advisers of the government. For the correction of above defects, it has appeared to be expedient and necessary, to place the Magistrates, Police, the Collector and other executive revenue officers, under the superintendence and control of Commissioners of Revenue and circuit; each vested with the charge, of such a moderate tract of the country, as may enable them, to be easy of access to the people and to confide to the said Commissioners, the powers now vested, in the courts of circuit, together with those, that belong to the Board of Revenue and further with a view to public economy, it has been deemed proper to abolish the office of Superintendent of police, the necessity of which, is superseded by the appointment of Commissioners".

The Superintendent of Police had been conferred considerable executive powers. This way, the executive police powers were combined, with the powers of the trying of the heinous cases. This step was taken, around the time and the year, when the British Parliament had passed the Metropolitan Police Act for London. This Act had provided for the appointment, of a full time police force, under its own Commissioner. The Commissioner of London Police, had no other duties like the judicial or revenue to perform. During 1828-1829, the total expenditure on the police and other judicial charges was nearly 65 lakh of rupees as against the revenue of 12,39,03,769 rupees. (Minutes of Evidence, Select Committee 1832. Volume 4). The Bengal Government issued Regulation No 11 of 1831 in which it authorised the Governor General in Council to vest any Tehsildar or Tehsildars with the powers, and exercise the powers of the Daroghas of police, and determine the limits of police jurisdiction. The Tehsildars could be authorised, to exercise the powers of the Chief Thanedar. He could exercise authority, on all the Thanas and village police establishments in his jurisdiction. Wherever this scheme was extended, the existing Thanedars were to be designated as Naib Daroghas.

Second British Parliamentary Select Committee on Police

Before renewing the Charter, of the East India Company in 1833, the British Parliament appointed a select committee, to enquire into the affairs of East India Company. The material placed before it was the evidence of the people, who had been connected with the affairs of the Company in India. It showed that the subordinate officials were very lowly paid and consequently were not only corrupt but also inefficient and oppressive. As the Commissioners and the Collectors, had to perform a multitude of duties, so their supervision, over the police, administration and other connected areas was ineffective. Mr. Hamilton on appearing before the Select Committee urged that the Commissioner and the Judge of the Circuit Court should be separate individuals. In his views, giving both the jobs, to one individual could lead to, many evils with a harmful effect. Another witness before the Committee said that already the Collectors had very heavy duties. Any further addition, could have only adverse effects, and in the conjunction of the two offices in the same individuals, one or the other office, is bound to suffer. About conferring the police powers on the Tehsildars, it was said: "The objective to vest Tehsildars and other subordinate native officers appears to me very serious. Conceiving, as I do, that they would be more likely to abuse their authority, even the present class of police officers. My own opinion, as to the best mode, of administering the internal affairs of our old established provinces, is that there should be a separate judge, a separate Collector and a separate Magistrate in each District." (Mr Bayley, WB, before the Select Committee, Minutes of Select Committee 1853, Volume 4, Judicial Report of the Indian Police Commission 1902-03).

Mr. Bayley also felt that a large number of criminal cases, emanated, in the want of regulations, explaining and recognising the different tenures, and of records defining the relative rights, interests and duties of the proprietors, tenants and cultivators of the soil. He urged for the maintenance of accurate records and regulations. Regarding the combination of the position of Magistrate and the Collector, it was said: "There is scarcely any principle in jurisprudence, more important, than the separation of these two offices. Their union is injurious, to offenders, to the community and the Magistrates. It is injurious to the offenders, because they are not tried by an unbiased judge, but by one, who will gain credit if they are convicted, whose opinion has been formed before the trial by a previous knowledge of the circumstances of the cases, who has himself been advising the police officers, how to conduct the cases. It is injurious to the community, because its interests are neglected because not only many accused but innocent persons are left to pine at the Sadar Kacheri, exhausting their little stock of money and debarred from the occupations by which their daily food is earned. And lastly, injurious to the Magistrates, because the hunting up of the thieves, is far from a dignified office, because it militates against his respectability and fixes upon him the title of the constable because it acquires for him an ill name, by overwhelming him with duties which are conflicting in their nature, and could not possibly be well performed." (Calcutta Review Volume 4, July-December, 1846, page 149-150). However, the union of the two offices was temporary and they were separated in 1827 during the time of Lord Auckland.

Suggestions and Instructions for Police Reforms

The Court suggested to the Government of India, to take steps, to make the administration, as little oppressive, as possible ,to the prosecutors and witnesses. It also advised, that Magistrates should hold their courts, in the interior also, so that the parties may get justice nearer their homes. It also urged that the evidence should be recorded in the language, it was given, rather than in Persian. Regarding the taking of deposition by the Daroghas, the Court felt that police officers, were unworthy of any such confidence, being reposed in them. The Court also pointed out, that they had become convinced, of the necessity of the Government discontinuing, to employ such a class of agents and of supplying their places by men of very different qualification and character. The court said " We desire that you will allow no other question, for none is of superior or of more pressing importance, nor financial consideration, for they should not be allowed to weigh, on such an emergency, to stand in the way of your deliberations, with a view, to a change, so urgently required".

British Perception on Indian Police in 19th Century

On receipt of the court directive, Sir Charles Metcalfe, circulated a number of questions, to assess the police performances. Mr Hawkins, giving his views said, "Devoid to a great extent of those moral qualifications, which are in themselves a guarantee, for the faithful discharge of public duties, have the persons usually selected, for office in the police department, had inducement held out to them, to keep them, in the way of uprightness and integrity? Have we endeavoured to compensate for the moral deficiency, by inducements of self-interest to a course of good conduct? Is not the true state, of the case, exactly the reverse? Look to the Police Daroghas, selected without reference to a qualification expected, to be incessantly on the move, for which he must keep a conveyance of some kind, in the receipt of a very inadequate salary, with no prospect of promotion, ever liable to the displeasure of the Magistrate, his immediate superior (a displeasure arising too frequently from chagrin and vexation), rather than strict inquiry and mature deliberation, constantly subjected to a change of masters, and in the event of dismissal from office, with every chance of employment in another district, in the same class of appointments; is it surprising that he should be found deficient, in the discharge of his public duties? That he should seek to enrich himself, than exert his endeavours faithfully, in behalf of whose benefit he is employed. Nearly the same observations, are applicable to the several subordinate classes of police officers, entertained by the government. The off hand way, of dismissing whole bodies of them, is one of the greatest vices of the present practice; and is in itself, no slight cause, of those very evils, which it is intended, to check. A Darogha has no confidence, in the permanency of his office; and while employed, he makes the most of his time in gathering together. All of his powers are uncertain. He does not know, when the order of his removal may arrive. The occurrence of a dacoity, or other serious offence, for which the Darogha is probably no more in fault, than the Magistrate himself, and which may occur at any hour, might be the cause of dismissal, especially if he fails to discover and apprehend the perpetrators. There is most pernicious practice, which I believe prevails generally, for fining police officers, heavily for the slightest errors. In such cases they will very seldom appeal, against the order of their employers, but will most assuredly make up, the deficiency, in their receipts in a far more objectionable way."

Mr. Lewis giving his views said: "The greatest impediment to the success of police operation in this country, was from the total want of co-operation, on the part of the people. There was a clear cleavage, between the regular police officer and the public, for whose benefit, the police was employed due to exaction on the one hand, and fear, ignorance and prejudice on the other." He also pointed out that the village community was rarely disposed to help the police in apprehending the criminals, however, dangerous or notorious. He also said that the village Chowkidar should be made serviceable and sound. He was a connecting link, between the police and the public. He should be treated well, so that he could be induced, to give valuable and useful information. Other points urged were, that there should be a separate officer, of the Magistrate and the Collector, so that there is a proper division of labour and responsibility, in the then existing system. It was vain to expect the Collector and the Magistrate, not to give, but secondary importance, to the police duties, as revenue duties were of primary importance. It was also urged, that since each Commissioner dealt with the police and police problems in his own way, uniformity in the directions and management and performance, had been lost. It tended to lower the efficiency of the police working. (Report 11-1-1837 Parliamentary papers 162 of 1835, pages 11-12, and pages 2-5).

Police Committee: Bengal

Acting on the despatch of the Court, and the enquiries instituted by Sir Charles Metcalfe, Lord Auckland constituted a Police Committee for rationalising the inputs received, for finding out the best means of improving the Moufissil Police. Its task was, to draw up a plan, for a more efficient organisation. The Committee was authorised, to examine all public officers, for any information and to examine any individual either in or out of service. The Committee amongst others had Mr. W.W Bird as President and F. J. Halliday, Judicial Secretary to the Government and P. C Smith and J. Lowis as members. (Proceeding 22-8-1837) No 2 & 3, 7-10-1837 and No 7 & 8 dated 24-10-1837 No 5 & 6; Letter to the court dated 1-10-1837. However, the Committee was told, that if the plan for improvement submitted by the Committee involved any great increase of expenditure, its implementation was likely to be delayed.

The Committee while submitting its report said: "As the inefficiency of that system is, in a great measure attributable to the inadequate scale, on which it has hitherto been carried on, no improvement without considerable expense will be practicable. Urgency was more than the extreme unpopularity... the grievous oppression connected with its operation, than from any increased disposition to crime on the part of the community at large." The Committee noted that there were defects everywhere, "The Magistrates are overwhelmed, the Daroghas and their subordinate officers are corrupt, the village watchmen are poor and degraded, and the community at large, oppressed and inconvenienced in various ways, are not only disinclined to afford aid to the police, but in most cases had rather submit quietly, to be robbed, than apply, to the police officers for assistance, to apprehend thieves or to recover the stolen property. The Committee also felt, that the efficiency of the offices, of the Judge and the Magistrate, would be increased, if the Superintendence of each department, was handed over to a separate functionary. Nothing can be worse than the Union. It is wrong in theory and evil in practice. (Appendix to report pp. 5.11.20 Selections from the records of Government papers relating to the Reforms of the Police of India).

Some Plain Speaking On Police

Mr. Dwarka Nath Tagore described, the police of the times in these words: "I think, that from Darogha, to the lowest peon, the whole of them, are a corrupt set of people; a single case could not be got out of their hands without paying money; the wealthy always gets advantage over the poor... When any report is called for, by the Magistrate from the Darogha, even in a true case, that report could not be obtained, without paying a large sum of money; and should the case be between the two rich parties, the richest or he (who) pays the highest, would get the report in his favour. If a *Jamandar* or peon is sent to a village for any enquiry, there is immediately, a tax levied by them, from all the ryots of the village, through the *Gamasthah* of the Zamindar. And this mode of extortion, has so long prevailed, as almost to give it the character of a just demand; so much so that not a single ryot, would ever make an objection to pay it; indeed they look upon it as an authorised tax. If a dacoity takes place in any neighbourhood, the Daroghas and all his people, will go about the villages and indiscriminately seize the inhabitants, innocent or culpable; and it often happens that persons so taken, although of the most suspicious character, in a particular transaction are released, on some money inducement, being given to the officers... In short nothing can be done, without paying for it, whenever they are called upon to interfere."

The Committee also felt, that the jurisdiction of the Magistrates, was too large, for building up, of any personal rapport, between the Magistrates and the people. This often led to very little or ineffective control over the Thanedars. As the areas, under the charge of the Magistrates was too large, the Magistrates could not visit the remote areas. The Committee recommended the gradual appointment, of Deputy or Assistant Magistrates, in different parts of the districts. It said: "No plan for controlling, the native officers of the police, at a distance, or of affording the people, of effectual protection, can be successful, which does not provide, for the distribution of functionaries, with powers of investigation and decision and of control throughout the District to reside amongst them, to satisfy them, that the Police exist for their benefit, as well as for our own, and to put an effectual stop, to the progress of extortion and misrule". The Committee felt, that it will be essential to eliminate those feelings, which dispose, the community at large, to regard being involved, with matters of police, as the worst misfortune.

Regarding the corruption and utter worthlessness, the Committee recommended graded increase in their salary. They suggested that steps be taken, for ensuring, that they are well treated, by the Magistrates. They are not removed from service, on flimsy, or insufficient grounds. "Unless these changes can be effected, and the office of Thanedar placed upon a footing, that will secure the services of respectable men, and put an end to the necessity, if we may so speak, under which they lie, of becoming the oppressors of the people, whom they are appointed to protect, it would be better, we are of opinion, to dispense with them altogether." The Committee recommended a system of promotion of every grade in the lower subordinates.

The Committee looked into the working of the Chowkidari and village police establishments. It considered it, as the most important subject, connected with the Police. The Committee described the Chowkidars a curse, instead of a blessing to the community. Commenting on the character and antecedents of the Chowkidars, the Committee said, that it was even a question, whether an order issued throughout the country, to apprehend and confine them, would not do, more to check, the theft and robbery, than any other measure, that could be adopted. They felt, therefore, that it was an urgent necessity, to have a thorough revision of this establishment, in order to place them, in a state of efficiency. The Committee felt, that the inefficiency of the police, was due to the lack of co-operation, on the part of the community in general, and the Zamindars in particular. "Perhaps the present defective state of the village police is chiefly owing to our own neglect. No rules have been framed, for defining the authority, to which they are to be subject, the duties they are to perform, the scale of remuneration to be received, the source from which it is to be derived, or the mode in which the payment was to be enforced. The fallacy, of condemning the system, for inefficiency, under such circumstances is obvious. Supposing the whole of the police, both regular and subsidiary, be taken into the hands of the government and transformed as proposed into a military body and supposing it to answer as an instrument of coercion and subjection, far better than the present establishment, with all their defects entirely removed, would it be desirable, thus to dispense, even if we could, with the cooperation of the people, to set their influence at defiance, and to act as if we had no hold upon the country but through the sword? Would it be politic to give up, without a further attempt, all hope of our conciliating them, or of impressing upon them, the conviction, that their benefit as well as our own, is the main object of our institutions?"

The majority in the Committee felt that: "to divest the Zamindars of all responsibility and interference and convert the village police into Thana Burkundazes, to be appointed, paid and regulated in all respects by the Magistrates, without the intervention, of either the village community, or of the landholders, would be to subvert at once the whole constitution of village society, to transform, the village watch as well as the Thana officers into military police, to re-impose, the vexatious interference, with its internal concerns, from which the government found it necessary, to relieve them by the enactment of Regulation II of 1832, to alienate more even than, at present the regard of the people, from the police and render the latter, still more an exclusive body, with which the community at large, are not only unwilling to cooperate, but regard with feeling of antipathy, which is an object of the greatest importance to us to endeavour, if possible to overcome."

According to the figures obtained by the Committee, there were a total of 1,30,305 Chowkidars and out of this 1130 were dismissed in 1835, 1836 and 1837. Out of this 19 were concerned in murder and *thugee,* 39 in burglary, 357 in robbery and theft, 42 in embezzlement or forgery, 55 in perjury, false evidence or false complaint, 28 in bribery, extortion or oppression, 96 in affrays, assault or wounding, 70 in being accessories to the crime and 178 in concealing crimes or aiding escapes and 246 for being bad characters or suspected of crimes. Also 37 of them were dismissed for contumacy, 33 for intoxication and 7 for being found sleeping on duty. (Parliamentary paper, of 1857, pages 47-48). The Committee recommended that the village police establishments should be revived. It included, araised allowance for the watchman, framing the conduct rules, as well as the powers of the village authorities and responsibilities. It urged that the Magistrates should have the powers to enforce the revised rules strictly. They should not interfere, in the privileges of the landholders and the village communities. They also suggested that the Zamindars, should be held primarily responsible, for the conduct of the Chowkidars. The Committee felt that an organized village watch, might become a valuable establishment, while the Zamindars would take a far greater interest than they do, or can help, in maintaining its efficiency. The responsibilities of the Zamindars would be real instead of nominal; they would compel the watchman to do their duty instead of conniving at their misconduct; the latter would have to serve one, instead of two masters; the loss of place would be a real punishment, and the situation having become more respectable would probably by degrees, be an object of desire, to others than the very lowest classes.

The situation does not seem to have changed, as a number of policemen, who have substituted the Chowkidars, are equally guilty of extortion, theft, robbery, murder and rude behaviour. No centralised information is available, as everywhere, there is a tendency to cover up. Infact, in place of the Zamindars protecting the criminals, the scenario has changed only to the extent, that now it is some present day politicians, who are themselves committing the same crime and also helping and protecting the guilty law enforcers.

The committee recommended that Regulation II of 1832 should not be replaced as people had generally approved of it. In India, no confidence can be placed in the lower officers of police. Their interference should be dispensed with, wherever it can be done with safety. They were against a system, which requires the interference of the police, on every trifling matter. It must inevitably be vexatious and unpopular. They also disapproved, the practice of the Magistrates' efficiency, being judged on the basis of convictions obtained. They suggested, that police should have all the powers, to deal with and against all classes of people, whether European or natives. They were not in favour of any special courts for the Europeans, for dealing with the criminal cases against them. The Committee expressed itself, against the practice of convicts, of being made to sleep in Thanas, or under the care of the Chowkidars, though this practice had existed for a long time. It said: "No system of police is entitled, to the smallest praise, which cannot be carried into effect, without exceeding the law, nor can Magistrate claim to be considered a good one, who is unable to keep the district in order without having recourse, to measures for which there is no legal sanction. It is needless for the legislatures to enact laws, if those, by whom they are administered, are allowed to disregard them, at pleasure and such a practice ought, we think, to be discountenanced in the most decided manner."

Revival of The Post of the Superintendent of Police (Equal to the Present Police Chief)

In the meantime, the Bengal Government decided to re-introduce the post of the Superintendent of Police to relieve the Revenue Commissioners of the pressure of the extra police work and for taking effective measures for introduction of an improved Mouffusil Police. (Bengal Government Resolution of 10-10-1837). Mr. F. C Smith was appointed the Superintendent of Police in the lower provinces. His yearly salary was Rs 50,000. He was given Rs 500 per month as travelling allowance. He commenced his work on 1st January, 1838. He was also given an office rent of Rs 200 per month. (Judicial letter to court 30-1-1838 and 20-7-1838). The Superintendent of Police appointed in those days, was almost the Inspector General of Police or the Director General of Police of modern times. He was asked by the government, to secure from the Magistrates, of each district, a list of heinous offences, against life and property, which had remained undetected, with a possible list of suspects and the steps taken to apprehend the possible offenders and the causes of failures. Lord Auckland in a letter to the court on 30-1-1838 (No 6), said that: "Change or extensive modification of a system long established, extending over a vast tract of the country, and employing a great number of instruments had been effected. In the quiet and satisfactory introduction of these measure, the happiness of the community was deeply involved. It was bound to be attended, with obstacles to success and charges of partial failure, if entrusted for execution, to different officers in each divisions."

Charter Act of 1833

The Charter Act of 1833 had added a legal member to the Council of the Governor General. It was enjoined on the Council to constitute: The Indian Law Commission to look into the jurisdiction, powers and rules of existing courts of justice and police establishments and all existing forms of judicial procedures, and into the nature and operation of all laws, whether they are civil or criminal, written or customary. The object of setting up of the Law Commission was that: "a general system of judicial establishment and police, to which all persons, whether Europeans or natives, may be subject, should be established at an early period; and that such laws as may be applicable in common to all classes of the inhabitants should be enacted, and that all laws and customs, having the force of law should be ascertained and consolidated and as occasion may require, amended". (R Muir, op.cit page 303). Lord Macauley was the first Legal Member of the Council. A Law Commission was appointed in 1835. This was the first major step in consolidating and codifying the laws of the country and in giving the country a common Penal Code, Criminal Procedure Code and Evidence Act. The Law Commission took up the work of preparing the Penal Code and other Codes connected with the criminal justice system. It may be pointed out here that the present Indian Penal Code is almost the same which was drafted during the British rule, with some modifications made from time to time. The same is true of Indian Evidence Act. The New Criminal Procedure Code introduced in 1973 is almost the old Criminal Procedure Code with minor changes made from time to time.

Non-implementation of Recommendations and Further Reforms

It was brought, to the notice of the Governor General, in August 1840, that the recommendation of Police

Committee Report till that time, had not been acted upon. The village police had been reduced to a "disgracefully useless state". Earlier Mr. Dampier had succeeded as Superintendent of Police to Mr. Smith. He considered it as a degrading condition of service in the police, where the Daroghas were not certain, as to how long, they will continue in service and what will be their tenure. He felt, that dismissal, had been made so common, in the case of those holding the office, that they had almost come to expect it any day. It had ceased to be, any more effective as a punishment. He told the Magistrates, to obtain his prior approval, before dismissing the police officers, above the rank of Burkundauze. He asked the Magistrates, to maintain a record of punishments, like reprimand, fine and temporary deprivation of office for period not exceeding six months. He also recommended a system of rewards, for police officers and higher pay scales. It will be interesting to quote the pay scale recommended. The pay for Mohurrir was recommended from Rs 25 to 30, Jamandar Rs 12 to 15, and Burkundauzes Rs 5 to 6 as the monthly pay. (Bengal Police Report for the first six months 1840).

Another reform introduced by Mr. Dampier was, non-recruitment of functionaries, beyond the prime of life. Mr. Speede, another Superintendent of Police, suggested the appointment of a Superintendent General of Police, for the whole province with four Divisional Superintendents. Each of them was to be given the charge of eight districts, with one or more Assistants. He suggested the merger of the police and village watch, into one body with a hierarchy of officers, like the Inspectors, Thanedars, etc. On account of the heavy expenditure involved, the proposal did not make any headway. According to Mr. Speede: "The main defect, of the police was, want of effective, sufficient and frequent surveillance, of all its Mofussil Officers." Mr. Dampier observed, in his report in 1841, that the police of the day, were too few in numbers, under little direct control and much harassed to get through the routine work, which came before them. He also felt, that it was useless to look for that systematic search after crime, which alone can be successful. He also mentioned that the Zamindars protected and sheltered the highway robbers and burglars for the lion's share of the spoil. The police were seen to be unwilling, or unable to cope with, the influence of these protectors. He also felt that the functioning of the police would improve, if its control was placed in the hands of the people, who could pay attention to it. He observed, that the Magistrates were too busy, with the court work. Daroghas were appointed by direct recruitment. He recommended that competent lower police officials should also be appointed as Daroghas. Mr. Dampier in his report of 1842 said: "Our police officers, do not know, how to act against dacoits. They are either totally deficient, in information, or else leagued with the upholders of these gangs, and are neither detective, protective or any thing else."

Other steps, taken to improve, the police included raising the salary of the Daroghas. On the recommendations of Mr. Bird, who had been the Chairman of the Police Committee of 1838, the Government of India, while approving the higher pay scales for the Daroghas, mentioned that they were "very desirous that the principles of the arrangement, should be carried still further, not only in respect to the Daroghas but to other class of police officers." However, when the Court, approved higher pay scales for Daroghas, it made it clear that in future, its previous sanction, would be essential for raising the pay scale of other ranks of police officers. The Court also disfavoured, the prevailing practice, of imposing heavy fines, on the native officers, as a punishment for acts of omission and commission. It felt that it was a degrading practice. It lowered them, in the estimation of the public. The Court also felt that such treatment and harsh conditions of service will naturally deter respectable people, from joining police and holding on to such jobs.

Similarly, Mr Dampier, as the Superintendent of police, Bengal, had felt that for the police system to be effective, it was essential, to improve the village watch system. It was physically impossible, to keep watch for all night, on a salary of Rs 3 per month, which was not paid very often. He also felt that the Regulation No. 22 of 1816 was wrong, which initially established the Chaukidari system. He suggested another far-reaching reform, that limits should be placed, against the appeals, in criminal offences. The interference by the judges, lowered the authority of the magistrates. It also affected the maintenance of peace and order, adversely. He also said, that increase in the salary and promotion possibilities, had a good effect. Good candidates had begun to come, forward to join the Police. But still increase in the salaries did not affect the old, inefficient Daroghas, who were still corrupt. He also felt that the system could improve, if the Magistrates encouraged honest and good Daroghas and avoided undue interference in their work.

About the police functioning, it was said, "The best security... for the correct and safe administration of justice, is in the doing all, that gives reasonable hope of success, towards employing an honest police, for the instituting of enquiries and collecting evidence, in regard to crimes committed. It cannot be too often, or too earnestly impressed upon the government, that it is not only the pay of the Darogha of a Thana that should be made sufficient for respectability. The *Mohurrirs* and *Jamandars* who and must be daily employed, (as in this case) with independent powers, are excessively underpaid. It cannot be a matter of surprise, that parties so paid, and exercising such great authority, under very little practical check, should be found to be open to temptation, and to lend themselves to the gratification of private malice."

Mr. Mills also said in his report— "The whole police system needs a change; but to remodel it effectively a considerable outlay and increase in expenditure must first be assented to, by the government and until that be done, it is useless to occupy space with a description of the reforms, which should be introduced. In the present system, there is one great and striking anomaly. The pay of a Darogha ranges from Rs 5 to 10 and that of a Mohurrir, who holds almost as many local investigations into crime, as the Darogha does, and performs other equally responsible duties, is only Rs 8 per month. I think that the police Mohurrir's pay should be raised at once to Rs 20 a month and the Jamandar's to Rs 12." (Parliamentary papers (191) of 1857, pages 109-110).

Policing in Bombay: Why Policing Was Poor?

Mr. Eliphinstone, on his appointment as Commissioner for Deccan instituted enquiries about the civil, criminal and police system. Regarding an efficient police he observed: "The principal causes, to which the disorders in Bengal have been attributed, are the over-population, and the consequent degradation and pusillanimity of the people; the general revolutions of property, in consequence of our revenue arrangements, which drove the upper classes, to disaffection and the lower of desperation, the want of employment to numerous classes, whether military or otherwise, who were maintained, by the native government; the abolition of the ancient system of police, in which besides, the usual bad effects, of a general change were included, the removal of responsibility from the Zamindars; the loss of their natural influence, an instrument of police; the loss of services, of the village watchman, the loss of a hold over that class, which is naturally disposed to plunder, and in some cases the necessity to which individuals of it were driven to turn robbers, from the resumption of their allowance; the separation of the revenue, magisterial, judicial and military powers by which all were weakened; the further weakness of each, from the checks imposed on it; the delays of trials, the difficulties of conviction, the inadequacy of punishment, the trouble and expense of prosecuting, and giving evidence; the restraints imposed by our maxims on the assumption of power, by individuals, which combined, with the dread of the Adalat, discouraged all from exertions, in support of the police; the want of an upper class among the natives, which could take the lead on such occasions; and to conclude the small number of European Magistrates, who supply the place, of the class last mentioned, their want of connection and communication, with the natives, and of knowledge of their language and character."

Mr. Eliphinstone also said: "Many of the evils, from which this country has hitnerto been exempted, are inseparable from the introduction of foreign government, but perhaps the greater may be avoided, by proper precautions. Many of the upper classes, must sink into comparative poverty and many of those, who were employed in the court and army must absolutely lose their bread." (Mr Elphinstone's Report 25-10-1819, East India Journal Volume 4, 1836, Pages 139-207).

On Policing in 1830

The Governor of Bombay, Sir John Malcolm observed in 1830 that with the extension of the new laws, it had become very difficult to establish a system of good policing. The people, for whom, these laws were framed came from different backgrounds, character and habits and they did not easily adopt themselves to the new liberal laws. He suggested that "Village system of policing should be strictiy maintained and restored, wherever it has decayed". He wanted the Village Patel to be well supported, and rendered responsible within his own circle. He also said: "The task of seizing the most notorious criminal is easy, compared to that of proving their guilt, according to the principles and the forms of our courts of justice. There is seldom, that full evidence they require, and the consequence is, the annual discharge of well known plunderers, to recommence their career of guilt, and to take ample vengeance on those, whom they suspect of having aided, in their apprehension. If our laws are not modified, to meet this great evil, it can alone be mitigated by a change in the executive branch, of the police in those provinces, that are inhibited, or subject to the inroads of predatory tribes.

The duties, of a Collector are too heavy, to admit of his giving the police, of such countries, that personal attention, which they require; and the changes on promotion and other causes, prevent the Assistant being a sufficient aid to him, in a branch which particularly demands, constant residence in disturbed and often unhealthy districts, jungles, etc. Added to this, that the Regiments, which are found, a serious bar to the establishment of a good police in our well cultivated and tranquil provinces, present obstacles that are almost insurmountable, to its establishment amid mountain and jungles, inhabited by races of rude and uncivilised men. We need not be surprised until some change is made, either at the increase of crime, or hardly that one year should pass without our being compelled, to employ a part of our regular force, in suppressing bodies of plunderers, who are too strong to be put down by the civil power." (Parliamentary papers of 162 of 1853 pages 88-89).

About the conditions, in the areas, now constituting Gujarat State, it was reported by Mr Ironside that due to extreme insecure conditions and occurrence of highway robberies, it was impossible to travel, from one village to another. He also said, that these conditions had occurred, because the old idea of holding the village community and the village Headman for prevention of offences, had been given up. He advised, that it would be better, to revert to the old system, of holding the landholders and the village Headman, responsible for the peace and prevention of offences there. Mr. Willoughby, A member of the Council also felt that the existing police was 'Wretchedly inefficient' and there was an urgent need for a 'radical reform of every branch of it'. It is requisite, that they should, very clearly lay it down, as a fundamental rule, that the Magistrate is to continue, being responsible, for the police of his Zilla. His responsibility is to be real, and efficient responsibility. From this, it was clear that this would reduce the position of the Superintendent to that of the Magistrate's deputy. He wanted the Superintendents to act as the eyes and the ears of the government, and to superintend the police under the general control and authority of the Collector and Magistrate of the Zilla, in the same manner as the Revenue or Judicial Commissioners superintend their respective branches of administration. "This will be manifest, if we only consider the light, in which all natives, will view the superintendent; if they see that he is the Magistrates' right-hand man for everything, relating to the police; that the Magistrate assists and supports him in every way, attends to all his suggestions, and does not interfere with him except when the interference, is really necessary and just. Contrast the position, the superintendent would under such circumstances hold, in the eyes of the community, with that of a man on inferior salary, without any prestige, from rank in his own service, with a virtually distinct and independent charge, whose proceedings are viewed with indifference, if not with some degree of jealously, by the Magistrate and his Assistants. There can be no doubt that in the latter case, whatever weights he might have from personal qualifications, he would have none from his position".

He was equally keen to maintain the influence of the Collector. It was felt, that without the police charge, the position of the Collector, would not remain paramount in the district. Unless, he continues to be responsible for the police of the Zilla, under his charge, in what will the Magistrate differ from the Judge except in the case of his jurisdiction? However, Mr Willoughby also said that the discipline, interior economy, and the distribution of the force should be left to the Superintendent of Police. About the dual responsibility and the running of the Police Department, "It will be neutralised if all parties act in harmony together for the good of the public service." (Minute 11-4-1851 Parliamentary papers 162 of 1853 pages 63 to 95).

Mr Willoughby also quoted the Madras Committee of 1805, the Courts orders of 1814 and Sir John Malcolm, Lord Falkland and other officers. One of the Magistrates mentioned that the police had been greatly neglected everywhere. "The root of the whole evil is the useless expenditure in legislation, neither homogenous to the character of the people nor suited a code of laws, that delights the thieves, rogues, and *Vakeels*. It is a stumbling block and rock of offence to all and grievous hindrance to the efficient administration of justice. The people may have some confidence in our honesty and desire, to do justice but they hold our courts in contempt. Look through the country and see who thrive and make fortunes; but a greater evil than the Code is the court of Sadar Adalat and their incessant fault finding with the Magistrates and reversal of decisions for defect of form... and so it will be to the end of the time, as long as the Bombay Judge tries the pursuant robber, and lets him off ,because his mothers' name is said to be Managua instead of Lingo. It may be very good law, but it is very bad justice... Some reliance must be placed in the judgement and discretion of the Magistrates and then the police may become a terror to evil doors and the praise of those who do well."

Mr. Willoughby quoted Sir James Mackintosh who had said that new code should be adopted to the peculiar interests and usages of the people. "Penal laws loosely enforced are lotteries in which the offenders speculate, and it is remarkable how accurately they calculate their chances of prosecution and escape."

3

POLICE INVESTIGATIONS

Police, in one form or the other has existed throughout the ages. In ancient times, as the population was limited, the administration was not a complicated affair. The problem of law and order, was not as serious then as it is now. Policing was simply a question of observing customs. Primarily, the question of maintaining order arose, during raids by foreigners. The British were the first, in India, to introduce system of laws, based on just and fair premises. They endeavoured to take out the scope of arbitrariness to the maximum extent possible. For the first time in the history, proper procedures were laid down, for the admissibility of the evidence, for investigating the cases and the punishments. The penalties for violations of laws were prescribed. If any thing, the law was slated, in favour of the accused. A person was presumed, to be innocent, until proved guilty in accordance with the procedure, laid down by the law. The State was almost put in the same position, as the accused. It had to prove its case, in reasonably independent tribunals, or the courts, before the guilt of a person could be proven and the punishment awarded.

In fact, the State was and is, still at a disadvantage, because neither the statements recorded by its investigating agency nor the confession, made before it, are admissible in law. Thus, theoretically and even actually, if an accused person committed a murder and confessed the same to the highest police functionary in the state, that is the Director General of Police, this confession, will not be admissible in law courts. The evidence of a top police officer is even worse than useless. But if such confession is made, before a criminal or a person, wanted by the law, this will be admissible and creditworthy, so far as our legal system is concerned. Apart from this, the State provides legal aid to the criminals, who cannot afford a lawyer of their own. This bounty is, against and at the expense of the taxpayer. Thus, the taxpayer not only has to pay for nabbing and prosecuting the criminal, but also for helping him to get out any legal harm, that may come his way. One can understand the citizen paying to get the guilty punished. But it appears a bit too thin for the citizen, paying for the accused to evade the punishment for crime committed by him. Thus, the double sufferer is the innocent citizen who has to pay twice for no fault of his own. The courts in the country are cluttered with the cases and due to the sheer larger volume of numbers, it is not possible to dispose off the present work load, for decades to come, even assuming, that no case is added, for the next ten years. The job of a judge is not only challenging but also a highly demanding one and in the interest of not only justice but also for his own conscience, a judge has to be satisfied about the guilt of the accused. A judge is a man, and man by nature has to be more answerable, to his own conscience, which is the highest judge, than any other authority. The question of laying down a quantitative target for disposal is a proposition, fraught with very dangerous consequences, not only for the accused, but also for the society as a whole.

At the same time, it is a fact that justice delayed is not only justice denied, but also justice murdered. If the cases are allowed to drag on, as is happening now, a stage is bound to come when the people will take the law in their own hands. There is a limit, to which the patience of the people can be stretched. The case of patience, being exhausted, happened in Bhagalpur in Bihar, when the entire town, went on strike, in favour of the policemen, who had allegedly been suspended, for committing atrocities on the dacoits. This was a case, where people had exhausted their patience, with the criminal justice system. They were in favour of a summary public trial, even though in the eyes of law, such a proposition has no place. This only highlights the need of law, to keep pace with the social changes.

Manning the Police Outpost

Police outpost is a curious institution. It generally consists of a Sub Inspector or Head Constable and some Constables. It has no legal authority to register a case. It is a poor substitute of a police station. It only communicates the offences which take place, in its jurisdiction. The Head Constable cannot investigate a case unless specially empowered or acting as the officer incharge of the police station. The outpost does not even have the strength to maintain the law and order, because one or two of the constables are used for sentry duty. This is one of the old practice continued, every where in India.

The Sentry on Duty: A Wasteful Practice

A person complained to a police constable on duty at an outpost about a quarrel. He requested his intervention in resolving the dispute. The police constable replied that as he was all alone, on sentry duty he could not leave the post. The complainant pleaded for immediate intervention, as the quarrel otherwise would assume serious proportion. The Constable true to the sentry duty, thought otherwise. He considered it more important, to stick to the outpost office, rather than to save a life. The complainant in desperation after having failed to persuade him to act, stabbed the Constable. The Constable survived the attack, after a dozen stitches, and a three weeks of agonising stay in the hospital. The point to be observed here is that the police is bogged down in routine duties laid down, by the antiquated orders, which nobody has thought fit to amend. While attending a course on the Trade Promotion in United Kingdom, I happened to visit a police station there. I found nobody on sentry duty. I heard the clutter of type writers. I found a Board on a counter with the words prominently written on it "Ring for attention," with a jingling bell kept on a side. I jingled the bell and a constable came out and said 'What can I do for you, Sir?' I just said that I also work for the Police Department in India and I just wanted to see a British Police Station. I asked him, that how it is, that nobody was on sentry duty, outside the police station? His counter question was 'What for?' I was rather hard put to explain, that it was kind of a watchman duty, to guard the police station against the thieves and criminals. He asked me as to what kind of protection the police could give to the people, if they could not guard their own police station, without a rifle in their hands. He asked me if the same job could not be done while sitting and doing some concrete work in the police station, instead of just standing outside, waiting for a possible criminal, to come and attack the police station? I agreed that there was lot of sense, in what he was saying. This is a simple reform, which has not been done for ages. One possible reason is, that in form, if not in content, the police is patterned on the army. The sentry duty is one of its abiding legacies.

There is no reason, as to why the vast manpower used, just for standing for sentry duty, cannot be diverted to real and effective policing, or for updating the police records, for effective control on crime and criminals. It is time for police to muster enough grit to dump some of the wasteful practices. Such practices should have been discarded long ago. Policing is becoming more and more difficult day by day, not only for the policemen, but for the public as well. The expectations of the people have been aroused, after the independence. They expect much more, from their democratically elected representatives, than from the civil servants. The civil servants have many times, to perform the work, of brakes. Nobody, ordinarily wants to be stopped and least of all the public representatives, because it is likely to give an impression of dependence, as well as leaning on the bureaucracy. Policemen get caught, in the whirlpool of the state policies, which they neither frame, nor have been consulted before they were framed. The responsibility of the implementation lies elsewhere, other than in the police department in this case.

Take for example the mass copying which takes place during the examinations. Have the authorities gone into the genesis of copying as to why, when and where it takes place? My discussions with the academicians reveals that this has never been done. Such an analysis would strike, at the root of our examination system. Our examination system is not a test of ability. It is a memory test. Some of us may have excellent ability, but not excellent memory.

Not even one student, indulging in copying has been asked, to give justification for his act. Academicians live a life of seclusion in an ivory tower of their own making. Some of the down to earth ideas, either do not occur to them, or are brushed aside, as being not the brainchild of academic thinking. At the drop of a hat the universities set up committees; but not even one university, has set up any committee to go into the entire gamut of copying during the examinations. This is due to the fact, that setting up of such a committee, will be considered an admission, of the open secret, of mass copying. We as a nation, somehow have come to believe, that by not accepting the existing evils, we can wish away their existence. This kind of wishful thinking away, of a problem does not lead us anywhere. On the contrary, it only aggravates the situation. The least that can be done, is to have a close, unbiased look at the problem from all sides and make an effort to find to a solution, in a time bound framework, rather than leave the question of improvement and reforms open, as it has been for over one century.

The Process of Investigation and Consistency of Evidence

Investigation is the first step in finding out truth. A complaint made to the police, of a cognisable offence, under the Indian Penal Code, can only lead to the investigation . During the investigation and in an effort to find out the truth, some angularities slip in, or are slipped in, to help the accused person. It brings a bad name to the police. The lapses of a few tarnish the entire department. Sometimes, the complainants exaggerate the gravity of the offences and falsely implicate individuals. This tendency finds pronounced expression, in mass participation offences, like riot cases. In such cases, the complainants try to involve all the male members of a family, including children of tender age, and old and infirm people. Different parts are attributed to the small children, and old people to implicate them in the criminal investigation and the cases. Often, the number of injuries, in an occurrence indicate the participation of a much smaller number of persons, than what are said, to have jointly taken part, in an attack. Another feature is, that investigating officer, almost invariably adheres to the version of the occurrence, as given in the First Information Report (FIR). This is irrespective of, his actual findings, in the investigation. The investigation officer is afraid of departing, in any manner, from the story set out in the First Information Report, however, false or improbable it may be. He is apprehensive, of failure of the case, in the court, on this account. He feels that it is more important for evidence to be consistent, than to be probable, and in accordance with the human nature.

The investigator fears the complainant. If the story of the complainant is not accepted in entirety and the investigator starts finding out what the truth in regard to an occurrence, and collect evidence in support of it, regardless of the desire of the complainant, the complainant might start a campaign of vilification against the investigator. There is a likelihood, of a spate of complaints against him to the superior officers. The higher authorities prefer the safe, conventional and time tested method of going to the court, with a case in accord, with the First Information Report and produce such evidence as supports it entirely, leaving the discovery of the truth to the court.

Determining the Criminality or Innocence of the Act

The Court has to depend, on the investigating agency, to lay bare the truth. Passing on the buck, is a wrong approach. It is an abandonment of the task of the investigator. It needs a courage of conviction, in the initial stages to put the matters right and insist on the truth, being brought out. The other defects are, the false implication, or the use of weapon, more dangerous than the accused carried. It is generally noticed that when the medical report, negates use of such a weapon, or the part played by the person, carrying it, are put before court the guilty are let off, because of the use of wrong weapon, attributed to him, or the wrong parts assigned to him. Occasionally, this kind of defect, recoils on the whole case. Doubts are cast, whether the occurrence was witnessed, by the persons claiming to have witnessed it, or that it happened under conditions, when the assailants were visible, or could be recognised. Other type of cases in which the accused too have been injured, though they themselves may have been aggressors and injuries may have been caused by the complainant and his men also are likely to have no prospects of success. This is so, as initially no effort is made, at the time of recording of the First Information Report, whether the other parties also received injuries at the relevant time.

The Clause of Injury: Complaint Vs Accused

It is also a fact, that the complainant will, rarely mention the fact, of the accused, having been injured. Even if he does so, the investigating officer seldom, makes an effort, to find the truth, as he himself wants to prove the guilt of the accused. Even if the informant, divulges this fact, to the investigation officer, the investigator omits to mention the fact in the records, leaving it to be denied, or explained according to the needs of the situation. The investigator seldom realises, that where both the parties in the fight have received injuries, the circumstances in which each party is injured is of vital importance. The criminality or the innocence of an act, has to be determined, not by the act itself, but mainly by the circumstances in which it was done. It is best to have, a fairly complete picture, of the entire occurrence in the First Information Report (FIR) itself. This is in order to allay any criticism that there was not only an omission to explain the injuries of the accused, but a studied attempt to conceal any fact. It has been observed, even during investigation, instead of frankly coming out with the case, that the accused persons also received injuries at the hand of the deceased or the complainant and their helpers, grossly improbable stories like the injuries having been accidentally received at the hands of their own party are introduced. In some cases, the fact of their having received injuries, is concealed and when the injuries are proved, by the entries made in the jail records, it becomes, too late, to explain. The investigating officer needd remember that if the accused are really aggressors and the prosecution really admits it and also the fact that the accused were also injured in the fighting, it would inspire more confidence in the mind of the courts. The case would have better chances of success.

Cases Ending in Acquittals

In case of *Baldeo Vs State* (1969 AIR pages 756) the Court observed:

"In a case, relating to a fight in which both the parties are proved to have received injuries and the injuries of either party cannot be regarded as negligible in number and nature, ascertainment of the manner, in which the fight began and developed, is essential for deciding the guilt or innocence of a party. In such a case, the acts done by a party, would not by themselves, show their criminality or justification, and they would take their legal complexion entirely from the circumstances, in which they are proved to have been done. Determination of the true sequence of events, therefore, becomes a matter of vital importance in a case of this kind and if the court, on consideration of all relevant matter, is in the end, left in a state of reasonable doubt and uncertainty as to the origin of the fight, and as to whether a situation had arisen in which the acts, with which a party is charged, became justified in law, the court cannot hold that party guilty."

Another type of case, which normally ends in acquittal is the one, in which there is a "free fight", between the parties, equally determined on their rights. They meet only for settling their avowed rights. When both the cross cases, are sent up for trial by the court, such cases end in acquittal. The reason is obvious, for the acquittals. The prosecution witnesses, in one case, are the accused in the other and vice versa. The witnesses in cross cases, tend not only to exaggerate but also indulge in falsehoods. They keep their safety in the cross cases in view. They attribute aggression to the other party and assume the role of injured innocence.

The Benefit of Doubt

Very rarely does an investigator, in such a case examine, or succeed in getting , an impartial witness. The result is, that such cases, end in unmerited and undeserved acquittals. There is no definite evidence, produced, before the court to reach any conclusion, regarding the truth of the matter. The result is, that benefit of doubt is given to the parties and the cases end in acquittal. The proper course for handling such cases, would be to find out independent witnesses. Such witnesses would be in a position to give the true version, of the incidents to the court. They can be produced as common eye-witnesses, even though their version, may conflict with the partisan witnesses in the court. This is the only way, in which the court can be assisted, to find out the truth. Cases relating to the quarrels and fights over the land and other properties, are very common. The acquittal in such cases, is common due to the inadequate attention paid to the revenue records to establish the rights of the parties. False records also lead to the benefit of doubt, being given by the court to the accused. Investigation in such cases, requires knowledge, of the village and other revenue or municipal records. Copies of the sameby the competent authority are the best evidence. The deficiencies in the investigation, have to be made good, before the case is filed before the Court.

Medico-legal Cases

In sex offences, one of the main causes of the failure, is the inadequate proof, of the age of the woman. The investigating officer should not go by the estimate of age, given by the parents, or the medical opinion, or even the x-rays. He should establish, it by producing the copies of the birth certificate. This is more so in cases, where the age is not very apparent. Care should be taken, to fix it, with exactitude, because in such cases, a very thin margin, divides the innocence, from the guilt.

In the medico legal cases, the medico-legal expert has an important role to play. A Commission noted that it was surprising that all medico-legal experts are empowered to do medico-legal work, irrespective of their experience. The majority of them, not only lacked experience but also did not have the benefit of necessary experience. The Commission observed, 'what strikes one as rather a strange, is that although medico-legal opinion forms the real battle ground of so many forensic contests, in court, and may prove the turning point, upon matters like cause and time of death, the age of injuries and the weapon of assault, there is no provision for any pre-service or in service training for medical officers. They have to draw, therefore, essentially upon the knowledge, gained by them, as students in the Medical College, where forensic medicine is one of the subjects of study in the third year of MBBS class. A Director of Health Services giving his evidence before the Commission said: "The subject of forensic medicine is taught in the third year of MBBS students by theory, lectures, demonstration including attendance at post-mortem examination. This is sufficient only, to give a basic idea to the students, about the subject. It is not adequate, to equip students, to do independent medico-legal work and post-mortems examination, on joining the Provisional Medical Service. The students, during their graduation period for MBBS, consider forensic medicine as a minor subject, and so their attention, comes to be diverted, to subjects like medicine, surgery, ophthalmology and they do not pay the same attention to forensic medicine."

Imperfections in the Medico Legal Cases

The knowledge of the medical expert in forensic medicine, in cases involving life and liberty of the people, accused of offences, is considered to be a matter of minor significance, during the period of medical education. Commenting on the nature of post-mortem examinations, Mr. Justice G. D Khosla observed in his book *The Murder of Mahatma*:

"I have always considered it a matter of regret that doctors in this country do not make, a more thorough and careful examination of a dead body suspected, or known to have been the result of criminal homicide. Except in the rare cases, relating to an important victim, the autopsy is carried out, with utmost reckless indifference, to scientific accuracy. A great deal depends, on the accurate and intelligent observation, of the conditions of the dead body, the nature, size and location of the injuries found upon it, the state of internal organs, the contents of the stomach and intestines, the presence of some poison or alcohol in the blood or tissues. Yet it is surprising, how frequently this basic information, is lacking, in a murder case. I have heard stories of actual job of dissection, being entrusted to the hospital sweeper, who calls out, the answers, to various questions, listed on the printed forms, intended for the doctor's post-mortem report. The doctor himself sits, at a table outside the mortuary, safe from the stench and infection of the dead body, and notes down the information shouted across to him."

Survey Committee on medico-legal practices in India observed that: "in most cases and particularly in putrified bodies, post-mortems are not conducted by the medical officers but are entrusted to a sweeper or a ward boy. A Police Commission observed that: "It is true, that examination of a decomposed body, is unpleasant, but the responsibility, of such a vital task, cannot be transferred to a sweeper, on that account. It must be performed, by the medical officer himself, with a full realisation of the fact, that thoroughness and care, with which he performs it, will go a long way in helping the court in dispensing justice."

Another witness incharge of the State Forensic Laboratory said : "Post-mortem reports, are often prepared, in a perfunctory manner and they do not contain details, of measurement of wounds, correct description of burning, blackening and tattooing. Due to inexperience or ignorance, the abraded skin, which gets blackened, in the course of time, is mistaken for blackening from powder. The perfunctory nature of work done, in regard to firearm injuries examination, is due to lack of experience and training, on the part of the medical officers, performing post-mortem examinations. I would suggest, that apart from the training, that students receive in medico-legal work, in their medical course, they should have at least one week's training in the Ballistic Section of the Forensic Science Laboratory."

Essentials for a Post-Mortem Report

A witness before a Commission indicated the imperfections in the medico-legal work in the following words: "In my opinion, the present forms prescribed, for the post-mortem examination and preparation, of injury report, are defective in some ways. Strangely enough, in the injury report, there is a column for mentioning the probable weapons, by which the injury was caused, but there is no such column in the post-mortem report form. Such a column is essential, for the post-mortem examination form as well. The data on which the information, regarding the age of the injured and the weapon, with which they are caused, are not mentioned, either in the post-mortem report, or in the injury report with the result, that it leads to useless cross examination and to the employment, of more conjectures, by the doctors. In my opinion, the data on which, all those matters are formed, should be mentioned. The data regarding the features of the dead body, on the basis of which, time since death, is determined, is not properly given in the post-mortem report. I think, it should give this data. A detailed description, of the contents, of the stomach, the small intestine and the large intestines and the bladder, seems to be absolutely necessary, and these details are entirely excluded in the post-mortem reports, that usually go to the court. The parts in which faecal matter, is found and the estimated quantity of the matter, should be invariably given. It should also be indicated, in which part, of the small intestine, his food had been found. The urine found in the bladder should be weighed and its quantity mentioned in the report.

The time since death, in my opinion, should be described, in terms of hours, upto 36 hours and thereafter in terms of days or parts thereof. Post-mortem examination reports, in regard to firearm injuries, are of a most unsatisfactory nature, and they often lead to wholly unmerited acquittals. The reports, do not show any proper appreciation, of the distinction between scorching, blackening and pencilling. No proper light, is thrown, in the post-mortem reports on the shape, direction of the injury and the track of the bullet. Doctors performing the post-mortem examination, and doing medico-legal work, have very inadequate idea, of dispersal and distances, or anything pertaining to ballistics.

Evils and Lapses in Handling Medico-Legal Cases

Regarding, the want of integrity, on large scale, in the medical officers, a lot of complaints, but without any legal evidence, are there. In one district, the Medical Officer, himself admitted, before the Commission, that it was the usual practice, for both, the accused and the complainant, in that district, to rush to the Medical Officer, soon after a murder, evidently, to offer temptation for a favourable report. Issue of false medical certificates, and preparation of wrong medical reports, was also, not said, to be unknown.

Another evil, which very much exists, is that very often, the accused gets injuries manufactured, after the occurrence, and in order to prove, that he received them, during the occurrence and thus support a false theory of self-defence, he manages, to have the age of the injuries, as mentioned in the report of the Jail Doctor, synchronise, with the date or time of the occurrence. It is essential, to have safeguards, against this evil practice, so as to avoid miscarriage of justice or attempts to pervert the course of justice. All cases of injuries, on the body of a person admitted to jail, should be immediately put up, before the Superintendent of jail by the jail doctor, or by another doctor, of the district hospital, nominated by the Superintendent of the Jail. He should check up the correctness of the entries, as early as possible. No consideration of overwork, or any other consideration, should be allowed to stand in the way of ensuring honesty and preventing failure of justice. Sometimes there is avoidable delay, in the writing of medico-legal reports, and their transmission to the police. This kind of delay, is not always due to negligence or overwork, but is deliberate and due to manipulations. Such a practice needs to be condemned. Severe steps, should be taken in dealing with the evil, and severe action should be taken against the medical officers indulging in such a malpractice. Careless or incorrect handling, of medico-legal cases, and the negligent post-mortem, can lead to miscarriage of justice.

The Shorey report on medico-legal cases has this to say: "The present position, in regard to the investigation, of medico-legal problems, is very unsatisfactory. Every medical practitioner, incharge of a remote dispensary, regardless of his qualifications and experience, is asked to undertake medico-legal post-mortem, in complicated cases of crime and he is liable to be held in question, thereafter, the presumption being that every medical man is competent to undertake these responsibilities".

It must be emphasised that the question of improving the quality of investigation, is invariably linked, to the amount of time an investigator can devote to the case.

Duties of a Sub-Inspector Investigator

Investigation is a laborious process. The amount of time spent is directly proportionate to his total workload. Beyond a humanly possible workload, the quality of the work is bound to suffer. The number of investigations which can reasonably be handled by an investigating officer should be fixed with reference to the capacity and quality of cases. At present the duties of the Sub-Inspector or officer incharge of a police post, are generally, as under:-

(i) Patrolling and surveillance over the bad characters.

(ii) To make law and order arrangements for various religious festivals and fairs, and VIP visits.

(iii) To conduct enquiries into the numerous complaints and representations of the public.

(iv) To make enquiries in respect of firearms licences applications.

(v) To serve court processes and execute warrants.

(vi) To make arrangements for elections to Parliament, State Assembly, Local bodies and panchayats.

(vii) To make security arrangements during the visit of the VIPs.

(viii) To handle communal or civil disturbances or other agitations as well as the students agitations and agitation of Government employees, and other section of the community.

(ix) To conduct morning parade for the staff and allocate duties to them and to ensure that the same are performed efficiently and well by the staff and to keep the staff under control and discipline.

(x) To make preparation and maintenance, of various crime records, of the Police Station, as laid down in various orders and the police manual.

(xi) To deal with law and order situations, which may arise from time to time, on various issues, not necessarily concerned with the police or policing directly.

(xii) To look after, the court cases of the Police Station.

(xiii) To conduct inquest into the cases of natural or suspicious deaths reported in his Police Station. He also has to look into those cases, which may give an impression of foul play, as the margin between the unnatural death and murder is very thin.

(xiv) To maintain liason with the local officers like the medical officer, the executive magistrate, the local respectable citizens of the locality.

(xv) To have the identification parades of the suspects and the accused conducted. He also has to have the stolen property identified.

(xvi) To ensure the safe custody of the arms and ammunition, government property and records.

The above list of the duties is only illustrative and not exhaustive. This indicates the heavy workload of the investigator, hardly leaving him any time, for sustained investigating work..

The Police Commission also noted as it was urged by the investigators themselves as well as senior police officers and others that even the norms of 60 to 75 investigations recommended by the UP Police Commission 1960-61 was on the high side and that even these norms have now been stretched almost to a breaking point. Against the heavy workload, heaped on the Sub-inspector of Police, the second UP Police Commission analysed the time available for the Sub-inspector to collect evidence which is the *raison d' etre* of the investigation. It observed: "In a year, a Sub-inspector can get 30 days earned leave and 24 days casual leave. We feel that this leave should be given to a sub-inspector, in view of the difficult and exciting nature, of his duties, which he has to perform, round the clock, but is not being given freely, as it should be owing to increasing pressure of duties and shortage of manpower.

Norms of Cases Inspected per Investigator

A sub-inspector is thus left with 311(365-30+24) days in a year. During this period he has mainly:

(1) to attend to the *'parivi'* of cases at the district headquarters which takes 52 days per year at an average rate of one day per week,

(2) to attend the monthly staff meeting at the District headquarters which takes another 12 days in a year,

(3) to make security and other law and order arrangements during fairs, festivals, VIP visits, agitations, flood, etc, which occupy atleast 24 days in a year at an average rate of 2 days per month.

An actual period of 311 - (52+12+24) = 223 days is only thus available to an investigator for completing 70 or 65 cases per year, as the case may be. Now even this period, gets further reduced with five days, a week, in most states, as it reduces, the availability of the Investigating Officer, on working days, for attending the court and the headquarters, assuming that he is not taking any holidays for this personal and family work. This means an average time of 2.9 to 3.7 days or approximately of only 3 days, is in effect available, to an investigator for completing the investigation. During this period of 3 days, per case for investigation, the investigating officer, has to visit the scene of crime, at least once, if not more, organise raids and searches, collect and pursue clues, prepare case diaries and other relevant documents, contact witnesses and comply with other procedural requirements of the investigation. Each of these steps, of investigation, is time consuming. It requires concentrated attention. Only then the quality of investigation can be improved. Obviously, this average period of 3 days per case, for investigation, is grossly inadequate, for a thorough and proper investigation.

One solution in big cities, with a population of over one lakh, where functional separation exists, between 'law and order' and investigation, the norms should be reduced to 60 cases for investigations per year per investigating officer. And in the urban and rural police stations, the norms should be 50 cases for investigations, per year per investigator. The strength of the investigators at each police station should be fixed in accordance with the norms suggested above or any other norm, which the Department or the Government may fix. The numerical strength, of investigators, at each police station should be, reviewed every year, by the government in consultation, with the State Police Chief so that the cases are investigated efficiently.

It is also seen, that the officers-in-charge, of the police stations and other officials, avoid taking up the investigation, in the initial stages. This tendency needs to be checked with a firm hand. It is only during the initial stages of investigation of heinous cases, the fate of the case is made or marred. In fact, as Director CBI, I had ordered, that at least one important or complicated case, per year, would be investigated by each Superintendent of Police, himself. This was to ensure, that the Superintendent of Police, is in touch with the ground reality and the pitfalls in the investigation. This considerably improved the quality of investigation. With the expanding scope of police investigations growing complexity of crime, and the continuous advances, in the methods of tackling them, there is a need for scientific and constant evaluation and up-gradation of the police procedures, practices and operations followed in the fields of investigation, prosecution and prevention of crime.

Permanent Body to Study Police Functions

It is essential to have systematic study into the police working, to discover facts and to arrive at certain conclusions and propositions. Such presumptions can be verified, either through future experiments, or by other data and statistics. The data for such a study, can be obtained through the police records, experiments, and observations. Each state should set up a permanent body for studying police functions and suggesting ways and means for increasing the functional efficiency of the police. Such a body can undertake various projects for study, for having a citizens friendly police force. It can be the extent and nature of the unreported crime, or study the police response time, to the public needs and complaints, and the common mistakes, as pointed out by the courts in police investigations. In short, such a body could be assigned the following functions:-

1. To study various factors having bearing on police administration both outside and inside the department and make specific recommendations capable of actual implementation. The idea of the study will be directed towards increasing the police operational efficiency.

2. To examine the effectiveness the utility of the present procedures, working methods in the police, equipment and techniques, and suggest ways of optimum utilisation of the existing personnel .

3. To study the court judgements, particularly the High and Supreme Courts and issue guidelines to the investigating officers based on the views and assessment of the High Courts .

4. To collect, classify and maintain proper records, of all information and literature of police interest and maintain liaison, with other similar or Non Governmental Organisations in the country so that the benefit of innovations in one place is passed on to the others in the country.

4

IMPROVING THE POLICE

Corruption in Police

Corruption and illegal gratification have become a very favourite topic for the public and the media. Every morning this subject, has been hitting the headlines, in the newspapers as well as being discussed in the Parliament. Corruption cannot exist, without co-operation, between the giver and the taker. Nobody will complain, when both the giver and the taker benefit. It is only in cases, where the pocket of a person is directly picked, without any corresponding benefit, to him, that complaints are made. The other cases, where the complaints arise are, if any particular person is forced, to part with something, against his wishes. There are many instances, where individuals are corrupted, without giving it the name of bribes. First they are tempted with smaller gifts, then gifts turn larger and this continues till the receiver begins to relish them.

Another form of corruption is underselling. Whereby a seller with the intention of benefiting somebody, charges almost negligible cost. It is one way of acquiring goods, for which otherwise, an unaffordable fortune, may be required to be spent. The reverse way is also prevalent whereby the seller gives more than what the purchaser, may get in the ordinary course—another recourse taken for indirect favours. One reason for the corruption is, an environment, where low wages and high cost of living co-exist with vast opportunities to make a fast buck. What is the reason for this widespread malady? And who is responsible for it? It is a fact, that we get the government, we deserve. This is particularly so, when it comes to eradicating corruption. It is impossible to fight this scourge, without public cooperation. There is a great reluctance, on the part of the people, to get themselves, involved in any court case. Whenever I have questioned and talked to the people, about their cooperation, in eradicating corruption or other evils, they reply, that this is the responsibility, of the government.

I was once, talking to a very senior police officer about corruption. He observed that the police should get witnesses, from the government departments, so that, they do not turn hostile later on. In one case, a transport minister of a State Government, got complaints about the receipt of bribes at the police outposts. He sought help from the complainant to trap the guilty. The Minister got reply from him, that he would be happy, if the Minister gave him a letter, saying, that the truck belonged to a friend of his and he should not be harassed. The complainant also said that by getting person trapped, he would make permanent enemies, in the transport department, who would pursue him, till his ruin. The Minister refused his request, not on the moral grounds but because he apprehended that the letter of recommendation from him would lead to questions in the Assembly. In any village or town, if ten or twenty young men could start a movement to end corruption, there is a strong possibility of keeping this malaise in check. The problem lies in the question of who will bell the cat? In cases of collusive corruption where both the giver and taker benefit, only the state can be the complainant. Corruption has been existing all the time. It may not be possible to eradicate totally, in one shot. But there should be no slackening of efforts to keep it under check. The remedy is an enlightened public, which should raise a howl, at the malpractices, and bowl out such elements, at the time of elections. The public spirited people, should expose it, as often as something comes to their notice.

At the same time, in the government, there should be simplification of procedures, leading to transparency and openness. For instance, decisions on the representation for economic policies could be taken openly, after public hearing of the issues. The decisions on applications of public, are taken in secrecy. A friend mentioned to me, that his work will come to stand still, if he did not keep almost everybody, in the Government, happy, contented and well greased. This includes the entire staff, right from the peon, for promptly taking his visiting card, inside to the boss, to the despatch clerk, who despatches official communication to his office. Whereas the lower subordinates are happy with the retainer amount starting from Rs. 500 to 3000, the higher ups are to be entertained in five star hotels or for shopping. This also includes shopping abroad. The businessmen do not regard it as corruption, but legitimate business promotion. Only when the rates, are raised too high, for kickbacks, it pinches. Very rarely any businessman makes complaints, as he passes on, the cost, to the consumers or his customers. The only way to cut corruption out is to have minimal rules.

The Remedy

The simplicity of rules and trusting the citizens, would go a long way, in maintaining purity, in the administration. It is a fact, that sometime rules and regulations, are so complicated, that it is only the experts, who can fill up various forms for applications. For export or import more than 100 documents has to be filled up during the period of the 1970's onwards. I doubt it very much, even now, if anybody can fill up, his own income tax form, without any expert's help. The bureaucracy in our country believes in making simple matters complicated. The result is, that common man, is left at the mercy of a few who prey upon him for any conceivable excuse or pretext. The remedy lies, in an enlightened and a vigilant public, a simple set of rules and regulations, responsive bureaucracy, open decision making process, and an accessible political executive dedicated to the task of a clean administration.

What can be done to Improve the Police

The policemen are never around when you need them most. The average citizen does not feel safe, going out late in the night from his house, or a citizen does not wish to go to a police station, for lodging complaint even in genuine cases. It reflects a state of affairs of contemporary policing in the country. The average citizen definitely expects more from the police than what he is getting now. The question as to what should be done and how it should be done provides the basis of all reforms. There is no doubt that changes are required, but how, when and what are the best methods, for determining the same, are the questions we have to pose ourselves. Changes do not necessarily come from within the departmental officials, but they can be imposed, by the elected leaders of the people, as suggested by the academic world. Many a time the suggestions for the change, no matter from what quarter they come are unrealistic, both from the practical point of view as well as the cost.

However, the sole objective of these efforts is to improve the police efficiency and to enable them to render best service to the citizens. There is no doubt about the objectives, but at present, it is a question of defining, what the citizen and the government expects from the police and how the police should go about its business, in rendering the same. The establishment of the police is evidently the recognition, by the society for the need of order. Police force thus becomes a part of the society, charged with the specific responsibility of maintaining peace and order. Requisite powers and authority is given to the police in order to maintain order in society. The police differs from an ordinary citizen, as it is their full time duty to see that the law is upheld and peace and order maintained.

Principles and Requirements for Efficient Police

The President's Commission (American President's Commission) observed in 1967:

"The quality of police services will not significantly improve, until higher educational requirements, are established for its personnel. The complexity of the police task, is as great as that of any profession. The performance of this task requires, more than physical process and common sense. Sworn personnel who, in various unpredictable situations, are required to make difficult judgements, should posses a sound knowledge of society and human behaviour. This can best be obtained through advanced education. The ultimate goal is that all personnel with general enforcement powers have Baccalaureate degrees."

Robert Peel, the Home Secretary of England was farsighted enough even in the nineteenth century to give a solution to the crime problem. The fundamental that guided him in the creation of the modern British Police Force have come to be known as Peel's Principles and are as valid today as when they are enunciated.

The principles are as follows:-

(i) The police must be stable, efficient and militarily organized under the government control.

(ii) The absence of crime will best prove the efficiency of the police.

(iii) Crime-news must be widely distributed.

(iv) Territorial distribution of the force by hours and shifts must be accomplished.

(v) No quality is more indispensable to an officer, than a perfect command of temper; a quite determined manner has more effect than violent action.

(vi) Good appearance commands respect.

(vii) Proper securing and training of personnel lies at the root of police efficiency.

(viii) Public safety requires that every policeman must be given a number.

(ix) Police headquarters should be centrally located and easily accessible to all the people.

(x) Policeman should be appointed on probation basis.

(xi) Police records are necessary for the correct distribution of police strength.

(xii) The best way to select men is to 'Size them up' and then find out what their neighbours think of them.

Based on the above principles, the British police which was created as a result of the passing of the Metropolitan Police Act of 1829, has become the model police for the world and the above principles are as valid for Indian police as when they were enunciated.

Our efforts in India are to be directed in the same direction in moulding the Indian police. It is relevant to quote here the observations of former Commissioner of Police, London, Sir Robert Mark who observed: "The Police is the best reflection of a society. If the society is tolerant, literate, human, the police will act accordingly."

Pandit Jawaharlal Nehru, the first Prime Minister of India had observed: "A strong army and efficient police, are likely to do more for Indian self-esteem and independence than any result that could possibly emerge from planning. The major problem in India is that of development, we must never lose sight of this objective. The army and police only provide the background because they create the condition in which that development is possible. In India there is a hangover of old days when the police was distrusted and considered as something apart from the citizen. This may be the attitude of suspicion, which has influenced the pattern of national planning in which the police does not fit in. All the countries hold strong views on the fact that a strong and efficient police service is necessary for the well-being of the community to a greater degree than another public service in peace time".

There cannot be any peace stability and development, in the society without proper law and order. It is only in a peaceful atmosphere that development, and progress of the country is possible. Cooperation between the police and the people is essential for an efficient criminal administration system in the country. The police perform many of their duties at great personal risk to themselves.

Role of the Central Government

Though under the Constitution, law and order is a state subject, the fact remains that Central Government has a very vital role to play in the same and in actual practice, the State Governments carry on the routine police work. In fact, in all major troubles and outbreaks of violence it is the Central Government which steps in with men and material to aid the states.

Since independence, the Central Government has taken up more and more responsibilities in assisting the State Governments for policing the country by creating new Central Police Organisations and by activating the old existing organisations like the Intelligence Bureau. The organisations created or strengthened since independence include the Border Security Force, the Central Reserve Police Force, the Railway Protection Force, the Central Industrial Security Force, the Indo-Tibetan Border Police, the Assam Rifles, the Central Bureau of Investigation (CBI), the Intelligence Bureau (I.B.). The other organisations under the control of central Government for assisting the states in the investigation of crime are: Central Forensic Institutes, Serologist to the Government of India, the Central Finger Print Bureau, the Master of Mints, the Examiner of Questioned Documents, the Master Indian Security Printing, the Inspector of Explosives, etc.

Another police power rested with the Central Government is the appointment of the IPS (Indian Police Services) officers. The Central Government determines the service conditions and appointments of the IPS officers and the cadre strength of various states. The State Governments cannot alter the service conditions of the IPS officers to their disadvantage. Another important police power of the Central Government is the grant of Police and National awards and supply and provisioning of arms and ammunition, wireless and vehicles to the police under various schemes. The Central Government also gives loans to the State Governments for the Police Housing Schemes of the States.

Besides, the Central Government through the Parliament is the sole authority to amend the basic police laws and Acts and the procedures in the country like the Indian Penal Code. The other important enactments coming exclusively under the purview of the Central Government are: The Arms Act, the Explosive Act, the Extradition Act, the Passport Act and other similar subjects, like the Essential Commodities Act. The administration of the police is intimately connected to the state work and the Central Legislation has primacy over the State Legislation, if any state chooses to enact the same.

Thus, the role of the Central Government in the maintenance of law and order and proper policing in the states is that of an active partner and not that of a passive spectator. In fact, when something goes wrong in the country in any sphere, people look up to the Central Government to set it right. The recommendations of the National Police Commission too tilt towards this centralisation. Since the Central Government has been playing a very vital role, in the policing of the country, it is desirable, as recommended by the National Police Commission, to have a committee to evaluate the police performance.

Monitoring and Evaluation of the Police

At present there is no evaluation of the police performance, in a state, except in the Annual Report of the Police Department. Some kind of a state committee, ideally of the state legislature, should periodically look into police functioning, and satisfy itself that the money spent on the police from the public exchequer, is well spent and procedural or other legal difficulties are rectified, wherever required. The suggestion of the National Police Commission to have a body both at the Central and State level on the pattern of the Law Commission to constantly monitor the legal difficulties and handicaps and suggest ways and means for remedying the same is essential to delete the unpractical laws and to remove bottlenecks and difficulties in the implementation of the others. This body could also serve as the brain trust of the police department and as well as the sounding board of new ideas. As on 31st December, 1999 over 3.2 crore of cases were pending in various courts. There is an urgent and dire need for the simplification of laws and judicial reforms to clear this heavy backlog, which is increasing day by day.

At present, the affluent can get away, with any crime by indulging in lengthy legal wrangles and procedures. They prolong the cases by appeals after appeals, not only during their lifetime but even going on to the next generation. It is time that something was done in this direction, else our democracy is likely to crumble, under the weight of crimes and criminals, who can get away, by taking advantage of the existing legal system in the country. The British Home office working group on training has laid down:

"All members of the Police Service, must be able to show, by their actions and attitudes that they are aware of the major sociological forces, which influence our way of life."

In fact, the *British Police Review* of 10th November, 1972 observed: "We may not yet be a unanimous nation of thieves, but we are plainly on the way." In the *Police Review* a British Policemen wrote for his colleagues and the next generation, "you are serving a society which in the main regards loyalty and patriotism as alien words.... a community wallowing in a sordid mass of crime and incredible greed." Those are the observations of the police about the perception of society about themselves and policing and how they sound like the observations about the Indian society. In fact, another British Police Officer, Superintendent Hung wrote as follows in *Police Review* of 6th April, 1973:

"There are conflicting interests, of groups in society, but no clear right and wrong. Examples may be drawn from the files of public order. So called freedom of speech, freedom to demonstration and protest are highly treasured. At the same time the small groups, recurrently annoy and inconvenience, much larger groups, who ask nothing more, than to be allowed, to go about their living in peace. A similar conflict is involved in strike pickets. In modern society there are many currents of opinion, sometimes converging, sometimes conflicting, there is strong support for liberalization of the laws controlling pornography. In all these situations like police action or inaction is bound to alienate a section of the public."

F. Roy Lewis in *A Force for the Future* wrote about the role of the police in the next ten years: "This is more common when the law is unclear and no majority view entrenched in the tradition. Against what are called 'consensus' crimes—murder, robbery, child molestation, and so on. The police can rely on cooperation, even in ulster. But the public consider a good many laws, to be something of a gamble, involving no reproach, or shame, if one is unlucky enough to be pinched. There is healthy aspect to this morality without it the people would be steeped in a growing sense of guilt. After every prosecution for a relatively minor crime, the police claim to lose three classes of former friends. They lose of course the accused: 'Why pick on me. Everybody is doing it. It is officious, malicious, unfair of the police.' They loose the victim: 'Why did you not prevent it. Why are you never around when you are really wanted. Getting him fined does not help me and besides, the lawyers have twisted it into a completely different case.' And they loose the witnesses. 'What an informal futile waste of time be sure I will not get involved again.'

The Strength of the Police

It is a well known fact that the strength of the police is subject to various factors like the state of the law, and the courts and post trial procedures. These are basically the prime determinants of the capacity of any given number of policemen in dealing with the crime.

The Indian Police also face the same handicaps, which the British do despite its excellent records of centuries, has not been able to overcome. At present, there are a number of Central Police Organisations, headed by the officers equal in status and pay to the secretaries to the Government of India or the Chief Secretaries to the State Governments. There is now a greater need than before for setting up of a coordination body of the Chiefs of Police, so that the development is uniform between the various police organisations and coordination problems are sorted out. In fact, a study team of the Administrative Reforms Commission, as early as in 1970, had recommended the constitution, of a Central Police Advisory Board. It is time that this recommendation was revived and implemented.

It is pertinent to quote Field Marshal Montgomery, who said in his memoirs:

"The raw material with which the General has to deal is men. The same is true in civil life. Managers of large industrial concerns have not always seemed to me to have understood this point. They think their raw material is iron ore, or cotton, or rubber, not men, but commodities, In conversation with them, I have disagreed and insisted that their basic raw material is men. Many Generals have also not fully grasped this vital matter, nor understood its full implication and that is one reason why some have failed.

I have always held the view that any army is not merely a collection of individuals with so many tanks, guns, machine guns, etc, and that the strength of the army is not just the total of all these things added together. The real strength of an army is, and must be far greater than the sum total of its parts, that extra strength is provided by morale, fighting spirit, mutual confidence, between the leaders and the led and especially with the high command, the quality of comradeship, and many other intangible spiritual qualities."

The raw material entering the police is equally important for doing its duties well. The persons entering the police are its assets and in the words of Edgar Hoover, Former Director of FBI: "No one is compelled to choose the profession of a police officer, but having chosen it, every one is obliged to perform its duties and live up to the high standards of its requirements. Compromise, personal feelings, animosities and prejudices have no place in professional police service. Honesty and integrity must ride in every cruiser, walk every beat, influence every command and answer every roll call. Good ethics must be in evidence, whenever and wherever duty calls, every minute of every day."

Presidential Commission on Law Enforcement and Administration of Justice set up by President Lyndon Johnson observed, "Crime does not look same, on the street, as it does in the Legislative Chamber. Many times a police officer has to act in difficult and fast moving situations and sometimes even a mild handling of situation, can bring about calamitous consequences. However, the efforts of the police should be never to abuse or sacrifice the use of his best judgement of discretion."

Accountability of the Police

It is also essential that police, should be accountable, for its actions. The National Police Commission said about it as follows: "Our experience in the preceding decades, (after independence), has shown that a constitutional system of government, based on democratic principles, cannot function without the support of an effective, efficient and accountable administration. Constitutionally, the political executive, i.e., the minister has been made accountable, for the performance of executive, under him. We feel, that such undiluted ministerial responsibility, is not, in the interest of either administrative efficiency or the people, sought to be served by the administration in the present conditions.

Responsibility of the political executive, or the cabinet in the Assembly, is too broad to afford relief, to the people, who have no access to the channels of power. It is, therefore, essential that the accountability of the bureaucratic executive at the various levels be defined and a degree of immediate proximity, to the people be introduced. The concept of anonymity of the bureaucratic executive cannot wish away the necessity for fixing his accountability, for the performance of his duties. While the above is true for the entire administrative machinery, it has an extra significance for the police organisation, which is entrusted with the task of preservation, of basic order in society which is essential for the stability of a Constitutional Government. Unlike the other executive wings of the Government, the police has maximum visibility. Visibility by itself waters down anonymity. The accountability of the police has to be viewed in this light.

Accountability means answerability, for the proper performance, of the assigned job. It means, not only the responsibility, to discharge duties, but also the satisfaction of the party for whose benefit the duties are being discharged. In a democratic society, each department including the police is ultimately accountable, for its performance, to the people. However, direct accountability, to the people in a society like ours, may prove difficult.

The Ministerial Responsibility

It has, therefore, been constitutionally laid down, that the public service is accountable to the elected representatives of the people through forums of Parliament and State Legislatures. In the modern world, ministerial responsibility of this kind, waters down the administrative efficiency and fails to provide the necessary satisfaction to the people. At present the concept of total anonymity, of the bureaucratic executive, and an undiluted ministerial responsibility, to the people, has resulted in distortions affecting police efficiency, and citizen's satisfaction. Unfortunately, therefore, the concept of ministerial responsibility has given the wrong impression to the political executive that they are authorised, to guide and intervene in all functions, of the police in all areas, regardless of such guidance or intervention being in accordance with, or in contravention of the law of the land. It is ultimately the people, who agents the police functionaries, and to whom they are ultimately accountable.

The process of police accountability, to the people, has suffered considerable distortion, in the recent past. Various pressure and elite groups, have come to develop in society having infinite expectations, from all government departments, including the police and seeking favours to the exclusion of legality and fair play. These are the members of the State and Central

Legislatures, the local bodies, important functionaries of the political parties, particularly the ruling ones, representatives of the local yellow press, other important persons of the locality and government servants holding important positions, who have desired, to divert the police accountability from the people to themselves. Police functionaries, therefore, also have tended, to shift their priorities to these pressure groups. This had obvious effect on the attitude of the common people themselves, who feel that the public services, including the police services, are meant to serve only the elitist group and in case they wish to avail any public service, they have to purchase it through illegal gratification, or secure exercise of pressure from power wielding sections of the society. Another distortion noticed is preferential attention of the police, to the urban areas, at the cost of rural areas. Since the urban population, is more vocal and more demanding, the police services have tended to neglect rural population. The rural areas are neglected except for completing the rituals of supervision and inspection. Therefore, the police appears to be out of touch with the problems and difficulties facing the vast majority of the people residing in the villages."

The Annual Administration Reports of the State Police performance is not enough for an objective assessment. It is based on statistics which, as we have more than once observed in our previous reports, are unreliable on account of the fact that there is considerable burking of crime. Further the Annual Administration Reports generally project only a quantitative assessment. It is not possible to have an accurate idea of the qualitative satisfaction of people from such reports. About the prevailing position in India, the National Police Commission said that their assessment is the same. The commission quoted Professor David H. Balyey as under: "In India today, a dual system of criminal justice has grown up, the one of the law and other of politics. With respect atleast to the police, decisions made by the police officials, about the application of law, are frequently subject to partisan review or direction by the elected representatives. The autonomy of the police officials, in specific and routine application, of law has been severally curtailed. This is not only true to law and order situations. People accused of crimes, have got into the habit, of appealing to political figures for remission from the sanctions of law. People officials, throughout India, have grown accustomed to calculating the likely political effect, of any enforcement action, they contemplate. Fearing for their careers and especially their postings, they have become anxious and cynical. But everywhere officers are expected to be held personally accountable by the politicians, even more than by superior officers, for enforcement action taken in the course of duty. Altogether, then the rule of law in modern India, the frame upon which justice hangs has been undermined by the rules of politics. Supervision in the name of democracy has eroded the foundations upon which the impartiality depends in a criminal justice system."

About the departmental accountability, it has been advised that a functionary in the department, at a particular level, should be held accountable only, with respect to functions and duties assigned to him. Conversely the accountability should not extend to duties over which, he has no direct control. Such duties and functions are assigned, to police officers at various levels, from time to time, by virtue of various laws and departmental rules. Great damage has been done by not taking note of this important principle and holding functionaries at each level, (e.g. SP, DIG and IG or DG) responsible for everything happening throughout their jurisdiction. To elaborate our point, the IG, or DG is responsible for generally maintaining integrity and morale of the force, personnel management, including the training of the personnel, etc. But he cannot be held responsible for each isolated incident, in a particular district, unless it is proved, that the particular incident occurred, because of some acts of omission or commission, on the part of the chief of the police, or such incidents have been widespread, and the latter has failed to react adequately. In a similar manner, it would be wrong to hold the SP or the SHO, accountable for each isolated incident, in their respective jurisdiction.

One of the Commission set up by the Government in 1977 observed: "Employing the police, to the advantage of any political party, is a sure source of subverting, the rule of law. The Government must not only seriously consider, but implement insulating the police from the politics of the country and employing it scrupulously on duties, for which alone it is by law intended." About policemen's apprehensions, of not yielding to the political pressures, imaginary fear of possible and probable consequences, for doing the right things, have done more harm than the known consequences, that actually may have followed, the performances of duties, on the right lines, by the government servants. In the final analysis, our country will be governed well or ill, by the competence and character of Government Officers. If they are content to be mere tools, and willing to lend themselves questionable objectives, there will never be dearth of unscrupulous operators. There is no substitute for a vigilant enquiring and enlightened public opinion, which keeps a close watch on the workings of the public servants. (Shah Commission of Enquiry, 26 April, 1978)

The above observations are as valid today as they were made almost twenty-five years back. It can be said with certainty that the amount of security and safety provided to the citizens will depend on the quality of the police officials. The quality of officers, naturally depends on the training, imparted to them. The scenario of the training is not a happy one. The Police Committee on training observed that "they visited a number of police training establishments in different parts of the country and our considered view is that police training, except in some of the Central Police Organisations, is currently in a state of general neglect. The training arrangements in the different States, are unsatisfactory qualitatively, as well as quantitatively. The number of police training institutions is inadequate to meet the needs of an expanding organisation. The strength of the force has increased substantially in every state, but the facilities available in institutions, have not kept pace, with this increase and in many cases, the duration of the training programme has been curtailed, to make it possible, to organise more than one course in a year. Even the buildings, which house many of these institutions, and the state of their maintenance and repair, are unworthy of a major organisation, of the government entrusted with vital functions. The most important reason for this situation of general neglect, seems to be the lack, of a genuine conviction about the value of training, on the part of the administration, including the upper ranks of the police service.

In recent years, law and order duties have tended to form the major part of police work, in most states. Harassed police officials, who are pressed for time, and are perennially short of men, use up their district pools as well as their training reserves. They are unwilling, to spare their men, for training except for the shortest of courses. In such an atmosphere, training has become a ritual, where new recruits, have to be put through a programme, which is sometimes shortened to half, or even less, of its normal duration, and where unwilling, and ill-equipped instructors, perform the necessary rites, of drilling and lecturing. So for bettering the quality of police functioning for the police of 21st century, the government and the police leaders will have to devise ways and means of making the training effective and attuned to meeting the challenges and needs of the people".

Grievances Against the Police

The following are the grievances of the people against the police. They are not without basis and have a ring of truth about them.

(i) They indulge in favouritism, do selective enforcement of laws. They function only when the influential or powerful people are involved.

(ii) The police are discourteous and use abusive languages, even to the persons who are aggrieved. The result is that even honest citizens avoid doing any thing for the law enforcement agencies. They avoid approaching the police even for genuine grievances.

(iii) The complaints of the poor, and uninfluential citizens, are not even taken cognisance of by the police. In this way, the redress of grievances, for the common man, at the hands of the police is next to impossible.

(iv) Police themselves do not comply with the laws. They do not discharge their duties as enjoined by law. and thus, bring law into ridicule. They also fabricate evidence, make out false cases against the public. They indulge in illegal methods, like the use of the third degree, beating, torturing, wrongful confinement, and detention of the people.

(v) The police are corrupt. It is impossible to move them to act even in genuine cases. It is easy for the rich to purchase the police inaction in cases, where the police should legitimately function as required by the laws of the land. People, do not trust police, to do the right.

The Government and the police leaders need to take into account complaints of the public more seriously, than they have done in the past. They should ensure that the police department's growth is not only in size, dimension and importance, but also , in its response to the grievance of the people. There is also a need to root out lethargy, indiscipline and incompetence from the department. A well informed and enlightened public, is the best guarantee for a responsive administration. It is time that police educate the citizens, as to what is expected of them, and what they can expect from them. Another point worth considering is to have viable small units, rather than unwieldy big units. This applies as much, to the police stations, as well as to the massive police organisation, having a strength running into hundreds of thousands. The massive increase in the strength of the para military organisations like CRPF and BSF and big states like UP, have posed serious problems of management. It also affects adversely the rapport of top officials with their men and their commanding officers. It has been observed, that in the giant sized organisations, the top man does not even know half of his officers personally. He may be able to recognise only a small number of them. It would just not be possible for any Director General to visit all the units of his organisation, if its size is unwieldy and too large.

The small units and manageable manpower, are more effective, in dealing with serious situations. Sometimes para military forces are deployed for dealing with law and order situations. A para miltary armed policeman, is not a police man, appointed under the Police Act. He is not vested, with any police powers, under the laws of the land or the police regulations. He is simply a soldier in uniform. The desirability of small and viable police units, needs to be explored both at the police station levels as well as at higher levels. It should also be considered whether there should be more than one police district at least in bigger states, that is to say that the states could be divided into two or three regions with separate Director General of Police. Presently, there is a tendency to create posts of Additional Officers like the Additional SHO, Additional Superintendents of Police, Additional Deputy Inspectors General of Police, Additional Director General of Police or Special Directors. It will be more desirable to create additional units, than create posts of additional officers. Many a time the officers so posted feel suffocated that they are never given full authority or responsibility. This leaves them in limbo. Quite often, government use this as a device to penalise upright or non compliant officers.

More than anything else, it is time that police officials, from the lowest to the highest concentrated on acquiring a slant of professionalism in the discharge of their duties. It should be amply clear to the meanest intelligence, that for improving the police image there is no substitute for performance. Sir Robert Mark, the former Commissioner of Police, London, once observed:

"The Police is the best reflection of a society. If the society is violent, so are the police, if the society is corrupt, so are the police, but if the society is tolerant, literate, human, the police will act accordingly."

My personal experience of working in the Central Para-Military Organisations, has been that the top man does not even know half of his officers. He may be able, to recognise only a small majority of them. It has, just not been possible, for any Director General of most Central Police Organisations, to visit all the units of his organisation even in a three to five years tenure. Small units and manageable manpower are more effective in dealing with serious situations, rather than large unwieldy organisations. An armed policeman, belonging to a Central Police Organisation or even the Defence services has neither any police powers under the laws of the land or knowledge of the police regulations. He is simply a soldier in uniform.

At present there is a tendency to create posts of additional officers like the Additional Superintendents of Police, Additional Deputy Inspectors Generals of Police and Additional Directors General of Police. It needs to be considered whether it will be desirable to create posts of Additional Officers. Many a time the officers posted to the additional posts so created have observed and felt that they cannot give their best in such situations, because, however, high their positions might be, they are never given full authority or responsibility and a feeling of dependence does remain in such charges. This is a trend set in all Government departments and needs to be curbed.

There is no doubt that the credibility and dependability of the police is at the lowest ebb. There is big gap between public expectation and the police performance. The common citizen takes the help of the police as the last resort. He fears the police, whereas criminals not only violate the law of the land with impunity, but also get elected to the law making bodies and hold the reign of the Government. The system still functions in colonial mould, to sustain the Government of the day in power. There is no doubt that it needs to be revamped, so that it becomes public friendly and effective in dealing with the crimes and criminals.

It is necessary that the existing weaknesses in the police are set right. One of the first Acts regulating the working of the police is the Madras District Police Act, 1859, which is still applicable in Tamil Nadu as well as in the Andhra area of Andhra Pradesh. This was immediately followed by the Indian Police Act of 1861. This Act is in force in all Union Territories and various other State Police Acts also, by and large, have followed the same provisions. The Calcutta Police Act and the Bombay Police Act followed in 1866 and 1869 respectively, and are still in operation.

Weaknesses of the Police

The major weaknesses of the police are:

The Police is not fair and impartial, in its dealing with the public in its attitudes, behaviour mind-set and investigation of crimes. The general impression among the public is that, it only takes care of the interests of the political and social elite. It is also believed that it is a tool subject to the manipulation by the party in power; There is also a feeling of prevalance of rampant corruption at various levels in the department and no case is ever registered without pressure or recommendations.

The Police Version of the Problems Faced

The police feel that they face some handicaps hence they do not come upto the expectations of the public for the following reasons. The handicaps include the distrust of the law in the police. The confessions, even to police officers are not admissible as evidence. There is no evidentiary value of a statement made before a police officer, irrespective of his rank. The police in developed countries, on the contrary are not distrusted. Terrorism is a major problem for the country. It has come on the centre stage of the country. There is no Central Law to fight terrorism and organised crime. The final outcome of any crime depends on the prosecution. Prosecution has become independent after 1973;

The Police are answerable to a multiplicity of agencies like the District Magistrates, Union Home Ministries, Administrators and various National Commissions. Other problems include the low morale due to low pay scales, harsh working conditions, very poor housing facilities and lack of public co-operation and delay in the disposal of the cases. The police feel that reform should be towards making more stringent laws and giving the police more powers and more resources. The police officials also strongly feel that there must be a check on arbitrary postings and transfers of police personnel. There must be a fixed tenure for all key players running the department. The general public feel that the police cannot be trusted. They should change their attitudes, behaviour and mind-set so that the public could trust them not to misbehave or come under the influence of the rich and powerful. They feel that at present the police cannot be trusted with any more powers, as it will add to the misery of the people.

It is a fact that the police officers are exposed to undesirable and unwarranted interference in postings and transfers, if they do not oblige people in powerful positions. Due to political interference, the command and control structure has totally collapsed in some States, the performance of police forces in other States has been much better. The attitudes and performance of the police force depends, to a great extent, on proper recruitment, need based training, interaction, support of the public, motivation, high morale of the force, and most importantantly, the leadership in the police department. However, all these facts are rendered meaningless unless the political leadership lends a helping hand in the State. Changes in the legal and organisational set up, which was created in by the Police Act of 1861, are badly required. Other factors which have affected the force are: slip-shod recommendations based recruitment in the force, improper management of manpower, lack of career planning, lack of appropriate training at all levels, both at induction or in-service, blocked avenues for promotion, lack of resources, sub-human living conditions, lack of prompt appreciation of work, and faith in numbers rather than on quality, faith in display of force and visibility to control law and order situations, have led to the present state of the Indian police. Quality has not been up to the mark, due to several factors.

Reasons for Poor Quality of Policing: The Detractors

A lot of duties, other than policing duties, have been passed on the police and naturally it affects their efficiency and detracts them from their main job of fighting crime. These duties include, deployment of police for conducting examinations, deployment of police at mega private events, like film shows and premieres, which are not really in the public domain, entrusting responsibility of a large variety of social legislation's to the police, responsibilities under the Forest Act, Wildlife Act, Child Marriages Act, Offences under the Excise Act, etc. The Police should be left to do their duties, of keeping the peace and order and the concerned departments should enforce the relevant Acts, or that private security agencies should be deployed for certain mega events organised by private organisers. However, the police needs to be relieved from some routine duties, which could be entrusted to concerned departments, though the police cannot and should not wash off its hands from all activities, which will have some relationship or cause a law and order or a crime situation. This is one way of bringing police and public together, and win their confidence, trust and co-operation. The role of police is bound to be expanding. The police should not shy away from undertaking any assignment expected of them by the society. However, the resources made available to the police, should be suitably enhanced to match the increased responsibilities entrusted to them.

A Few Suggestions

The police in India is recruited, trained and equipped for maintenance of law and order. The problem facing the country and the internal security are extremely challenging. A normal policeman, is not trained, to confront the problems of internal security. It would be only wise, if the present day challenges to the internal security, especially posed by Pakistan extremist groups and the religious fundamentalists are also included in the training syllabus of Police. For meeting such challenges, meaningfully and effectively, the society and the country need a highly motivated, professionally trained, infrastructurally self-sufficient and a well equipped police force. This is a paramount national requirement for the maintenance of integrity and sovereignty of the country. The present day policeman does not evoke any respect. He projects a bad and sloppy image of the entire force. The police force generally consists of over 85% constabulary. Opportunities being extremely limited, most of them cannot hope to rise beyond the level they were recruited.

1. There is a need to have more opportunities for them to rise in the force, so that at least 50 percent of them finally retire as Sub-Inspectors. There is a need to go in for more recruitment of Sub-inspectors, from within the force, so that depending upon the qualifications, a constable could hope to go in for being inducted as a sub-inspector within the first five to ten years of his service. Recruitment to constabulary could be restricted, so that it becomes more of an officer oriented force. We need a thinking police man, who can show their mettle in the investigation, intelligence gathering, and in maintaining law and order. The existing constabulary should be re-trained. Every policeman should be put through training every five years. It is more important at the level of constables, so that they imbibe the right attitudes to work. Those who do not successfully complete the training should be weeded out.

2. All promotions should be subject to successfully undergoing and passing the mandatory training programmes. Community policing should be encouraged.

3. The politicisation of police, and the consequential transfers are the undoing of the department. There have been brazen and blatant interference, leading to an average tenure of SPs and SHO's in some States from 15 days to 3-4 months. Misuse of the power of transfers, is freely exercised in many States. SHOs transfers are being ordered by the Chief Ministers/ Ministers in some States. This had led to the line of command in the police force, completely breaking. There is an urgent need to stem the situation. There is a need of a transparent transfer policy, which should be continued irrespective of change in the government. No committees and no laws

can do it. What is required is a political consensus and to play the game of transfers fairly.

4. In our country, due to a number of factors, including caste and communal reasons, maintenance of public order is a high priority job for the police. This leads to neglect of investigation, which is given a low priority. Staff earmarked for investigation, even in states, where there is a separation of crime and law and order gets drafted to do law and order and sundry duties, in an emergency. Such emergencies arise quite frequently. It is desirable to have a separation of investigation and law and order functions, so that the investigation work does not suffer. I had a personal experience of this as Deputy Commissioner of Police, dealing with crime in the city of Bangalore in 1973. I noticed that it was easy for the crime SI to stand on the road for law and order work, than to spend hours together on the painful work of investigation. At the district level, the District Police Chief should have an Additional SP, exclusively dealing with crime and investigation. The Police should be encouraged to use forensic science and aids to the investigation. There should be an encouragement for specialisation, amongst the officers, as well as greater professionalism. More than that their professionalism should be utilised in the channels, in which they might have acquired expertise. The morale of the trained force can be kept high only by proper career planning, and, by inculcating a sense of values amongst the members of the force.

5. There is an urgent need in the changing world, that the Police should have people trained in every area of policing, like prevention of crime, investigation of crime, intelligence, security, traffic, vigilance, etc. For a top class investigation, there is need to develop specialised cells to deal with each of the major crimes, like kidnapping, extortion, murder, car thefts, organised crime, cyber crime, economic crime, etc. The present age of specialisation makes sense to encourage specialisation.

Unless police departments make conscious and serious efforts at specialisation, they would not be able to tackle the emerging sophisticated crime situation.

6. Police have no authority to investigate non-cognisable offences in the India Penal Code. In the absence of powers to investigate, these provisions have almost remained as dead letters in the Statute. But they are misused by some policemen for extorting money and harassing public, as there is a thin margin between cognisable and non-cognisable offences. In some police stations, the police has to interfere in such cases to avoid more serious fracas. There is a need to remove this distinction.

7. In the interest of providing a quicker and effective response to certain offences having inter-state, national and international ramifications, they should be declared as federal offences and the CBI should be the investigation authority. I am aware that this will not be to the liking of the States, as this will amount to their having to shed certain powers. But the national interests and nation should come first and for this purpose, the PM should try to create a political consensus for amendment of the Constitution.

TADA, the law dealing with terrorism has lapsed and there is no special law to deal with terrorism. Terrorism, gangsterism and underworld dons are posing a big threat to the country. A distinction needs to be made between a murder in property dispute and a contract killing. Distinction should be made in the procedures and punishments to be awarded for a murder in a drunken brawl and an explosion caused by a terrorist killing scores of people, like the Bombay blasts of 1992. Both are violations of human rights, but have a feature of their own. We can strongly enforce and recommend, The Human Right Act, as well as equally effective special laws to fight terrorism. Stringent laws do act as strong deterrents, if enforced effectively and fairly. The accountability of police presently is very diffused and vague. Police authorities complain that there are many commissions, which keep on questioning their actions, leaving them hardly any time to concentrate on their job. The fact remains that every executive action or executive authority in a democracy has to be accountable to various statutory and non-statutory bodies, which perform the watchdog duties and act as checks and balances.

These bodies only look into certain limited aspects of police work, when there are complaints that police have been remiss in the discharge of their duties. Everybody, even the Prime Minister and the Chief Ministers are accountable. The police accountability, is the accountability to the head of the department, to the government, who is accountable, to the tax payer for the efficient use of resources placed at the disposal of the police. Tax payers have a right to demand and complain if necessary whether their money spent on the police is giving the required returns and whether the police are upholding the laws of the land and provide satisfaction to the people for whose sake they are supposed to exist and work. The police officers should not be touchy, when they are called upon to assure and explain to the Government and the people at large that they are doing a good job.

Law and order and police are State Subjects under our Constitution. Most recommendations to improve the police have to be accepted and implemented by the State Governments. However, Government of India can always set an example through models for better policing in the Union Territories, under its control.

One good example is worth millions of commissions and committees and communications sent. No State Government is going to say no to improving the police, as where there is a will, there is always a way.

The Union Home Ministry has to set up norms and standards of performance, for the entire country. It has been providing support for training of the IPS officers in establishing data bases for prevention and detection of crimes (NCRB, National Crime Records Bureau). It has been encouraging computerisation and faster communication by having organisations facilitating Police Wire Less Coordination like National Informatic Centre which has also been extending financial support for modernising the State Police Forces. The funding for modernisation currently stands at Rs. 1000 crores per year, and it is likely to go up. Thus, the Government of India is making strides to bring about improvements and innovations in the police force. It is obvious that this alone will not help unless the entire system works in a new gear.

There is a need to have a package of in the criminal justice system, including in the prosecution, as well as in the judiciary, the prison administration and the legal system itself. The public is not only disillusioned with the criminal justice system, including the working of the police departments, but also our legal system and the delay in the disposal of cases. However, most of the criticism for all the ills is levelled at the police department, as it is they who initiate the process. It is essential to overhaul thoroughly all the components of the criminal justice system . A few statistics would reveal dramatically the failure of the system. The disposal percentage of IPC cases by courts (trials completed), which was 30.3% in 1961 declined to almost half, i.e. 15.8% in 1998 this rate had a corresponding decline from 64.8% in 1961 to 37.4% in 1998 this rate is still lower for serious crimes. The government should initiate a comprehensive reform process quickly in consultation with the Chief Justice of India, so that the entire system changes. The new focus should be on the reform of criminal justice administration in the next decade, like the country focused on the economic reform system from 1991. Reform as a lone component of an integral system will not yield the desired results. But it will be better than nothing if at least efforts are started for reforms in the police service. More than anything else, it is of the utmost importance that police officials from the lowest to the highest concentrate on becoming professionally competent in their duties for bettering the police image. Sir Robert Mark, the former Commissioner of police, London, once observed; "The police is the best reflection of a society. If the society is violent so is the police; if the society is corrupt, so is the police, but if the society is tolerant, literate, human, the police will act accordingly."

5

COMMUNAL RIOTS

Communal problems, which occasionally erupt into communal riots have existed for a long time. But at times, the occurrences at some place have not only been prolonged but also shed a lot of blood. The police is blamed, for not handling the situation, well and tactfully. It may be mentioned that the problem of handling communal riots which in a way is a social problem, cannot be set apart from the general state of the administration. It cannot be separated especially from functioning of the police department and its major policies of recruitment, promotions, postings and transfers. The National Police Commission (1977-81) observed: "In some of the case studies undertaken by the National Police Commission, it came out in some detail that in many cases of troubled cities, the police and the magistracy, just withdrew, when anti-social groups indulged in violent crimes. The deployment of Magistrates on such occasions appears to have been reduced to almost a farce."

There is a tendency amongst the officers, to avoid taking responsibility in dealing with the situation. They either avoid going to the trouble spot, or even when they happen to be present there, they do not order the use of force, though the situation may require it. Or they do a shade better, by slipping away from the scene, leaving the force and its junior officers leaderless. This reaction of the officers is a calculated decision on their part, to avoid facing any commission or any inquiry. It is generally not, a reflex action out of cowardice. In view of the difficulties, they may face, later on, they consider it prudent to avoid getting involved in ordering the use of force. It is only those officers, who have taken some action in dealing with the situation who are accused of all sorts of allegations. It is they, who have to face harassment and humiliation in the inquiries that follow. The real villain who allows the situation to deteriorate by not taking firm action, in the initial stage, to control the situation manages to go free, by his inaction. For dealing with the situations, as they arise, it is essential that officers act, on their own, in their best judgement. They should not seek instructions from higher quarters, where none are necessary. A number of commissions of inquiries have gone into the genesis of some of the riots in recent years. They have stressed, again and again, the need for effective and prompt action and contradicting rumours, about communal incidents, as they add fuel, to the riots.

The contradictions of the rumours should be made in such a way that it will generate the confidence of the people in the administration for correcting the situation. An authoritarian demand and pre-emptory command for public for co-operation cannot deliver the results. The law abiding and peaceful citizens will extend cooperation, if the necessary climate is created. The Criminal and Election Laws (Amendment) Act, 1969 contains provisions for controlling and checking of prejudicial publications. In spite of the availability of legal power under this Act for controlling objectionable publications in the Press, very little action or no action under the law is generally taken by the State Governments, to deal with the situations. While no government in a democratic system, should restrict the freedom of the press, the government should not abrogate its functions, if mischievous reporting in the Press is likely to lead to a breach of the public peace. The Criminal Law (Amendment) Act, 1972 (Act No 31) of 1972 introduced a new Section 153-B in the Indian Penal Code. It makes imputations, assertions, etc, prejudicial to national integration, an offence punishable with imprisonment which may extend upto three years or with fine or with both. Thus, legal provisions are available for controlling prejudicial publications and other activities prejudicial to national integration and public order. It is important that in important and sensitive matters, the State Governments and local administration should act impartially. They should use every weapon in their legal armoury, to fight obnoxious propaganda, prejudicial to the maintenance of communal harmony.

The police should have an updated list of anti-social elements in the communally sensitive areas, along with a list of the policemen, who can identify them. Great care should be taken that, in the list no law abiding citizens are included in it, to settle old disputes and controversies. In the event of a riot having occurred, a thorough investigation and successful prosecution of a crime will prevent further riots and crimes. It will further discourage, potential mischief makers in future. A stringent punishment, will act as a prevention for future. It will make the potential criminal realise that crime does not pay. The problem of communal riots cannot be isolated and separated from the general law and order situation and enforcement in a state. A strict and impartial law enforcement on a day to day basis can reduce the chances of a prolonged communal riot. The National Integration Council has suggested that the District Magistrate and Superintendent of Police, should be made personally responsible for prompt action, to prevent and stop communal disturbances. Jagan Mohan Reddy Commission felt that moral and cultural education should be inculcated in the youth, so as to imbibe in them, a sense of toleration and to broaden their outlook. The concept of a secular state is compatible with the moral aspect of religion. The political leaders, should inculcate the idea of oneness, in all sections of the people of India.

The problem of communal strifes must be solved by political and social leaders, as it is they who can initiate action and create conditions and prescribe norms to inculcate that feeling and achieve harmony and make for a better society.

Antoech Commission & Madon Commission felt that:

> "The most effective way, of bringing down a disturbance, which has taken a serious turn, or is about to take a serious turn, is to use firearms. Police firing should never take place in the air, and should not be long delayed. The police should not be afraid of judicial inquiries. The police should open fire, on the most determined part of the mob, keeping their arms low, so as to avoid, taking life, as far as possible. In every case of police firing, the government need not accept, the demand of a judicial or public inquiry."

The long term measures lie, with the social and political leaders, in the country. However, the police on its part has to ensure that all laws must be enforced equally and equitably for all people. There should not be select few, who receive preferential treatment or selected groups or religious denominations, singled out for particularly harsh or unjust treatment.

Dealing with Religious Fracas

Parliamentary democracy is sought to be derailed by mixing politics with religion. As a result, the communalism has moved to the centre stage of national politics. Whether it is Ram-Janam-Bhoomi, Babari Masjid, Muslim personal law or cow-protection, religious conversions with or without foreign influences, all these issues, have the potential of sparkling off communal riots. The fissiparous and divisive forces are out to weaken the national solidarity and sovereignty of the country. The most convenient tool with these forces, is to whip up communal feelings, during a festival. These trends do not auger well, for the unity and integrity of our country. Past experiences suggest, that the communal riots have erupted, mostly coinciding with religious processions. It is of paramount importance, to lay down some guidelines, which could be useful to the District Superintendents of Police, their Circle Officers and others concerned. However, the guidelines can never cater, to all kinds of situations or contingencies.Therefore, these will vary from place to place, time to time and situation to situation.

Policing the Religious Processions

In the past, provocative gestures, have led to serious communal riots. The genesis of the trouble, could be the religious processions, taken out by members of different communities. Policing of religious processions, is of great importance for the maintenance of communal harmony, peace and law and order. The object of policing processions should be (i) to give a sense of security to the processionists, as well as to the general public; (ii) to ensure proper observance of schedules and movement by processionists; (iii) to ensure safe and secure passage of the procession.

These objectives can be achieved, provided police arrangements, are formulated methodically and executed in a planned manner. The police officers and men, should not only be impartial, but should also appear, to be impartial, in their attitudes and actions. This will enable them, to win the confidence, of the members of different communities. A body of men, comprising more than five persons, moving through a public thoroughfare in observance with any religious rite/ritual can be termed as a religious procession. There are various classifications of religious processions.

Classification of Processions

Many processions of Hindus, Muslims, Sikhs, Christians, Jains and Buddhists, are taken out on fixed dates and routes. They are pre-arranged according to the prevalent traditions and customs. These are organized by religious bodies and have more or less fixed timings. These have a definite destination. Prominent examples of religious processions are:-

(i) Processions taken out during Dussehra by Hindus
(ii) Ramnavmi processions
(iii) Janamashtami processions
(iv) Durga Pooja idol immersion processions
(v) Kali Pooja idol immersion processions
(vi) Saraswati Pooja Idol immersion processions
(vii) Ganesh Chaturthi processions
(viii) Holi processions
(ix) Ravidas Jayanti processions
(x) Ambedkar Jayanti processions though it commemorates one of the recent political leaders, but it has acquired a religious nature.
(xi) Processions of Sikh in honour of their Gurus
(xii) Sobha Yatra, Rath Yatra, Jal Yatra, etc.
(xiii) Eid-Milad-un-Nabi procession
(xiv) Moharram processions and their various variations

Occasional Religious Processions

These are not regular annual features. These processions are taken out to commemorate special events for example:

a) installation of new idols in a temple
b) to commemorate centenary of any saint or any religious event;
c) processions taken out during periodical occurrences like Kumbh Mela, etc.

Protest Processions on Religious Issues

Recently a number of processions have been taken out either in protest against alleged atrocities on co-religionists or in support of the cause of their faith, for example: (i) The processions taken out against alleged atrocities on Christians (ii) Processions taken out on the issues of Ram-Janam-Bhumi / Babari Masjid (iii) Funeral processions of assassinated religious leaders, taken out by the deceased co-religionists (iv) The processions to protest against the arrest of Political Leaders.

Reasons for Processions Turning into Riots

These processions, require special police arrangements because of their nature. As the elements of animus already exist, these processions can easily turn, into a violent agitation, leading to riots. They call for, well thought out police arrangements, as otherwise, they can snowball into any law and order situation.

This can take place due to the following reasons:

(i) Irresponsible and emotionally surcharged leadership, may direct the procession, against persons of other faiths, in order to seek revenge, for real or imaginary wrongs.

(ii) Any provocation, either caused by persons within the procession, to persons of other communities, or caused to the processionists, by members of the other communities, like music before the mosques, reciting or singing , throwing of unclean articles like pork, beef that may hurt the religious sentiments of a community, on the procession.

(iii) Change in routes and timings, causing trouble to other communities.

(iv) Coinciding of two processions, of different faiths, or different factions, of the same faith, on the same route.

(v) Passing of the procession, by the side of any *Pandal* or platform, where rituals of other faiths, are being carried out.

(vi) Violation of sanctity of any religious place before the procession is taken out, or during the procession.

(vii) Use of offensive placards, or raising of offensive slogans during the procession.

Police Arrangements to Counter any Eventualities during Processions

The police arrangements should cover: (a) Pre-procession preparations; (b) Arrangements during the processions; and (c) Post procession analysis and appraisal.

Pre-Procession Arrangement

The incharge of the area, should prepare a calendar, which will consist of, all regular, organised traditional religious processions. However, no calendar of occasional or protest processions can be made. These will have to be dealt with, as and when they are taken out.The police officers should prepare calendars, for their own areas. Religious processions vary from place to place and hence no uniform calendar can be prepared for the entire state. This calendar, should be kept under the table top, and displayed prominently in the police station, so that every day, the staff including the official incharge, are able to glance it. This way no procession will be lost sight off. They should be entered in a register, to be called festival register. Before any procession is due, the register should be studied, well in advance, to find out various implications. After perusing the festival register, the routes of procession, should be physically checked by officers, and in cases of important processions, personally by Superintendent of Police, It would be desirable if the concerned Magistrate is also taken along.

The inspection of route should take place, a few days in advance, so that in case any obstruction has come up, the same could be removed. The removal of any obstruction, in close proximity, to the event, is well-neigh impossible. However, if it is done sufficiently in advance, then generally there is least opposition. For example, if a 'Peepal' tree branch which has come up on the route fixed for Tazia procession is cut, during Moharram days, it can create protest from the Hindus. Contrarily, if a *Mahavat* is directed, discreetly to take his elephant, two months in advance, on the spot and get the branch eaten up, by the elephant, it would not create any opposition, and the purpose would be served.

The organisers of processions should be contacted, in advance, so that their plans and programmes, are known for better planning. Personal contact with the organisers, creates a personal rapport between them and the police. It helps in tiding over many delicate situations. Sometimes, especially during Dussehra and Moharram, Akharas participate in the procession, and carry blunt and sharp-edged weapons, without licence. Their licences should be checked. Most of the Akharas do not possess any licence. Sometimes they resist the idea of licence. However, if the organisers are contacted a month in advance, this can be straightened out. Some permanent marking should be affixed to these weapons, so that these are not replaced, at the time of procession.

Valuable assistance can be obtained from voluntary bodies. They should be contacted in advance. Generally Peace Committee meetings, should be held, a few days in advance, of the event. The help of voluntary bodies like Mohalla Defence Committees, Peace Committees or Civil Defence Committees should be enlisted. Details of volunteers, for various sections of processions, should be prepared. There should be an attempt, to create a group of influential and well meaning persons, who can act, as intermediaries, between police and processionists. Any direct intervention of police, can lead to confrontations. Influential persons of the area, specially those belonging, to the same faith, will prove to be very useful.

Many a time, there are elements, which are not directly concerned with the processions but have an important bearing on it for example, idol makers of Durga, Kali,

Ganesh, Saraswati or Tazia-makers. There is a growing tendency of increasing the size of idols or Tazia, every year, by the organisers of the processions, to beat their rivals taking out similar processions. If these people are contacted before the event, they can be briefed, about the clear specifications based on previous year's measurements. They could be requested, to adhere to the same. A fortnight before the installation of the idols, Bazar Band Masters, shop-keepers hiring out loud speakers, float-makers, etc, should be contacted, and told about their expected conduct and role, during the procession.

The police staff duty charts, with clear assignments, of each person, at a specific area or route procession, should be prepared. The staff should be briefed in advance A site plan prepared to a scale, on a hard board, showing sensitive points on the route, tall buildings, traffic intersections, etc, would be very useful and should be prepared for every police station. If possible, sand models, should be prepared. These will be useful for briefing of the men. Video graphing the route will be more helpful. It will make things very clear. Arrangements for traffic diversion should be well thought out and necessary publicity given through newspapers or posters, TV, Radio about the programme. It will help avoiding congestion and inconvenience to the public. The possibility of disturbance, during the procession should be accepted, as a likely risk. Contingency plans must be made to tackle it by; (i) diversion of procession, on to a safer route, in case of major breakout of trouble; (ii) rushing of fire brigade, in case of acts or arson; (iii) abandoning of, the route of processionists, to prevent their committing arson or looting. It has been observed, that many a time, if a just or unjust demand, of the processionists, is not met by the administration, they leave the idols/ Tazias on the route, as protest and leave the procession. This creates a very delicate situation, as any direct attempt by police, to remove them, would invite allegations of sacrilege. In such cases, help of the intermediary and voluntary bodies, should be sought.

The contingency plan should also cater for scotching rumours, isolations, or segregation of troubled areas, taking possession of a large number of cycles, or other vehicles, *chappals* and others articles left behind, at the time of panic or police action. The method for their disposal, can also be planned in advance. Similarly the place of interception of the procession, if required, should also be decided earlier. In the pre-procession stage it should be ensured, that provision of fire brigade, and ambulance for medical cover is made. Similarly weapons to be carried, alongwith ammunition; tear smoke shells, should be circulated in advance. It would be desirable, to have a public address system for directing the procession, or scotching communal rumours, etc. Some policemen, could be provided with loud hailers, while accompanying the procession. Action plan should include, rounding up, in advance of anti-social elements. The complacent attitude of the officers should be discouraged. All developments of interest, must be reported to the senior officers, through the fastest means available. Any attempts of suppression of information should be viewed seriously. Rehearsal, for dealing with any possible riot, should be done, atleast a fortnight in advance. Any rehearsal close to the event, might create panic. The riot equipment boxes should be checked up and brought upto-date. Some help-centres may be set up, on the route of processions, to render medical help, to the old and infirm persons, or those sustaining injuries during the procession. Wherever curfew is proposed, the service of Notices U/S 30 of the Police Act or orders U/S 144 Cr.P.C should be given atleast a week in advance and signatures of organisers must be obtained. Special vigil should be exercised on the anti-social, anti-national and communal elements. Preventive arrests wherever necessary should be made in advance.

The police should become more visible, tone up the routine duties, like checking up hotels, *dharamshalas,* railway stations, bus stations, liquor shops, arms and ammunition dealers, and cinemahalls, etc. However, it should be done very carefully and tactfully. Any highhandedness, during these checking, can prove counter-productive. It may create trouble during the processions. Men should be briefed, in general as well as on the spot. It would be more useful, if the Section Commander/Station Officers are briefed. They should be checked on the spot, to find out, whether they possess full knowledge, about the duties to be performed or not. The men should wear proper shoes, so that their mobility is quick and efficient. They should also be briefed, not to carry any arms, other than the government arms. Men should be briefed, to identify the organisers, and other important functionaries, for a better rapport. Some special tricks can also be devised, in advance, to defuse building up of tension. For example, if a member of the one particular community objects, to cutting of telephone wires while the other community is hesitant to bend the Tazia during procession, the ground should be dug suitably, to facilitate the passage of Tazia, without cutting the wires. Senior officers must brief the policemen; not to nurse, any bias or prejudice, against any community. This will help, in rebutting the allegation, that policemen of one community have shown vengeance, or are guilty of inaction, against another community. The following points must be made known to every policeman on duty:

(i) The background of the procession legends and traditions associated with it.

(ii) Time Schedule;

(iii) Route and sensitive points on the routes;

(iv) Organisers and other personalities connected with the procession;

(v) Elements and developments to be watched carefully;

(vi) Communication available to them, if any telephone is available near their duty points, the same should be known by them, apart from the wireless or cellular phones; and

(vii) Emergency Plans.

For most of the processions, enforcement is required, atleast for sometime in advance. The required reinforcement, should be calculated, so that there is no confusion, before the event and reinforcements are available.

Arrangements during the Procession

The posting of men should be done, atleast one hour in advance, so that they become familiar with the spot. In this way, they can keep a watch, on the movements of people, who form the procession. While checking uptodate information, should be given to men on the spot. During these hours, the policemen and the volunteers would be able to know each other by face and name. This would ensure better cooperation between them. At the head of the procession, besides the regular force, small squads of policemen either with motor Vehicles, motor cycles or cycles or mounted police should be kept. They should function as the alerting teams and precede the procession. They should go, five to seven minutes in advance, altering all the policemen on duty, to stop or divert the traffic and sharpen their vigilance. Special attention should be given to the tail end, of the procession. Generally trouble starts, after the main body of the procession, has passed the sensitive spot. Hence, proper control, over the last portion of procession, needs to be maintained. Wherever feasible, a police officer and magistrate in a vehicle should be in the front, and rear of the procession. During processions there is a tendency among policemen to speak up simultaneously. This jams up the Radio traffic and urgent messages get blocked. Hence, all persons handling Radio equipment should be trained to maintain proper Radio discipline. Other Radio Stations should also observe silence during the procession time. It is not possible to man all the openings on the routes in any city. However, tactical deployment, even on a skeletal basis, can help in sensitive areas, especially on rooftops. Roof top duty should be assigned in pairs. The force posted there should be provided binoculars and wireless sets after training in the use of simple code, or walkie-talkies or flag signalling. For these duties, the best men should be selected. They would be working, as watchmen for the entire force. Use of video cameras, placed strategically, will deter miscreants and also faithfully record the conduct of procession. It would also be useful subsequently, for training, briefing purposes and evidentiary purposes. These Video Cameras, should be located, in such a manner, that various portions of processions, as well as locality, are filmed simultaneously. For large processions, four to six Video Cameras, would suffice. Close Circuit TV, would enable the senior officers, at the control room, to monitor the procession. Open and concealed, use of tape-recorders would also help in deterring irresponsible elements, from indulging in provocative slogan shouting.

The Reserve Force with full proper equipment should be positioned before hand. The officers incharge of various sections of procession should be fully aware, of their positions and strength. Alongwith this reserve force, some local leaders of various communities, should also be collected. In case it is necessary, their services may be utilised, on need basis to control the procession without resorting to the use of force. Otherwise at the time of emergency, precious time would be wasted in searching and locating them. Response time of the reserve force should be fixed. The response time, should also take into account, the likely time to be taken, if the movement is to be done on foot. It would be useful, to carry out mock exercises, for summoning the Reserve Force, to check their efficiency, in arriving at the allocated place.

Arrangements after Dispersal of Procession

Generally after a procession has reached its destination, the policemen think, that their task has been completed. They leave their duty posts, or slacken their vigilance. This has to be guarded against. In fact greater vigilance is required, as persons returning individually, or in small groups, after dispersal of the procession, become more vulnerable, to mischief-mongers. Atleast for one hour after the dispersal, the staff on duty should be alert. If procession is to start or continue in night-time, then proper lighting arrangements should be ensured. Throughout the route, alternate supply of electricity, should be provided to meet the exigency in case of any sabotage or break down of regular electric supply.

Post-Procession Analysis and Appraisal

At present only brief reports are given, and the emphasis is, only on the strength of force, deployed on the occasion. As a result, the complete picture of a procession does not emerge from these entries. The local Intelligence Unit should also maintain a permanent record if possible regarding these processions, in which they should put in their reports. Guidelines for future improvements should also be prepared and kept for future use. A detailed scrutiny of the police arrangements should be carried out to draw lessons for future. It would be better to computerise all the plans, schemes, details of personnel to be deployed and other arrangement

Conclusion-Do's and Don'ts

1. Collect details of plans and programmes of the procession in advance.
2. Collect all information about the elements opposed to the procession and their preparation in this behalf.

3. Identify all possible places, where obstructions to the procession are anticipated.
4. Acquire full knowledge, about existing animus, irritants, between the major communities of the area.
5. Analyse communal incidents, in advance, that resulted in riots, during the religious processions.
6. The route of the procession must be marked in advance.
7. Keep the procession route as small as possible.
8. Keep vigil over the religious publications, declarations, and speeches made on loudspeakers
9. Prepare list of communal elements and their financiers/helpers and keep them under close watch.
10. Deploy the force, according to the size of the procession.
11. Stagger procession, in-groups of 100, or less, to ensure effective control over them.
12. The organisers should be given some identification, discs and their addresses should be noted.
13. Do not permit loudspeakers, alongwith the procession.
14. Do not permit playing of music, before the places of worship.
15. Do not promulgate Section 144 Cr.P.C, if it can not be enforced.
16. Do not allow provocative slogans of one religion, against the other. The orders on this behalf should be promulgated in advance.
17. Do not allow arms which are not required to be carried, with the procession, according to the religious rituals.

18. Do not allow vehicles other than the one carrying idols.
19. Do not allow animals alongwith the procession.
20. Keep a check on persons owning pigeries. Movement of pigs should be kept under effective watch.
21. Cater for long duty hours, by the policemen. Arrangements for food packets/ water stalls, etc, should be made for them.

6

CRIMES AND DEVELOPMENT

Every developing nation has to pay the price of development and one price tag is the increase in crime. Industrialization also gives rise to new economic and political conflicts. Unless there is an anticipation and preparation to meet this kind of situation in a developing society, the tensions are bound to increase leading to a serious situation affecting all sections of society.

The process of change in socio-economic and political order sometimes can give a psychological shock. The price of development has been paid by the countries all over the world and the process of social and economic transformation gets complicated depending upon the period in which it takes place. Change is the immutable law of life and all nations whether they are capitalists or socialists, experience it. The experience of change is contingent on any particular ideology.

In India also there has been transformation, though the process has been painfully slow. Industrialisation in recent times has affected the social structure. One effect of the transformation has been that the principle of institutional legitimacy has been considerably diluted. Expectations of the people have been aroused as a result of change, which is coming over the Indian Polity. Crime faithfully follows the development, though development by itself is not criminogeneric. Development leads to the migration of people from the rural to the urban areas and increase in literacy rates. Mass education makes the common man aware of his rights and an educated man can approach the higher officers for the redress of his grievances effectively.

Another effect of the phenomenon of the urbanisation is the growing impersonalisation in the day to day conduct of human affairs too. Whenever there are riots, the shops and cars are damaged, though their owners have nothing to do with the issue in dispute. Poverty breeds crime and accentuates in this situation. It is the impersonalisation, which helps the crime. Anything which is the symbol of prosperity, becomes the target of attack. Crime is the product of: (1) motivation, and (2) opportunity. Unless these factors aid, no criminal can indulge in any crime. Generally speaking, the crimes are committed in the awareness area of the criminal. For dealing with the crime and criminal and riots situations, the police presence at the flag marches has a limited role, at the best having the effect of a sedative. Any Police Crime Prevention strategy, will have to lay a great stress, on strengthening the police stations both quantitatively and qualitatively.

Criminals and gangsters are not born over-night. They start by committing marginal crimes, like bootlegging and prostitution, unlike serious crimes like murder. In such cases, the *prima facie* victimless nature of the crimes, of marginal category, tends to reduce the involvement of the society. Most of these marginal crimes, are aimed at meeting economic ends. Such criminal acts (the marginal crimes like smuggling, bootlegging, prostitution) provide services and goods which though illegitimate, have a demand. A section of the society, has a vested interest, in such crimes. Enormous discretion is available to the police functionaries at grassroot level in handling such crimes and the senior officers of the police department also do not regard the occurrence of such crime as a threat to the existing set-up and at the best they have only a mildly intolerant attitude of such crimes. Sometimes even the policies behind marginal crimes are not clear. For instance if gambling is immoral, then why are there state run lotteries or race courses which provide a good deal of revenue to the government. Similarly if the consumption of liquor is a health hazard, then why do we have state liquor selling shops.

Thus concepts of social or marginal crime undergo changes due to societal friction, caste considerations and religious frictions.

Reforming the Inadequacies of Police

There cannot be prevalance of peace, stability and development in society without proper law and order. Jawaharlal Nehru observed: "A strong army and efficient police are likely to do more for Indian self esteem and Independence than any result that could possibly come from planning. The major problem in India is that of development, we must never lose sight of that objective. The army and the police only provide the background, because they create the conditions in which that development is possible.... In India there is hangover of old days when the police was distrusted and considered, as something apart from the citizen. This may be the attitude of suspicion, which has influenced the pattern of national planning, in which the police does not fit in. All the countries hold strong and efficient police service, which is necessary for the well being of the community, to a greater degree, than any other public service in peace time".

Is the police coming upto the expectations of the people? Do common people perceive, as to what policemen expect from them and of them? Are the two parties satisfied with each others' performance and whether something more can be done?

No other executive wing of the government has come in for so much criticism as police. Despite the fact that the present police system was given its shape by the colonial rulers, its inadequacies and shortcomings had been the subject matter of intensive debates even then. Mr Dampier, Superintendent of Police for Bengal, which included at that time the present Bangladesh, West Bengal, Assam, Orissa and Bihar had made very pointing observations regarding the state of affairs, way back in 1840, which has been quoted in this book in the beginning.

In fact, the police is only a part of the criminal justice system in the country. It can only take the suspect/ accused before the court of the law and it is for the courts to judge the guilt and award punishment. The gathering of evidence depends only on the cooperation and assistance given by the people. This is a very old problem and it was highlighted as early as in 1830 by the then Governor of Bombay, Sir John Malcom quoted earlier in this book.

Non-cooperation by Citizens

Incidentally, the same laws are operational even now though these observations were made 170 years ago. Now the question arises why people do not cooperate with the criminal justice system in providing the necessary assistance. The police alone cannot deliver the goods unless reforms in all the wings of the criminal justice system, like the Judicial and Prosecution system are effected. The drawbacks in the existing criminal justice system are best explained by a letter written by a District and Sessions Judge, to the National Police Commission who said:

"The biggest single hurdle which inhibits the citizen from coming forward to help the police is the deplorable conditions prevailing in the courts of law. The lot of witnesses appearing on behalf of the State against a criminal is certainly pitiable. More often than not the case in which he is to appear is adjourned on one pretext or the other.

"This is invariably done at the end of the day after keeping the witness waiting for the whole day. While fixing the next date the convenience of all concerned, except the witness is kept in view. If the witness fails to turn up on the next date, coercive steps are taken against him. If he appears on the adjourned date, the chances are that the case will be adjourned again."

"When ultimately the evidence is recorded, the witness is browbeaten by an overzealous defence counsel or declared hostile or unreliable by the prosecution. After undergoing this agonizing experience, the witness is not compensated for the loss of the earning of the day. Even the out of pocket expenses incurred by him are seldom reimbursed."

"The most difficult problem faced by a witness in our courts is the complete lack of any amenity or facility to make the long wait bearable. What to talk of drinking water, and urinals, etc., in most courts, there is no place where a man can sit unless he forgets all about his dignity and squats on the floor of the verandah or under a tree. The sight of people sitting under the blazing sun or in torrential rain is also not so uncommon, as it may seem to be. Chairs and benches for the conveniences of the witnesses are nowhere available.

"It is small wonder then that disinterested persons fight shy of extending a helping hand to the police and only those persons agree to come to its aid who have an axe to grind. A man going to the railway station or a bus stand to catch a train or to board a bus has to spend an hour or so. Yet he demands and gets basic amenities like drinking water, and a place to sit, but a man who has to wait for 5 to 6 hours in a court of law is not provided with any of these facilities.

"The plight of a witness is further aggravated by the fact that he is required to prick up his ears so as not to miss his name being called in a most unceremonious manner by the court usher. A prisoner suffers for some acts of commission but a witness suffers for no fault of his own. All his troubles arise because he was unfortunate enough to be on the spot when the crime was being committed and at the same time "foolish" enough to remain there till the arrival of the police. It is for these reasons that people do not take the victim of a road accident to hospital or come to the help of a lady, whose purse or gold chain is being snatched in front of their eyes. If some person offers help in such cases, he is to appear as a witness in a court and has to suffer not only indignities and inconveniences but also has to spend time and money for doing so. Sometimes the witnesses incur the wrath of hardened criminals and are deprived of their lives or limbs."

Thus, unless reforms are brought about in all the limbs of the criminal justice system, the improvement in one will not be of much consequence. It is for the reformers to take up the challenge and unshackle the system from the past burden of laws, traditions and customs which have outlived their utility in the present age.

7

TERRORISM AND ORGANISED CRIME

Organisation is a fact of life. Every crime has some kind of planning and organisation, behind it, though it may be the handiwork of one man. Even a thief burgling a house, has to plan his crime and escape routes in advance. Terror means extreme fear or governance by intimidation. Among the universally accepted features, are governing, by terror of capital punishment, and the law of private defence, which gives all citizens the right to kill to defend life and property. Dictionary, however, defines terrorism as an organised system of intimidation, especially for narrow political ends. Bank robberies, bombings, kidnappings and hijackings of aircrafts, are all categorised as terrorist acts. Most of these activities are unrelated to any philosophy of revolutionary action. The use of force is legally and morally justified. However, according to provisions of general international law, in the legitimate resistance to oppression and tyranny, acts of terror both governmental and private are prohibited by international human rights documents. The terrorist may be often willing to sacrifice his own life. The terrorist anticipates retaliation from the government forces. Very rarely, he may be naive enough, to think that the government will not strike back.

But a civilised government feels, that they have a responsibility to ensure that both over-reaction and under reaction are avoided in dealing with the terrorist. It is essential that both the officials and public, at large are educated, with the ideas relevant to the positive approach.

The Human Rights Activists feel that no one be encouraged to take a blindly authoritarian view, even while using force against force. The answer to the question, whether terrorism at all poses, a threat to India's body politic, is positively yes, without giving in to any fear psychosis. Whatever happens, the world over, has its repercussions in India and vice-versa. Hence, we have to look at the background in more detail. My intention here is not to justify terrorism, but to try to understand the phenomenon.

Definitions

T. P. Thornation distinguishes between 'enforcement terror' and 'agitational terror'. Enforcement terror is used by those in power and wish to suppress challenges to their authority. The agitational terror is used by the terrorists who wish to disrupt the existing order and ascend to political power themselves. It is the same as 'the regime of terror' and 'the siege of terror'. Terrorism, in short is designed to influence political behaviour by extra-normal means, entailing the use or threat of violence.

Terrorism may achieve political ends by, either mobilising sympathy or by immobilising the forces, of the authorities. But the authorities have the initial advantage because of the inertia, which characterises the normal political relationship between authority and citizenry. There is a distinction between four types of terrorism: criminal, psychic, war, and political terrorism. Political terror are isolated acts, which are neither systematic nor organised. They are often difficult to prevent. Therefore, neither an isolated act, nor a series of random acts, is terrorism. On the other hand, political terrorism, is a sustained policy of organised terror, either on the part of the state, or a movement or faction entailing some organisational structure. There is some kind of theory or ideology of terror, however rudimentary or preposterous, behind the actions. Political terrorism can be revolutionary terrorism, sub-revolutionary terrorism, and repressive terrorism. The first type seeks total change. The second type seeks more limited goals such as forcing the government to change its policy on some issues, punishing specific officials or retaliating against specific government actions. The third type is defined as the systematic use of terroristic acts of violence for the purpose of suppressing groups, individuals, or forms of behaviour deemed to be undesirable by the oppressor. Repressive terrorism was practised by Adolf Hitler's state, in the past. Now, it is the Afghan Taliban, doing the same. Political terrorism can be defined, in one way as the use of threat or use of violence, by an individual or a group, whether acting for or in opposition, to established authority. Their action is designed to create extreme anxiety and/ or fear-inducing effects, in a target group larger than the immediate victims. The purpose is to coerce that group, into acceding to the political demands of the perpetrators. Even when terrorist acts, are apparently directed at killing innocent people, yet terrorism as a deliberate means is to acheive end.

Political Philosophy of Violence

Since the dawn of history man has used violence against his own kind. During the past fifty years, mankind has survived about 1500 armed conflicts all over the world. Theoretical justification for all this violence can be seen in socialism-communalism; radical nationalism-fascism; and anarchism-syndicalism. These theories do not consistently uphold violence as the only infallible tool. They all preached violence at some point, for gaining their objective. It is necessary to have a brief look at these theories relevant to India.

Karl Marx declared that the purposes of society are essentially economic. Economic and technological relationships define social and political structures and determine the patterns of change. The dominant class in any society is that, which controls the means of production. The rest of the population, is dependent upon the controlling group for survival. They can be organised, manipulated, and exploited by the dominant class. But such societies, are inherently unstable because of their class character. The state is an integral part of the political and legal order. Its class character can be changed, through class struggles, peaceful where possible, violent where not, before the forces of production, can be liberated from the quest, for more and more profit and utilised for the benefit of the entire community, in which the economic exploitation, of man by man is no longer possible. Marx believed that the movement towards socialism, is a movement towards democracy. Political democracy must be strongly defended, against all detractors and enemies but from the point of view of democracy as a way of life, it is necessary but not sufficient. Political democracy must be used, to achieve complete democracy, by extending democratic values of the principles, into economic and social life.

The objective of the Soviet, Chinese, Cuban and other contemporary revolutions (also regarded as extensions of the revolutionary tradition beginning with the American and French revolutions) was not merely to replace the government, but to change the social system and improve human dignity of their citizens. Lenin, Mao Tsetung, and Che Guevara— all point out the distinction between, on the one hand, terrorist acts aimed at limited and specific results, and on the other hand revolutionary struggle of the masses, which alone can achieve any notable improvement in the life of the masses. Their tactical rationale, aimed at planning the seeds of revolution in traditional agrarian societies, where political consciousness is low and the dominant elite are well-entrenched, with the poverty-stricken masses steeped in inhuman ignorance.

Fascism is a 20th century political movement originating in Italy. Social and economic backwardness, fear of communist revolution and frustrated national ambitions, following World War I encouraged its growth. Fascism rejects ideas of individual liberty and equality. It is characterised by ideas of national superiority, racial purity, authoritarian leadership and the virtual absence of a social message. In fascism the political demands and aims, far outweigh any social aim. The main object is to come by political power for the sake of a dictatorial cult figure, (or figures) who is/ are confident, of manipulating the masses.

Religious Philosophy of Violence

Since the purpose is to discuss the phenomenon of terrorism and not to justify it, we should also briefly examine the attitude of the various religions to violence and terror. Jehovah the God of the Hebrews was a God of holiness, love, power and wisdom as well as great dread and wrath who inflicted terrible punishments on those who ignored the way of life he set before them. Early Christians, following Paul, insisted upon the Christians, the duty of obedience to the ruler, who was considered to be God's instrument for repressing evil "The powers that be, are ordained by God" and "submit yourselves to every ordinance of man for the Lord's sake" were Paul's guidelines for early Christians. Augustine (350-430 AD), stressed that the authority of all rulers is derived from God. Recognising that one who kills another in obedience to God's direct command is not guilty of a sinful murder, Augustine also upheld the divine right of kings.

Saint Isidore of Seville (560-636 AD) however distinguished between kings and tyrants and urged that the title "King" belongs to him who governs rightly. Saint Thomas Aquinas (1225-74 AD) regarded sedition as a moral sin. He did not consider it seditious to resist a tyrant. But Aquinas opposed private action against a tyrant. He urged appealing to the higher authorities. Though ultimate authority stems from God, immediate authority, comes from the common will, of the community. Luther (1483-1546) had contempt, for the dignity of princes, but he denounced resistance. Calvin (1509-64) was also opposed, to resistance of authority, but followers such as John Knox (1514-72) urged resistance, where religious belief was threatened. The Koran lays down, "You shall not kill any man whom Allah has forbidden you to kill, except for a just cause" (17; 32 to 37). "The true servant of the Merciful are those who do not kill for a just cause (manslaughter is forbidden by Him)", (Chapter II 20 and 30).

In the *Gita* Lord Krishna reveals to Arjuna, "it (the soul) is not born and it does not die. It is birthless, constant eternal and ancient; it is not slain when the body is slain — there is no greater good fortune for a Kshatriaya than a righteous battle" (Chapter II 20 to 31). Thiru Valluvar says in the *Kural*, "It is a soldier's virtue to be pitiless in battle. But when an enemy is in distress, to render him help, is the edge of the soldier's sword" (i.e. kindness to a foe in distress cuts him to the quick). Again, "of what use is it, to die amidst weeping relatives, and of age or sickness? One should eagerly seek a death. This is followed by a different kind of tears, tears of grateful admiration from the eyes of the kind whom one served." Thus, all religions approve of killings, executed in obedience to law or God's direct command. Some terrorists believe, that failing God's direct command, the next best thing is, the command of priests, or some other charismatic fascist, who may be called a saint. If every terrorist had the benefit of personal counsel, from a Sri Krishna, then there will be no danger, at all, to society. Then it will be possible to say that those who got killed really deserved to die. The priest's blessings may suffice to solve the ethical problem for some terrorists themselves. But, will the authorities be justified in exploiting the ethical issue to persuade the public at large that terrorism is not a legitimate tactic even if, in some cases, the cause in which it is used may be legitimate one? The answer has to be an emphatic 'No' to any such killing by any group.

Mahatma Gandhi's and Sri Aurobindo's Ahimsa

According to Sri Aurobindo "To abstain, to sit silent, to protest by non-intervention But abstention will not help. It will not prevent the fulfilment of the destroying will, but rather by the lacunae, it creates increased confusion. Even without the cries, the Godhead, my will of destruction would still be accomplished... No real peace can be, till the heart of man deserves peace; the law of Vishnu cannot prevail, till the debt to Rudra is paid. Christ and Buddha have come and gone, but it is Rudra who still holds the world, in the hollow of his hand".

Our problem is to comprehend violence and not justify it. But in view of Gandhian experience, it is difficult, indeed to acknowledge, that violence has a role, at all to play in public affairs. In this respect we have to note the sharp divergence between Sri Aurobindo's views and those of Mahatma Gandhi, who sought to raise Ahimsa or non-violence to the level of an eternal moral principle. 'The choice by a subject nation, of the means it will use, for vindicating its liberty, wrote Sri Aurobindo, is best determined by the circumstances of its servitude. One of the courses open, to an oppressed nation, is that of armed revolt... This is the old time-honoured method which the oppressed or enslaved have always adopted by preference in the past and will adopt in the future if they see any chance of success.'

Sri Aurobindo did advocate for his Nationalist Party a policy of passive resistance. This was by no means based on any moral aversion to the use of force. He put it as follows: "The present circumstances in India seem to point to passive resistance as our most natural and suitable weapon. In other words, passive resistance is advocated, as a tactical manoeuvre, as the best policy, to use at that particular juncture in the struggle against the British.' He wrote, 'It is the common habit of established Government, and especially those which are themselves oppressors, to brand all violent methods, in subject peoples and communities as criminal and wicked... But no nation yet has listened, to the cant of the oppressor, when itself put to the test, and the general conscience of humanity approves the refusal. Under certain circumstances, a civil struggle becomes in reality, a battle, and the morality of war is different from the morality of peace. To shrink from bloodshed and violence under such circumstances is a weakness deserving as severe a rebuke as Sri Krishna addressed to Arjuna when he shrank from the colossal civil slaughter on the field of Kurukshetra. Liberty is the life breath of a nation; and when the life is attacked, when it is sought to suppress all chances of breathing by violent pressure, and every means of self-preservation becomes right and justifiable - just as it is lawful for a man who is being strangled to rid himself of the pressure on his throat by any means in his power. It is the nature of the pressure, which determines the nature of the resistance'.

According to Dr Karan Singh:

'For Sri Aurbindo the deliverance of the motherland from foreign rule was the one paramount, overriding consideration. To this end all means were admissible, including violence, specially when the foreigners themselves were in India as the result of forcible conquest'. At this point we have also to take due note of the fact that when terrorist outrages were on the increase in 1909, Sri Aurobindo had come to the conclusion that as the Nationalist Party was powerless to stem the rising tide of terrorism, they could only suspend their own strictly lawful and peaceful activities and let the Government deal, as best, as it could, with the situation that its own policies had created. It is very important to understand that Sri Aurobindo's spiritual nationalism, has nothing at all common, with fascist ideas about racial and national superiority. True, he adapted the ancient mystic and religious concept of the divinity of the motherland, to the political requirements of India. He was convinced that India must be free, not for herself alone, but for benefit of entire mankind, for whom she had a spiritual message. India does not rise as other nations do, for self or, when she is strong to trample, on the weak. She is rising to shed the eternal light, entrusted to her over the world. India has always existed for humanity and not for herself, and it is for humanity and not for herself that she must be great... Our idea of patriotism proceeds on the basis of love and brotherhood and it looks beyond the unity of the nation and envisages the ultimate unity of mankind'.

Sri Aurobindo's *Essays on the Gita* at length in the context of the suggestion advanced by scholars as for instance, Alan F Sewell, that behavioural sciences can play a part in solving the terrorist problem, the psychological content of the *Gita* and the psychotherapeutic session administered to Arjuna are of immense significance. Dealing with terrorism, requires a firm determination, to show who is the stronger side.

Philosophy of the Constitution

It is best to remember that terrorism in India today, has passed through the various phases, from the use of crude weapons to RDX and AK 47 rifles and tactics like mass killings by bomb blasts and hijacking of the National Airlines' Aircrafts. We have a Constitution based on principles of justice, social, economic and political, liberty of thought, expression, belief and worship; equality of status and of opportunity; and fraternity assuring the dignity of the individual and the unity of the nation. Protection of interest of minorities has received specific attention in the Constitution. Universal adult franchise has been established. The Directive Principles of State Policy, aim at social and economic development with political democracy as the base. The Constitution of India provides safeguards, for expression of criticism, dissent and protest. But it is as a matter of concern that it also appears to have enabled fascist elements, to organise themselves. This speaks of deficiencies in understanding and implementing of the Constitutional provisions. The Constitution itself, needs a review, to meet the challenge of the times. It is essential to have a look very briefly at the different movements resorting to violence and terrorism, in the country in recent times. There are the insurgencies in greater Assam that is to say in the present day Assam, Nagaland and Mizoram as well as in Manipur and Tripura (and also the movement in Jharkhand) the Naxalite activities in Bihar, Madhya Pradesh and Andhra Pradesh and Jammu and Kashmir. The Punjab had extremism eating into its vitals for over a decade. It ended, when it found, that the State had broken its back.

As for the tribal insurgencies in the North-east, their origin is generally attributed to influence of Western Christian missionaries. The fact is, that tribals have gained an awareness of their regional and ethnic identity. The foreign influence, to subserve its interests has not hesitated to turn tribal frustrations, against the Government of independent India. In part, the tribal resentments, were caused by the unwarranted superior racial attitudes, adopted by the non-tribals including businessmen and officials. However, the tribals were never oppressed, by force or any rights guaranteed by the Constitution. The tribals are genuine minorities of India and any action to educate the majority to be gracious, and munificent, to the minorities should be encouraged and appreciated. At the same time, the efforts have to be made to get the tribals join the mainstream of national life.

As for the Naxalites their ideological predicament is well-known. They are alienated from the main Marxist movement, by their rigid adherence to the sole efficacy of violent means, to achieve their objectives. The different Naxalites groups, are engaged in peddling their own interpretations, of Marxism-Leninism-Maoism. It may become possible, to harness their idealism, by sufficiently well informed action, education, and motivation. A combined approach only can help. To fight the sorrow in the world, a truly spiritual army having no political objectives, representing peace and purity, will carry swords of truth *(sathya)* march along the path of righteousness *(dharma)* and use the most effective ammunition of all, love *(prema)* to exterminate evil and kill all hate. The efficacy of this *prema* is to be demonstrated through *seva*. This *manav seva* (service of humanity), has no bounds of religion, nation, caste, creed, or colour. As for the caste and communal violence, these are a far cry, from any realisation of the fact of unity of creation preached by Sri Krishna and the ideal of human unity preached by Karl Marx or Gandhi or Sri Aurobindo. The difference between statesmen and short sighted political leaders is nowhere seen, more clearly, than in their attitudes, to the age old communal problem. The statesmen view the poverty of the masses, as a common problem to be solved, but petty politicians find justification in Muslim poverty, Christian poverty, Hindu poverty, and so on. Statesmanship demand recognition of the fact that people belonging to all religions are bound, to live together in this country, in future as was in the past. Any amount of terrorism is not going to suffice to exterminate religious minorities.

Suggestions to Counter Terrorism

We should attempt to find long-term solutions to the underlying causes of terrorism by boldly acknowledging the inequities in society providing the objective causes of terrorism. Some suggestions are as follows:

(a) Increase the size and powers of the security forces.

(b) Introduce capital punishment for terrorist activities.

(c) Enact legislations limiting rights of assembly and increasing controls over the public by means of identification cards, etc.

(d) Establish a third force to cope with terrorist attacks. This involves policy decisions about the role of the police in anti-terrorist operations; about how early to commit military forces and civil military relations.

(e) Announce a policy of 'no negotiations' with terrorists.

(f) Increase physical and peripheral security.

(g) Introduce press censorship to control sensationalism.

(h) Introduce pros internment without trials.

(i) Special legislation authorising the above or other measures

(j) Make it illegal for individuals or private organisations to pay ransom to terrorists.

(k) Promote international treaties providing for extradition or trial of captured hijackers, etc.

(l) Research and develop alternatives to hostage negotiations.

(m) Involve the so called Human Rights Activists to ensure that terrorist group be encouraged to adhere to the norms of Human Rights.

(n) Develop and deploy highly intrusive technologies as pre-emptive moves, e.g. monitoring and surveillance.

Since we are dealing with human behaviour, the policy makers must assess the contribution that can be made by the behavioural sciences. Effective measures need to be taken for stopping the flow of external aid to the terrorist. This will include all forms of diplomatic efforts designed to preclude the terrorists gaining further foreign support.

8

POLICE DISCRETION

Police organisations, all over the world, are managed in a semi-military fashion. They are organised and structured as such. The individual policeman, does not get the opportunity to express himself fully, as the organisations are run along authoritarian lines. These days the police officers, in India, have to function both in emergency and normal situations, requiring them to take prompt decisions. Quite often, the decisions and actions of the police, are influenced by well-established and developed policies, of administration, and directives and orders issued. The purpose of the police organisation and criminal justice system is, to provide protection to society, from the depredations of the individuals, as well as the high handedness of the society and enforcement agencies It is also a fact that there is a growing amount of dissatisfaction with the judicial delays and the courts are considered not the dispensers of quick justice at all times. By law, the police have no discretion in doing their duty, as it is strictly enjoined that every police officer must apprehend all persons whom he is legally authorised to apprehend and for excercising arrest sufficient ground exists.

Social Responsibilities of the Police

Duties of the Police Officers: "It shall be the duty of every police officer promptly to obey and execute all orders and warranty lawfully issued by him by any competent authority; to collect and communicate intelligence affecting the public nuisance; to detect and bring offenders to justice and apprehend, and for whose apprehension sufficient ground exists, and it shall be lawful for every police officer, for any of the purposes mentioned in this section, without a warrant, to enter and inspect any drinking shop, gaming house or other place of resort, for loose and disorderly character." Thus, it may be seen that specific duties are assigned to the police, under the law of the land, and the scope of the discretion is rather limited as the word "shall" in the language of Section 23 of the Police Act, of 1861 it reflects. However, the social responsibility, cast on the police, have added a new dimension, to the police work and relationship with the society. The organised police is defined "as a response to the problems of social science in modern societies" by David J Bordua in the *International Encyclopaedia of Social Science.* The expectations of the society, from the police are infinite, including in their social sphere, with which the Police ordinarily, have nothing to do. The people requisition the services of the police for all kinds of jobs, like rescue of people's cats and other pets from the wells or the removal of a dead dog or dead body from the roadside, or to trace the missing child or elopement of the girl with her boy friend, or complaints against the neighbours for throwing rubbish or hanging clothes at their place earmarked for somebody else, for preventing cruelty to the animals, or practice of untouchability, or prevention of publication of harmful publications. It is worthwhile to mention, that the police are called upon to enforce, amongst other works, the following social legislation:

1. Children Act, 1960
2. Public Gambling Act, 1867
3. Untouchability Act
4. Reformatory Schools Act, 1897
5. Opium Act 1878

6. Dangerous Drugs Act, 1930
7. Suppression of Immoral Traffic in Women's and Girls Act, 1956
8. Drugs and Magic Remedies (Objectionable Advertisement) Act, 1954
9. Young Person's (Harmful publications) Act, 1956
10. Prevention of Corruption Act
11. Prevention of Cruelty to the Animals Act
12. Wild Birds and Animals Protection Act, 1912
13. Probation of Offenders Act, 1955
14. Narcotics and Psychotropic Substances Act.
15. Suppression of Immoral Traffic in Women's and Girls Act.

The above list, which is only illustrative and not exhaustive, indicates the new social responsibilities, which have been enjoined on the Police Force of the modern days, apart from assisting, in calamities like fire fighting, controlling traffic, floods cyclones, and earthquakes. However, there are limitations, to what the police can accomplish in spheres like Anti-Dowry or enforcement o Prohibition or other social spheres. By the sheer weight of the social legislation, and the plethora of laws, the police is called upon to enforce, it is no wonder, that the actual police work, of prevention and detection, of crime suffers a great deal. More often than not, the latest statutes are not available with the local police. A few decades ago, a law was passed against video piracy, banning the use of video cassettes of Indian Films not approved by the Central Board of Censors. I, as the police chief of my area, wanted to enforce it. I could not get even the Act and Rules which had been passed. When approached, even the local office of the Central Board of Film Censors and ministry of information and broadcasting said that they had not been supplied with any copies of the Acts and Rules. They had also come to know about such a law only from the newspapers.

The Use of Discretion by Police

It is also true that in present day, society there is no respite, from dangers emanating from various quarters, in unpredictable situations. At the face of it, there appears to be justification for widening the field of police activities. This is, how it should be, to ensure enjoyment, of the fundamental rights, as enshrined in the Constitution. The police has to be careful, in balancing the rights of the people, so that, the rights of some individuals, do not violate the rights of others. In some matters, the police tend to use their discretion, to assess whether the breach of the law is only technical. However, use of discretion, can lead to the misuse of responsibility. In any case, the atmosphere in the country, is such, that it does not inspire the police to use their discretion, lest they be misunderstood. Like the rest of the administration, the police also tend, to play safe and not take chances for inviting allegations. More often then not, they do not use their discretion, and let the cases, even weak and unsubstantiated ones, to be taken to the courts, so that the blame for not punishing the wrong doers does not stick to them.

To serve democracy, the police system has to contribute, to the upholding of the principles of liberty, equality and freedom of expression. They have a paramount ethical and moral responsibility to ensure that enforcement and non-enforcement of the laws is done impartially and equally, without regard to the social standing, religion, caste, creed or class. This is the only way, in which the police can earn the respect of all sections of the society. David H. Bailey in his book *The Limits of Police Reforms* says in connection with the situation and use of discretion in Japan: "There, the obligation, to make police behaviour, conform to the high standards, has been entrusted, primarily to the police, keeping external supervision in reserve, in the event self-regulation fails. The foundations, on which the effective self-regulation rests, in Japan, is pride of the policemen, in their identity. Knowing that they are well respected by the pubic, policemen view aberrant behaviour on the part of a fellow officer, as letting down their side. The organisation continually cautions about slipshod ways. The life of a Japanese officer is filled with admonitions, lectures, and exhortations about what it means to a policeman. Moral meetings are held regularly and even small mistakes are thoroughly discussed and strictly punished".

To ensure, that justice is done properly, in some countries, the police has been placed under the Department of Justice. The police is required to function under the Rules of Law. Supreme Court observed: "Crime is contagious. If the Government servant becomes a law breaker, it breeds contempt for the law... To declare that in the administration of criminal law, the ends justify the means, —is to declare, that the Government servant may commit crime, in order to secure the conviction of a private criminal — would bring terrible retribution. Against this pernicious doctrine, the court must resolutely set its face. It is better that some criminals should escape the law than that the government officer should play an ignoble part. This however, should not be interpreted, to mean that the police, are being told to fold up their hands and remain passive, when anti-social elements, suddenly grow in wealth. Instead they should be active and intelligent enough to track down those, who hold the nation's wealth, peace and security in jeopardy. The only insistence is that means must also be as good as ends." (Prem Chand Vs. Union of India, 1981, Cr. L J 5 (SC). The above land-mark judgement of the Supreme Court is a clear indication of the direction on which the police should function and exercise its discretion, that is in conformity with the laws and spirit of liberal understanding of the issues. Sir Harold Scott, a former commissioner of police, London Metropolitan Police observed: "Successive generations of police officers have been schooled to regard themselves not as masters, but as servants of the public. They have been taught, that even when prosecuting a case against an offender, they must be scrupulously fair, and that when they have put up a case before the court, their duty is done; and they are not concerned with the verdict. If there is anything to be said, in favour of the accused, it must not be withheld from the court after conviction".

The television, radio, and press have added a new dimension to the activities of the police. They are constantly under watch. The policeman more often than not is called upon to take decisions on the spot, and is liable to be exposed to public criticism. He is damned either way for taking a decision or for not taking a decision. This is the predicament he faces. In his job he has to do tight rope walking and strike a balance between the demands of the citizens and the often vexatious political interference. To some, he appears to be taking too drastic an action, in some situations and to some he appears not to be taking action at all, for the same situation. He has to do all this within the four corners of law and still exercise his discretion for the betterment of society and still come upto the expectations of the people. The role of the policeman is basically coercive in the enforcement of the laws. Yet it is expected of him, not to enforce it, in some situations. With a vigilant press and ever active citizen's groups, the work of the police is under constant close examination. His failures to come upto the people's expectations, can no longer be hidden under the carpet.

But can the present day policeman come upto the public expectations, without the change in the basic structure of the police set up. The role of the police has to be emphasised as "service" rather than a "force". The police bosses expect passive obedience and instant submission and non questioning by the subordinates. The existing paramilitary model of the police, needs to be revamped and changed, to bring it in a shape, wherein even the junior most functionary will be in a position to exercise discretion, without being fettered by the expectations of his seniors. It is absolutely essential, that the police set-up structured on the basis of 1861 Police Act should be changed. It needs to be remodelled to meet the challenges and demands of the 21st Century. One way it can be done is by providing proper training at the time of initial entry. Later on, it has to be followed up, by in service training and orientation courses, to change and mould his attitudes, towards the people and society. Such courses, even otherwise are also necessary for the growth and development of policemen, apart from emphasising the changed role of the police. The police are an integral part of the civic life, with powers to work in such a way, that they can be of real service to the people. Policemen are citizens in uniform. Their primary job is prevention and detection of crime, apprehension of the criminals and maintenance of law and order. As members of the society, their duties and social responsibilities, should also extend to rendering of such social service to the people as may be needed by them.

Promoting Police—Public Cooperation through Politeness and Good Manners

Normally, a public man coming to the police station has a sense of deprivation and grievance and rarely any public man, comes for a courtesy call, to the police station. During times when he has lost some property, or has suffered distress, his first and foremost requirement is sympathy. Every policeman should learn, to be courteous and sympathetic in his dealing with the common man who comes in contact with him. It must be made incumbent on every policeman to be courteous and polite, as courtesy does not cost anything, but repays itself in the goodwill of the police. Patient hearings, sympathetic response, and politeness in conversation are essential, in any interaction with the public. Expressions like "May I help you? Sir," "Gentleman", "Please", "Thanks", "Can I do anything for you" create a very healthy atmosphere and good impression, besides making the working pleasant. It needs to be emphasised to the policemen, that even, if they are not able to render any effective help when asked for, they have no right, or reason to be discourteous and curt in their behaviours. Bad behaviour and discourtesy, are a stumbling block to the spirit of service. Good and courteous behaviour, will generate police-public co-operation and improve the image of the police. Good manners, are in no way incompatible, with the work of the police, and the enforcement of the law. They only help in smoothening the rough angles.

It is essential, that senior police officers should not slur over, the delinquency of the subordinate police officials. But, at the same time, to keep up the morale of the force, it will be absolutely essential for them not only to punish on merit, but also reward on merit. They have to learn, to shun groupism based either on caste or religion or favourites. They should be unapproachable as well as uninfluenceable in the matters, pertaining to the discipline in the force. The American National Advisory Commission on Criminal Justice System observed: "The quality of personnel selected for the police service determines the character of police performance and ultimately the quality of police leadership. Too frequently, the people who possess, the necessary qualities do not apply for the job on their own. They must be recruited. Carefully selected police personnel, are the foundations, upon which successful police administration is built. When a department fails to function properly, the cause is found, in its law entrance standards or inferior or improper selection methods. Because of the enormity of the task of policing a community, it is necessary to emphasise the fact, that the best human material, in the country is none too good for the police service. That statement made decades ago is still true. A police force is only as competent and effective as its personnel are. (*Standards and Goals,* 1973)

It is clear that the quality and quantity of the police personnel are interrelated. The quality requirement, obviously affects and restricts, the number of police personnel available for the job. High standards, naturally narrow down, the number of people, eligible for the job. Attracting qualified candidates, for the police job, is an important aspect of the police recruitment. It will affect the functioning of the police vis-a-vis the public, and the quality of the service rendered to the people. For improving police and public interaction, specific areas will have to be earmarked for the conduct governing the police action, and use of discretion. Professor Peter F Druker observed in his Book *Management Tasks, Responsibility and Practices* that: "achievement is never possible except for the specific, limited and clearly defined targets in business as well as in service institutions". It is essential to cut out those roles for the police, which are no longer valid today. It is important to include the activities, which the society has added, as new police responsibilities. As the duties of the police have increased manifold, it is essential to define the priorities in the police work and set new objectives. Only a professional approach to working can enable the policemen to discharge their duties to the satisfaction of the people as well as to their satisfaction. It is only in this way that the police can be effective and render service to the society

Another dilemma the police face are the divergent views of the society on Crime. As Roy Lewis wrote in *A Force for the Future:*

"This is more common when the law is unclear and no majority view has entrenched the tradition. Against what are called Consensus Crimes— murder, robbery, child molestation and so on— the Police can rely on co-operation even in Ulster. But the public consider good many laws to be something of a gamble, involving no reproach or shame, if one is unlucky enough, to be pinched. There is a healthy, aspect to this amorality, — without it the people would be steeped in a growing sense of guilt".

After having joined the Force, it is essential both for the men and their leaders, to deliver the goods and to discharge the trust, reposed in them by the society. In the words of the former Director of the Federal Bureau of Investigation of the United States of America: "No one is compelled to choose the profession of a police officer, but having chosen it, every one is obliged to perform his duties and live upto the high standards of its requirements. Compromise, personal feelings, animosities, and prejudices, have no place in professional police service. Honesty and integrity must ride in every cruiser, walk every beat, influence every command, and answer every roll call. Good ethics must be in evidence whenever and wherever duty calls, every minute of the day." It is not, that that administration is not aware, of the difficulties of the police. President's Commission on Law Enforcement and Administration of Justice set up by President Lyndon Johnson observed: "Crime does not look the same on the street, as it does in the Legislative Chamber. Many times, a police officer has to act in difficult and fast moving situations and sometimes even a mild handling of the situation, can bring about calamitous consequences. However, the efforts of the police should be, never to abuse or sacrifice the use of his best judgement or discretion and act in a discriminating way, but with common sense and discretion."

The police have to do a tight rope walking in India, whether it is the use of discretion for the good or otherwise of the society. Professor David. H. Bailey observed regarding the prevailing situation in India today as under: "In India today, a dual system of criminal justice has grown up — the one of law and other of politics. With respect at least to the police, decisions made by the police officials about the application of law, are frequently subject to partisan, review of direction by the elected representatives. The autonomy of the police officials, in specific and routine application of laws, has been severely curtailed. This is not only true of law and order situation. People accused of crime have got into the habit, of appealing to political figures, for remissions from the sanctions of law. Police officials throughout India have grown accustomed, to calculating the likely political effect to any enforcement action they contemplate. Fearing for their careers and especially their postings, they have become anxious and cynical".

9

ACCOUNTABILITY OF THE PROSECUTING AGENCIES

Performance of the Prosecuting Machinery

In a democratic set-up, the punishment for any crime, can be awarded only, by following the due process of law. If any law has been violated, then action has to be taken, against accused person, by registering a case against him. After the case is registered, it is investigated and charge-sheeted, if found to be true. The police as an organisation, can only take the accused, before the court. Once the case is sent up to the court, it is for the prosecution agency to properly marshal the evidence, law and other aspects of the case .The efficient investigation alone, cannot lead to the offenders, being brought to book. It needs to be followed up, by equally efficient prosecution. Despite this, many true cases, have been ending in acquittal. This question has been examined by a number of commissions for taking possible remedial steps. In most of the States, the prosecution agency, has been totally separated from the police under its own Director of Prosecution.

Position in Uttar Pradesh

The UP Police Commission (1970-71 pp. 512-17) noted that the performance of the prosecuting machinery was far from satisfactory.

The Chief Justice of Allahabad High Court, Shri S K Verma deposed before the Commission saying: "At every level, the prosecution of the State cases is of poor quality and that is one of the reasons for the scandalous number of acquittals in the districts." Another witness, a former Advocate General of UP told the Police Commission: "At most of the places today, the District Government Counsel and the Assistant District Government Counsel are unsatisfactory. The observations of other important witnesses were: "Generally, the prosecution of the serious cases is unsatisfactory (Lakshmi Chand Acharya, Criminal Lawyer and Former Minister of Law and Justice). "District Government Counsel and other state Counsels do not take adequate pains, and Prosecution of cases both at the level of the Magistrate and the Sessions Court is unsatisfactory". (Home Secretary UP A. K Mustafa p. 513) and "Standard of prosecutions, both in courts of sessions and magistrates, is extremely poor, in respect of vast majority of cases." (IGP UP, Islam Ahmed) The Commission noted, the lapses of inefficiency, want of adequate knowledge of law, lack of sense of duty and insufficient application to their appointed work, on the part of the prosecution agency. At the level of the Magistrate's Courts, mostly inefficiency and inadequate knowledge of law, amenability to outside influences and corruption, were also associated with the prosecution agency.

It was also urged before the Commission, that the appointment of the Government Counsels, based on the extraneous factors, was the undoing of the prosecution agency. One witness stated: "It is a fact that appointment of the District Government Counsel and the Assistant District Government Counsel, has in recent years, become a matter of patronage by the minister of local people. It has been unanimously found, that recommendations made by the District Judge and the District Magistrate, particularly the District Magistrate are based on political influences... There have been cases, in which a Minister appointed, a person, as District Government Counsel, who had no pending case in court either on civil or criminal or revenue side at the time of his appointment." Almost similar conditions were pointed out to the first UP Police Commission (1960-61). It observed: "Several instances have been cited before us, of the cases in which appointments, of the District Government Counsel have been made, on considerations other than those of merit. Occasionally, influence has been brought, to bear over, on the District Magistrates. Such cases have lowered the prestige of the office of the District Government Counsel, in the eyes of the public and have done great harm to the criminal administration. Beside this it has been complained that in some cases, the District Government Counsel, being a local man, has been influenced on behalf of the accused."...

"One thing, which has struck us, is the lack of an integral connection, between the agencies, for prosecution working at different levels. Some District Government Counsels have complained, that they had experienced difficulty, in getting the assistance of the investigating officers, especially if he had been transferred, to another district. On the other hand, the investigating officers have complained, that the District Government Counsels, have been reluctant, in checking witnesses, before producing them in the court."

In committal proceedings, there's no link between the District Government Counsel and the Public Prosecutor. We were given instances of cases, in which despite repeated efforts, the Government Advocate at the High Court, could get no response, from the District. For the year 1960 alone, the Advocate General has given 27 such instances. Similarly there were counter complaints, that on numerous occasions, when the District authorities wanted to be kept informed, about dates and progress of the cases, in the High Court, they could not get the information. This indeed is a very sorry state of affairs and clearly shows the need for having closer connection, between the agencies at the different levels."

About the panel of lawyers, it was observed "Both at the High Court and at the Sessions Court, there exists system of panel of lawyers, who attend to the overflow of work, which the Government Counsels, cannot attend to personally. We have received innumerable complaints, about the working of the panels of the Sessions and High Courts, both from the Judges and the Bar. Generally, brief-less lawyers, are put on panels, and failure of many Government cases are due to their inefficiency."

Prosecution in Bihar

Another Commission, (Bihar Police Commission, 1961) observed: "Agreeing with the large volume of evidence available to them, the Commission have formed the opinion, that the existing system of prosecution, in the Magisterial and the Sessions Courts, have also not worked as it might have. The Commission recommends, that the entire prosecuting agency in the district, should be reconstituted, as a Department of the Government under a whole time Public Prosecutor, who should be designated as Chief Public Prosecutor and District Director of Public Prosecutions. The Law Commission of India had made similar recommendations and suggested that he should be classed, as a Law Officer of Government. It was also suggested, that he is not to be deemed, as a part of the police department. He should be an independent official, responsible to the State Government.

Functions of District Director Public Prosecution

It suggested following functions of the District Director of Public Prosecution. He should be the head of the prosecuting machinery in the district and exercise administrative control over all the prosecutors in the sessions and magisterial courts of the district. He should arrange for the prosecution, of all cognisable cases, through the prosecuting agency, and distribute the work among all public prosecutors. He should himself conduct important prosecutions. He should advise the police department or other departments at the district level, on the legal aspects of a case, at any stage of investigation. His advice will be, particularly helpful, in difficult and important cases, involving charges of conspiracy, fraud and forgery, cases based on circumstantial evidence and evidence gathered, from account books, specially of business firms or corporations. In important and difficult cases, he may, with the approval of the State Government, obtained through the State Director of Prosecution, engage an Advocate as Special Public Prosecutor to appear, in the Sessions and Magisterial Courts, on behalf of the State. Such a contingency should become more and more remote with the reorganisation... suggested... The Commission has been informed that large sums of money are spent every year, in engaging Special Public Prosecutors.

He should directly receive, by name from the police investigating officers, copies of the First Information Reports, final forms and other reports in the special report cases. The Superintendent of Police, will forward case diaries of such cases to him. He will scrutinise these reports, and the case diaries with a view, to offering appropriate instructions, to the investigating officers, for removing the defects, if any. In all other cognisable cases, he should receive copies of 'Briefs' in chargesheet cases, and of the final reports. He will scrutinise every chargesheet, before it is laid in the court. In case of any difficulty or lacunae in the prosecution cases, it should be possible, to remedy it by further investigation. His scrutiny of the final reports, should also ensure, that there are adequate grounds, for abstaining, from sending the case to the court. He should examine all cases, by acquittals or cases, where there is conviction only for a minor offence, the accused having been acquitted, of a more serious charge. This will enable him to find out the causes of acquittal and devise methods to avoid miscarriage of justice. He should encourage the prosecutors, to consult him freely in all cases of difficulty.

In all above scheme of control, the responsibility for ensuring that all cases are properly prepared and conducted in the court, will rest in the District Director of Prosecution. The Superintendent of Police will be responsible only, for ensuring that the District Director of Prosecution and other Prosecutors, are properly briefed, and given every reasonable assistance in studying records and briefs. The Superintendent of Police, will no longer be responsible, for the way, the prosecutor conducts the cases. It also suggested that the District Director of Prosecution, should also be responsible for the cases in the Sessions court, and not only supervise the prosecution, but also take in hand, the more important and difficult cases. It observed that: "The delay in the disposal of cases relating to cases relating to traffic offences is also reported to be serious. Numerous difficulties have been pointed out, and the most important is that quite frequently the accused remain untracked". It found the present day enforcement of traffic laws, and rules to be grossly unsatisfactory and of late, people are justifiably exercised over the failure of the authorities to punish this new class offenders. The Commission suggested the setting up of Mobile Courts and their operating on the trunk routes and roads and in large cities, to deal with the traffic offences on the spot and with expedition. It was also brought to the notice of the Commission, by a number of witnesses including the senior police officers, that records of cases ending in acquittals or awards of inadequate sentences, are not properly scrutinised and promptly followed up; and sometimes in well merited cases, appeals are not preferred... Some Superintendents of Police informed the Commission, that in a number of instances copies of judgement could not be made available despite persistent efforts and attempts. The Commission felt, that in the then existing situation, it was difficult to apportion blame, as the co-operation of several agencies was required.

Prosecution in West Bengal

About the prosecution of cases, another Commission (the West Bengal Police Commission, 1960-61) observed that the standard of prosecution was low in the courts due to (i) low standard of efficiency and (ii) delay caused by several factors. It also observed that "Many complaints have been received by us, regarding the time a case generally takes, to reach completion. Many adjournments are to be given by the courts. The usual causes of delay, are piecemeal hearings, non-attendance of witnesses, and police officers summoned to appear, neglect, by officer incharge of police stations, to send in time, the copies of case diaries, and other necessary documents to the court, and the required copies for the accused and the paucity of prosecuting officers." It also observed that the prosecuting officers should be responsible, for the attendance of the witnesses, in court on the date fixed for the examination.

As regards police officers, whose evidence is required, magistrates have complained, that they do not appear and often give other work to be attended to as the excuse for non-attendance. A few magistrates find it necessary sometimes, to issue warrants, against such police officers; and one District Magistrate has given an instance, where even after the issue of a warrant, the police officer, against whom it was issued, failed to attend. Such cases are generally, brought to the notice of the Superintendents, but magistrates have complained, that they are not informed of the action taken, in such cases. Failure of witnesses, to attend the hearing, for which they are summoned, is generally ascribed to their reluctance, owing to the discomfort incidental to attendance, the probability of their having to attend again and again waiting for long hours each time and the inadequacy of the diet and travelling allowance. It urged that no witnesses should be unnecessarily detained and a witness should be paid his diet and travelling allowance as soon as the court has finished with him. Regarding the piecemeal hearings the reason given was that the court officers had to attend to other duties.

Prosecution in Tamil Nadu

The Commission noted that in Tamilnadu, the then Madras State, the trial is not postponed, even if the prosecutor is absent and the witnesses are examined as per the chargesheet, if they are present. It felt that it would be useful, if similar instructions are issued in the State of West Bengal. Regarding the disposal of traffic offences, it suggested the taking of advantage of Section 130 of the Motor Vehicles Act, which provides for the accused, to plead guilty, to the charge, by registered letter, and remit it to the court, such sums, as the court may specify. By taking advantage of the above Section, a lot of time of the court is saved.

(2) Where an accused person is guilty and remits the sum specified, no further proceedings in respect of the offence shall be taken against him. It recommended the introduction of similar enactments in the State of West Bengal.

The Union Law Commission, had also considered the larger question, whether such a procedure, can be extended, to a wider class of offences. This question was also considered in England by a Departmental Committee on the summary trial of minor offences, which came to the conclusion that a change should be made in the law concerning enabling the defendant charged with a minor offence to enter a plea of guilty without appearing before the court where the offence is necessarily triable by a Magistrate and the proceedings were initiated by a summon. The recommendations of the Committee were implemented in the form of the passing of the Magistrate's

Courts Act, 1957. There are a large number of petty offences, mostly of a technical nature, in which the imposition of a fine would meet the ends of the justice. There is a likelihood, that the accused would plead guilty to them, leading to clearing of the backlog. There is a need to introduce such provision in our country also.

Prosecution in Madhya Pradesh

The Madhya Pradesh Commission also looked into the prosecution of cases and suggested changes in the handling of cases and the appointment of a State Director of Prosecution incharge of the prosecution in the State. He could either be a senior member of the Bar or retired or serving senior District Judge. Two or three assistants of the grade of Assistant District Judges or Government pleaders could assist him and their members could be increased depending upon the work. The following duties could be assigned to him.

1. He will be the head of the prosecution machinery in the State and advise the Government pleaders and police prosecutors and supervise their work in the conduct of the prosecution.

2. He will scrutinise judgements in cases of acquittals and advise about the filing appeal or otherwise. He will also prepare a note about defects noticed in the methods of investigators, as pointed out by various courts, and suggest ways of improvement.

3. He will advise the police department, on legal aspects, of cases, at any stage of proceedings.

4. He will supervise investigation in important cases and examine all final reports, in which the investigating officer, does not process further action, in heinous and important offences.

5. The Director and his Assistants may appear and themselves conduct selected cases in Sessions Courts.

6. He will organise the training of Assistant Police Prosecutors.

It was also suggested that investigating officers may consult the State Director of Prosecution at the stage of investigation of important cases and wherever there is a doubt regarding the advisability of putting up a case in court, the Superintendent of Police may refer the matter to the State Director, for his opinion.

Regarding, the agency to prosecute cases, in the Sessions Court, the practice of engaging advocates on payment, has been adversely criticised. Some of the District Judges examined by the Commission, also felt, that Government pleaders, do not devote sufficient time, and attention to their work. It was also stated, that the work of the Government pleaders, is not supervised and there is no standard or agency to judge, the merit of the work or their performance. In the case of private litigants, an advocate, is anxious to see, that he satisfies his client. In the case of the Government, not much consideration exists and the Government pleaders can neglect their work with impunity. It was also brought to its notice that selection of Government pleaders, is not always done on merit, and political considerations weigh in their appointment. It was also pointed out, that Government pleaders engaged on part time basis, do not feel themselves responsible, to any one. It was also complained, that the Government Advocates, are allowed private practice. They exploit the situation, and secure briefs from private litigants on high fees, in consideration of doing some service to them in Government cases. Another drawback, apart from lack of supervision, is the absence of any provision of office and the provision of inadequate office allowance. It was expected that the appointment of the State Director of Prosecution would go a long way in rectifying the lapses.

A similar post of the Director of Prosecution exists in England. He is appointed by the Home Secretary after consultation with the Attorney General and must be a barrister or a solicitor of not less than ten years of standing. His Department, consists of a staff, of about thirty qualified men, who act as solicitors and instruct counsel. The staff is not recruited, in the same way, as the ordinary body of the civil servants; it is for the most part, made up of barristers who have practised, for a short time and have come to prefer a steadier occupation.... He acts, under the general superintendence and general direction, of the Attorney General and in practice, enjoys a large measure of independence. His duty is, to prosecute in all the more serious classes, of indictable offence. There are certain categories of offences, which the police are required to report to him, for his intervention. He is obliged to prosecute, in case of murder and in cases referred to him, by a Government Department, provided he considers, they justify the institution of criminal proceedings. It is also his duty, to give advice asked or unasked, to Chief Constable and other chief officers of the state.

Crime Administration

It may be mentioned that crime administration work, can be divided into three stages. Each is an important and necessary adjunct to the other two. One cannot be result oriented and effective without the other two. The three stages are:

(i) Prevention of crime

(ii) Detection of crime and apprehension of the offender; and

(iii) Prosecution of the offenders in a duly constituted court of law with the objective of getting the guilty punished and convicted.

Each, of the above mentioned components, of the criminal administration is important. Each must function properly for effective results and ends. In one sense the prosecution work is most important. If the criminals are acquitted after committing crime, due to shortcomings in the prosecution, the labour of the police, in preventing, detecting and apprehending criminals, would come to a naught. It is equally essential, to pay as much attention to the prosecution. As per Section 61 of the Criminal Procedure Code, it is laid down: "No police officer shall detain in custody, a person arrested, without a warrant, for a longer period than, under all the circumstances of the case, is reasonable and such period shall not, in the absence of a special order of the Magistrate under section 167 exceed 24 hours, exclusive of the time necessary for the journey from the place of arrest to the Magistrate's court." After a person is arrested, on specific allegations and charge, he has to be released on bail, if the offence is bailable and the accused person is in a position to offer surety, or he has to be produced, before the nearest Magistrate, within 24 hours of the arrest. The options, open to the Magistrate, are either to remand the accused person, to the police custody, or judicial custody, or release him on bail. In the meantime, the police has to take action as per section 173 (I) of the Criminal Procedure Code which enjoins:

"Every investigation under this chapter shall be completed without unnecessary delay, and as soon as it is completed, the officer-in-charge of the police station shall forward to a Magistrate empowered to take cognisance of the offence on police report in the form prescribed by the State Government, setting forth the names of the parties, the nature of the information and the names of the persons who appear to be acquainted with the circumstances of the case..." Thus, under section 173 of the Criminal Procedure Code, it is enjoined on the police to conduct investigation of the cases promptly. The final report, to the court, can be of two types,— one in which the police can say, that either they have been able to detect a case, or have been unable, to apprehend the offenders, or the other, in which the police have been able to detect the case and apprehend the offenders. It is the duty of the prosecution agency to place all the facts before the Magistrate and obtain his order. In the cases where the crime is detected and the accused have been apprehended, the Magistrate may take cognisance, fix a date for trial issue necessary summons to the people concerned and the witnesses, to appear for the case. The prosecution agency, has to ensure, that the accused persons, are given copies, of all the evidence, which the prosecution proposes to produce. It has to be ready for the proper presentation of the case in the court as and when summoned by it.

When the police submits a report, in the case where they have not been able to trace an accused person or there is not enough evidence to warrant the trial of an accused person, the Magistrate normally accepts the final report. It is for the prosecution agency, to scrutinise the diaries, and decide whether there is enough evidence available for charging an accused person, and whether any further evidence will be available as required to secure the prosecution of the accused persons.

Prosecution of Cases in Delhi

Delhi Police Commission also looked into the prosecution of cases and observed: "The Law Commission and the various State Police Commissions who have gone into the matter, have held that the prosecuting agencies, in the various states, are not upto the mark, and much of the failure of police cases, in courts, is due to defective handling by the prosecution agency. Though different commissions have made different recommendations about the prosecuting agency, they are all unanimous, of the view, that the agency requires to be radically improved..." The Criminal Procedure Code requires that the trial of a criminal case should be completed promptly. Unfortunately, the experience in Delhi has been that cases have remained pending, for many months, and often for over a year.

The Magistrates allege that:

(i) The Police do not produce witnesses.

(ii) They do not execute the summons.

(iii) There are not enough prosecuting officers to prosecute the cases.

(iv) They themselves, as also the prosecutors, are often called away to perform executive duties. (This is changed now Judicial officials have no executive duties Dube.

The police say that

(i) there are unnecessary adjournments and very often the case is postponed.

(ii) The witnesses are thereby harassed and they get discouraged;

(iii) The witnesses are not paid adequate compensation for the day lost, in attending the court;

(iv) There is no proper arrangement, for the accommodation of the witnesses, while they wait to be called for their examination.

(v) Court attendance is most unpopular, and so the witnesses evade the service of summons.

(vi) Summons and warrants are often received too late, or with insufficient particulars, and so their service before the prescribed date becomes impracticable.

The prosecution agency alleges that

(i) There are not enough Magistrates, with the result that case load is too heavy, and this leads to frequent adjournments.

(ii) The prosecuting staff is insufficient, and each prosecutor, has to run from one court, to another, every day to prosecute cases.

(iii) Due to frequent absence of Magistrates on executive duty, cases are repeatedly postponed. (This does not apply to Judicial Magistrate)

(iv) The prosecutors are often mobilised for executive duties; and (It was at that time But not now)

(v) The police do not pay much attention to the service of summons or warrants.

The Lieutenant Governor, of Delhi was of the view that

(a) delays were caused by a combination of all the above factors and were most of all due to:

(b) Lack of proper arrangement of the work by the Magistrates; and

(c) Non-service of summons

The Commission was told at that time there were about 40 Magistrates trying police cases on whole time basis, and this number was considered most inadequate for meeting the needs of quick justice. Regarding the workload which a full time Judicial Magistrate should be assigned, should not exceed 300 police, cases per year and also 400 miscellaneous cases (non-cognisable) under the various local laws and special laws per time Magistrate. (The above figure is based on a survey conducted by Justice Kanihya Singh of Patna High Court and referred to by Bihar Police Commission as mentioned in the report of Delhi Police Commission 1966-68, pages 368 para 9). The Commission recommended that 300 should be the optimum load of criminal cases to be tried by a full time magistrate as accepted by Bihar Police Commission. A study observed: "The work of the police in bringing offenders to justice can be rendered ineffective, through the faulty conduct of cases in court. The police share, in any general discredit, which is brought on the law, by an apparent defect in the conduct of a prosecution in the court... Therefore, it is a matter of close concern for the police, that prosecution should be properly conducted."

The twin object of the administration of justice is (1) to secure that the guilty does not escape unpunished; and (2) to ensure that the innocent are not punished. The prevention and detection of the crime and the apprehension of the criminal are very important functions of the criminal justice. The prosecution is equally important. The entire work of detection and apprehension of crime will be undone, if the criminals and offenders are acquitted, due to shortcomings, in the prosecution. It will not be out of place, to mention that entire work of the police, and its effectiveness will be undone, if the guilty escape due to faults in the prosecution and the presentation of cases in the court. The extent of convictions secured is a rough and dependable test, of the efficiency of prosecution agency.

Filing of Appeal: Inhibiting Factors

The offences triable by the Sessions Court are fairly serious cases. The Session Judge, is at the top of the hierarchy of the subordinate criminal courts in the country. The Sessions Courts have the power to call for and examine the proceedings, of any lower courts, located within its jurisdiction for satisfying, as to the correctness, legality or propriety of any findings, sentence or order passed and to direct the District Magistrate or any other Magistrate to make enquiry into any complaint, dismissed under Section 203 or 204 (4). The powers of the Session Court are identical to the High Court under Sections 401 and 397 of the Cr.P.C. The study also noticed that the prosecutors were reluctant to file appeals as it involves additional burden without any additional remuneration.

Other factors inhibiting the filing of appeal are as under as per the study:

1. The Public Prosecutors' advice to file an appeal, is sometimes held up, or not acted upon.

2. The present procedure of the Public Prosecutor submitting his opinion to the District Magistrate, who in

turn forwards the Public Prosecutor's opinion, alongwith his report, for the consideration of the State Government, makes it lengthy, cumbersome and time-consuming.

3. The Public Prosecutor feels dejected if his opinion is not acted upon.

4. The lengthy and circuitous procedure, in filing an appeal, gives to the interested parties sufficient time to bring to bear sufficient influence, for not filing it.

5. Sometimes, by the time copies of judgement sought to be appealed are received, the case becomes time-barred.

It was noticed that, in some cases the Public Prosecutor, acted with zeal and ability, which were found deficient in other cases. By watching the actual trial, an impression was gathered, that greater stress ought to be laid by the Public Prosecutors in the preparation of their cases. This is true both about the examination and cross-examination of witnesses as well as about some other aspects of the trial, especially arguments. In other words, much more stress is required, to be laid, on the 'home work' by the Public Prosecutor than is generally done now. At present there is no serious attempt, at the pre-trial, preparation of the cases by the public prosecutors. The witnesses, which the police wants to put in, the witness box, are not briefed or prepared by the public prosecutors. No regular system exists for taking the advice of the public prosecutor before the witness is examined in the court. This is a serious handicap, which results in the prosecution witnesses, being demoralised by the defence. In sharp contrast to the thorough preparation by the defence, before the trial starts, the prosecution does not follow such a practice. One of the reasons for frequent acquittals is the lack of pre-trial preparation of cases. There is greater need for better co-ordination between the public prosecutors and the police.

Prosecution in England

About the prosecution system in England, though the police carries on the prosecution, the system of prosecution is not uniform. In some cases, the prosecution is launched at the instance of the Attorney General, and in other cases, the prosecution is launched by the Board of Trade. The police prosecution is, in the nature of, prosecution launched by the private citizens. According to the study, the police conducts the prosecution, in not very grave cases. The Royal Commission in its report, deprecated the zeal of police officers, in conducting the prosecution themselves, and recommended that except in petty cases, solicitors must be employed. The study pointed out, that in England there are no regular channels of launching and conducting prosecution. Daniel O Devlin sums up the role of prosecutor in the following words: "A prosecuting counsel will never press for a conviction (as a defending counsel will fight for an acquittal) but he rather considers himself a Minister of Justice whose duty it is, to lay all the facts, to help at the truth, and whose only interest is that justice is done."

Prosecution in the United States

So far as the US is concerned there are two parallel systems existing, one relating to Federal offences, and the other to state offences. Each federation unit, has its own peculiar prosecuting system. However, the general pattern is common... District Attorney, who is elected, conducts prosecutions in the US. The office of the District Attorney has its own investigating agency, which is well equipped, in all respects, in some cases. Regarding the role of the Prosecutor, the Law Commission observed in its 14th Report: "The prosecution of the accused is to be conducted with the utmost fairness. In undertaking the prosecution, the State is not actuated by any motive of revenge, but seeks only to protect the community. There should not, therefore, be any unseemly eagerness for, or grasping at a conviction. A public prosecutor should be, personally indifferent, to the result of a case...Even in the exercise of the power, to withdraw from a prosecution, he is controlled to a large extent, by the District Magistrate or the Superintendent of Police. On account of the practice that has prevailed for a long time, the Public Prosecutor has come to occupy a subordinate position. Even when he is aware of the defect in the prosecution evidence, he is not in a position to influence, the future course of the prosecution. He is rarely consulted, at the crucial stages of investigation and has no opportunity of guiding the investigation agency in the matter of gathering relevant evidence.

A large number of complaints never come to the courts, for the reason that the police after investigation report them, to be not worth proceeding, upon the grounds of insufficient evidence or legal difficulties...The Public Prosecutor is unable, to interfere, in any of these matters, being regarded more or less as a subordinate official under the control of the District Magistrate and the District Superintendent of Police."

Limitations of the Prosecution Agency

The study conducted mentioned the following limitations and defects of the prosecution agency:

1. Generally, there is lack of clear understanding, as to the factors, germane to the job, requirements of the public prosecutor's office.

2. The present general pattern, of selection of the public prosecutor, at the District level is unsatisfactory.

3. The engagement of the Public Prosecutor on tenure basis and on payment of the fee on daily basis has led to neglect and indifference on the part of the public prosecutor, which has been further aggravated by:

(a) The lure of private practice;

(b) Absence of overall review and supervision of the public prosecutors' work, and the lack of sense of accountability;

(c) The lack of counsel, co-ordination, and liaison between the public prosecutor and the police has an adverse effect on the entire years;

(d) The amorphous position of the public prosecutor has led to the weakness of the system;

(e) The equipment's and grounding of the public prosecutor in the principles of criminal jurisprudence requires improvement;

(f) The level of examination-in-chief and cross-examination, by the Public prosecutor is poor and the defence benefits from it.

(g) The quality of, preparation of cases, by the public prosecutor needs improvement;

(h) While the defence counsel, almost invariably, visits the scene of occurrence to acquaint himself with the situation, the public prosecutor, never visits the scene, except when the court makes a local inspection.

The above quoted study also included the perusal of the judicial records to identify the factors, which contribute to the acquittals, directly or indirectly. The study took up 50 cases where the reasons for acquittal were (1) due defective exposition of law 15; (2) in-adroit handling of evidence or record 16; (3) in-aptness in bringing proper evidence on record 12; (4) other reasons 7. It is clear, that the defective exposition of law, is one single largest, factor, leading to the acquittal of cases. It noted, that in one case, the Public Prosecutor did not properly appreciate and put across to the court the true meaning of the concept "obscene publication" and the result was that the trial court understood an obscene publication to be the one which must invariably contain the description of the actual process of sexual intercourse. This view was, diametrically opposite, to what has been settled, through well-known cases decided by the Supreme Court. In another case, the study attributed the acquittal, to the misapprehension of the true effect of the laws relating to accomplice evidence, as laid down by the Supreme Court in Sarwan Singh vs State of Punjab; 1957 SCR. The decision of the trial court was based, on the erroneous belief, that each and every material particular of the prosecution story must be corroborated independently. Trial court in another case could not appreciate that the burden of proving the right of self-defence lies, under Section 105 of the Evidence Act on the accused. In yet another case, it appears that the public prosecutor did not point out to the court, that according to law common intention, amongst the accused, need not be established, before the incident takes place, but can spring up at the nick of the moment when the incident actually takes place. Another glaring instance of neglect, was, that the prosecutor failed to point out, that the impugned book (*Lady Chatterly's Lover,* the copies of which were seized, in a raid carried out on the accused bookstall) had already been held, to be an obscene book by the Supreme Court in Ranjit Udesh vs State of Maharashtra. The acquittal of the accused, in another case, was based on misinterpretation of a point of law, that the statement of the accused under Section 118 was hit by Section 25 of the Evidence Act, although the Supreme Court had held the contrary view.

In another category of cases, the evidence was brought on record, but it was not marshalled properly, before the court, or it was excluded, due to the wrong interpretation of a point of law. For example, in one case a witness was disbelieved merely on the ground, that he himself was addicted to Satta when his presence at the place of occurrence, was even admitted by the accused. The prosecutor, failed to point out, that at its worst, such evidence could be scrutinised very carefully. In another case involving serious offence under the Official Secrets

Act, the trial court refused to rely on the confession; there was ample evidence of the Air Force officials, sketches of air fields and installations, etc, recovered from the Pakistani national who did not carry any passport and had contacts with the Pakistani agents. The prosecution failed to marshal evidence, with the result that the case ended in acquittal. The prosecution in another case, did not bring to the notice of the court that in all cases direct evidence need not exist and in very case adverse inference should not be drawn against the prosecution, for the non-examination of the accomplice.

In a serious case, involving murder of two persons, where every link in the story was established, the prosecution failed to analyse, sift, and marshal the evidence properly, to fix and attribute, the fatal injuries to a particular accused person. In another case, the public prosecutor failed to point out, that the evidence of a particular witness, should not have been left out; a short delay in lodging the FIR, is not fatal to a case, and with respect to the tainted testimony, all that was required to be done, was a careful scrutiny. Regarding inaptness, in bringing proper evidence, on record, the study quoted a case of counterfeiting of dollar notes. The study mentioned, that prosecution made a fatal error, of not establishing, that the premises, from where recovery was made, was the residence of the accused himself. In another case involving murder, no effort was made, to bring any corroborating evidence. In another case, the prosecution failed to examine, even the complainant and the doctors, who had attended upon the victim and who had actually been examined in the committal proceedings.

According to the above study of 50 cases conducted by Shri D C Pandy, Associate Research Professor, Indian Law Institute and Shri Subhodh Markandya, Advocate, the under-mentioned conclusions emerged:

1. The defective exposition of law, by the public prosecutor accounts for the acquittal in as many as 30%

cases. Apart from the quantitative significance of this factor, qualitatively also, its importance cannot be minimised. The knowledge of law, of the Public Prosecutor as reflected in the scrutiny of the judicial records, needs considerable improvement and updating. In some of the cases examined under this category, the Public Prosecutor misunderstood or gave a version which was divergent from or diametrically opposite to what had actually been, laid down by the Supreme Court. An impression would not be wrong, that in those cases, no attempt whatsoever was made by the Public Prosecutor to understand and expound before the court true legal position.

2. As many as 16 (32%) cases accounted, for the acquittal, on the ground of failure, to sift or marshal the evidence, already existing on record. The shortcoming of the public prosecutors also needs to be remedied, if the performance of the prosecuting agency, at the session's level is to be improved. The public prosecutor will have to master this art of sifting, marshalling and presenting, before the court, the evidence already brought on record.

3. In the third category namely, "Inapt evidence" as many as 12 cases, which account for 24%, of the acquitted cases were noticed. The Public Prosecutor will have to pay keen attention to such factors, as ingredients of the offences, charged and the foolproof manner, in which each ingredient, has to be proved, by bringing the relevant evidence, oral and documentary, on record.

4. Another category accounts for as many as 14% cases. These are the cases, where if the police had consulted the prosecutor, the time and labour spent on prosecution, could have been avoided, as it would have been examined in detail, whether it was essential to launch the prosecution.

There is a lot of scope, for improvement in the quality of preparation, of cases by the prosecuting agency. The equipment and the public grounding of the Public Prosecutors in the principles of criminal jurisprudence and the level of examination-in-chief and cross examination requires improvement.

Law Commission's Observations

The Law Commission also suggested, the need for effective co-ordination between the prosecutors and the police, and observed in its 14th report "One of the causes of defective investigation which often result in acquittals is the lack of legal assistance at the stage of investigation... In the present set-up of things, there is hardly any contact, between the investigation officer and the State Counsel during the investigation and it is, therefore, essential that the case should be discussed thread-bare between them before its presentation in court. The Working Group on Police Administration set up by the Administrative Reforms Commission (1966) observed: "Investigation and prosecution process, as are non-committal and cannot be separated when enforcing the criminal law. The agencies of investigation and prosecution are closely inter-linked and any separation of the two, is bound to cause friction, as a result of which, the interest of state prosecution will suffer. In the process, the society will stand to lose. Both the agencies must work for a common purpose and there should be close co-operation and co-ordination between them. Public Prosecutors, who are not associated with the police, are inclined to be casual and cases are not wanting when, for want of effective supervision, they have made uncalled for concessions, even on matters of fact, without consulting the SP."

The lack of rapport between the Prosecutor and the police, is not only, confined to India. This problem exists even in the US. The US President's Commission on law enforcement (Task Force Report: The Police: US Government Printing Office, Washington, noted that very few prosecutors' offices endeavour to provide legal counsel, to the police: excepting a few departments, which employ legal advisers, most police forces receive only sporadic legal advice and ordinarily the communication between the Prosecutor and the police is non-existent".

The study commissioned suggested that the public prosecutor must be a full time government servant without any right to private practice, either civil or criminal. The following duties were suggested in the case of the public prosecutors:

(i) To head the entire machinery of prosecution at the district level;

(ii) To conduct the trials at the sessions level;

(iii) To arrange for the prosecution of all sessions cases, which the Public Prosecutor is not conducting personally and to distribute work amongst additional public prosecutors;

(iv) To scrutinise the evidence, before the case is actually filed in the court;

(v) To conduct pre-trial testing of witnesses;

(vi) To scrutinise the cases, triable in the Sessions Court, in which the police decide, not to initiate prosecution;

(vii) To examine all cases of acquittal and cases where the accused are convicted only, of a minor offence and acquitted of more serious ones;

(viii) To render legal advice, to the Police Department at any stage of the criminal proceedings, including the stage of investigation; and

(ix) To give advice, as to preferring appeals, and draft petitions/memoranda of appeal.

Director of Public Prosecution: Functions

In its Fourteenth Report, the Law Commission suggested the appointment of a full time Director of Public Prosecution in each district, as a full time Government Servant, directly responsible to the State Government and in control of the entire prosecution machinery in the district. The function envisaged in the words of the Law Commission were as under:

1. He should be, the head of the entire prosecuting machinery, in the district and exercise administrative control over all the Prosecutors in the Sessions Courts and in the Magisterial courts of the districts.

2. He should arrange for the prosecution of all cognisable cases through Assistant Public Prosecutors and distribute the work among them. He should himself conduct important prosecutions.

3. He should receive copies of the FIR in all cognisable cases and also case diaries and other reports which are at present sent to Magistrate's Courts and are seldom looked into by them.

4. Every police chargesheet, before it is laid in the court, should be scrutinised in his department, so that in case any difficulty or lacuna exists, in the prosecution case, it should be possible to remedy it, by further investigation on the lines, indicated by his department.

5. He should advise the police department, other government departments at the district level, on the legal aspects of a case, at any stage of criminal proceedings, including the stage of investigation. His advice will be particularly helpful in difficult and important cases, like cases involving charges of conspiracy, fraud and forgery, cases based on circumstantial evidence and evidence gathered from account books, especially of firms or corporations.

6. For important and difficult cases, he may with the approval of the State Government, engage advocates, as Special Public Prosecutor, to appear in Sessions Courts or even in Magisterial courts on behalf of the state.

7. Cases, in which the Police Department, decides not to initiate prosecution, should similarly be scrutinised by his department.

He should examine all cases of acquittals, or cases where there is a conviction only for a minor offence, the accused having been acquitted of more serious offences. This will enable him, to find out the cause of acquittal, and devise methods to avoid miscarriage of justice.

The study of Pandey and Markhandaya suggested that the Public Prosecutors should be appointed by selection through the State Public Service Commission. After recruitment, they should be put through a short term orientation course in the Police Training College to acquaint them with Police Procedures, investigation techniques, and forensic science. He should have a suitable status, within Class I, of the State Civil Service. It also suggested, that present barrier standing in the way of the way of the police, seeking the legal advice of the Public Prosecutor especially during investigation, should be removed. Close liaison between the investigation and the Public Prosecutor, should be established. The study suggested, that at the State level, there should be the Director of Prosecution under the Home Department, responsible for conducting prosecution, in all the sessions cases and his duties should be as under:

1. To advise the police, at the state level, on legal matters at any stage of proceedings;

2. To exercise control and supervision, over the Public Prosecutors;

3. To scrutinise all final reports, in which the police does not propose, any further action, especially in the case of heinous and important offences;

4. To organise the training, of Public Prosecutors;

5. To scrutinise sessions cases, which end in acquittal, in which the Public Prosecutor does not propose, to prefer any appeal; and

6. To prepare such aids, as departmental manuals, on Court room procedures, etc, and bulletins on the court

decisions and legislative enactment's in simple language, for the use of the police officers.

The National Police Commission also looked into the working of prosecuting agency (National Police Commission, 1977, Fourth Report pages 23-25) and observed: "The ultimate success of police investigation depends on the efficiency of the prosecuting agency in marshalling the evidence and presenting it in the court in a convincing and effective manner. The success of a Prosecutor in handling this work depends on his mastery over the facts of the case, as ascertained during investigation, and his appreciation of the logical sequence and significance of the different bits of evidence for presentation in the court. This calls for good measure of co-operation and interaction, between the investigating staff and the prosecuting agency, when the case becomes ripe, for laying chargesheet in the court and also during the entire process of trial in the court.

This mutual co-operation and total involvement in the conduct of proceedings in court was effected easily when both were part and parcel of the district police set up in the old days...

With coming into force of amended Criminal Procedure Code, 1973, a feeling appears to have grown, among the prosecuting staff, in the States, that they form an independent wing of the criminal justice system and are not under the police set-up. This has led to a general weakening of the structure, at the district level, and lack of co-ordination, between the subordinate police officers, actually concerned, with the production of witnesses, and marshalling of evidence in court".

During the course of tours of States and discussion with Judges, Magistrates, General Administrators, Police Officers, Members of the Bar and the Representatives of the public, it was uniformly stressed, that there was growing lack of co-operation, between the investigating officers and the prosecuting staff, frequently resulting in the un-preparedness of the prosecuting staff, to handle cases in court and the consequent delay in proceedings. The investigating and prosecuting staff, tend to blame each other, for lack of interest, in piloting cases, properly in court. It felt, that an important reason, for the failure of some cases, in court is the existing lack of co-operation and team spirit between the investigating staff and the prosecuting agency. It noted, that this malady has remained, despite exhortations and instructions from the Government and the administrative heads concerned through departmental manuals and circulars. It felt, that it is essential, to evolve new arrangements and institutionalise it, on proper footing to secure the required measure of co-ordination, in the prosecution and investigating agency, for the successful conduct of prosecution in the court.

The generally unsatisfactory performance, of the prosecuting staff, is also linked, with the fact, that their service conditions, are not good enough to attract the best talent, from the Bar to induce them, to join the cadre of the Assistant Public Prosecutor, and the lack of facilities like accommodation, library and clerical assistance for handling a variety of work connected with the prosecution in the court. There is no efficient system, of supervision, at the District level, over the day to day work, of the prosecutors. Appointments, to the level of Public Prosecutor from the local Bar, are mostly made under directions, from the political executive. The Public Prosecutors appointed, do not always carry with them, adequate professional ability and competence to enthuse, the subordinate prosecuting staff, with appropriate advice and guidance in specific cases.

The National Police Commission suggested that the post of the Assistant Public Prosecutors, Additional Public Prosecutors, and Public Prosecutors, should be so formulated, as to provide a regular career structure to the incumbents, for the Entire State as one unit. A proper supervisory structure, with its own hierarchy at the regional level, as Deputy Director and a Director at State level, should be developed with an idea of having effective supervision over the work of the subordinate staff, of the prosecuting agency, and for ensuring co-ordination. It also suggested that the Public Prosecutor at the District level should be responsible for the efficient functioning of the subordinate staff of the prosecuting agency and should be given necessary supervisory control over them. He should also be provided with appropriate office accommodation, library and ministerial staff to perform the supervisory role effectively.

The Public Prosecutor and the subordinate prosecuting staff, should be made responsible, not only for conducting prosecution, but also for giving legal advice to the police, in any matter, general, or special, arising out of investigation or trials. The prosecuting staff, should function, as Legal Advisors, to the Police Department. This role, should be emphasised, in the departmental instructions, and a necessary and suitable section or sub-section should be included in the Criminal Procedure Code, specifying this role. At the apex, the state Director of Prosecution, should function, as the Head, of the local wing of the police set-up. The National Police Commission observed that:

"We are convinced, that such an arrangement is absolutely necessary, to bring about close co-ordination and co-operation, between the prosecuting staff and the investigating staff, down the line, and also to enable, a joint monitoring and evaluation of their performance from time to time. The arrangement as envisaged above, would also ensure, professional accountability at all levels. To bring about an additional measure of objectivity and detachment in the functioning of the legal wing, it may be laid down that the post of Director of Prosecution, shall be filled on deputation basis, for a specified term, by drawing officers of appropriate rank on deputation from the law department or the State Judiciary. There can be an additional post, at the State level called Additional Director of Prosecution, which will be the highest career post, available for the regular prosecuting cadres, to reach by promotion.

Pay scales and service conditions of the prosecuting staff, may be so determined, as to be sufficiently attractive for good talent, from the Bar to seek appointment in the cadre. Apart from the initial training of Assistant Public Prosecutor which should include adequate instructions to enable them to understand the details of police working, particularly in regard to investigations, there should be periodic in-service training to make them up to date in their knowledge of police methodology and case law. The prosecuting staff, would normally become aware, of the facts of case, when it gets ripe for laying chargesheet. The prosecuting staff, should be consulted, before doing so. At that time, it shall be the duty of the prosecuting staff, to scrutinise carefully, the course of investigation, assess the evidence gathered, identify points that may require further clarification, by securing additional evidence, which may be available, and generally ensure completeness of the investigation work. While the prosecuting staff will be entitled, to give their opinion, freely in specific cases, the decision, regarding the laying of the charge-sheet, in the case, shall be the responsibility, of the investigating agency. Apart from the availability, of the services, of the prosecuting staff, to scrutinise the evidence and tender advice, if any, regarding further investigation, when the case gets ripe, for filing the charge sheet, there would be a need, for a whole time functionary, of the rank of the Assistant Public Prosecutor, free from prosecution work in courts to function as the Legal Advisor to the Superintendent of Police in each district, for giving him legal opinion and advice in specific cases, as also other general matters, relating to criminal work in the district from time to time. The Deputy Director of

Prosecution at the regional level and the Additional Director of Prosecution and the Director of Prosecution at the State level shall perform a similar function to aid and advise the Deputy Inspector General of Police, and Inspector General of Police respectively."

It also felt, that the constitution and formation of the prosecuting cadres, into a separate legal wing to function under a Director of Prosecution as an integral part of the State Police set up as envisaged by it might require an amendment of Section 25 of Cr. P.C. It suggested that after the existing subsection (3) in Section 25, the following may be added as subsection (4) - "(4) Nothing contained in this section, shall preclude the State Government, from conferring on the Inspector General of Police, and the Deputy Inspector General of Police, the powers of administrative control and supervision over the Public Prosecutor, Additional Public Prosecutor and Assistant Public Prosecutors appointed by it." The Uttar Pradesh Government has already made such an amendment, as a local amendment for the State.

Since the National Police Commission made the above recommendations, the scenario in the country has totally changed. No amount of acceptance of any recommendations can rectify the situation, unless adequate steps are taken to increase the number of judges and Magistrates trying the cases. It was estimated by the American Commission that there should be at least 50 judges per million population. America has 160 judges per million population. Even UK has more than 110. Whereas in India, it is only 10.5 judges per million population. Long term and short terms steps need to be taken. The most important need, as of today, appears to be, to increase the number of judges for trial of cases. Unless that is done, there is no possibility of liquidating the heavy backlog of the court cases.

10

POLITICAL INTERFERENCE

The interference, by the political executive in the police working is generally mentioned, as one of the causes of the deterioration in the law enforcement in the country. The National Police Commission observed:

"After long years of tradition, of law enforcement subject to the executive will, under the British Rule, the Police entered their new role, in independent India, in 1947. The Foreign power was replaced by a political party, that came up through the democratic process, as laid down in our Constitution. For a time, the things went well without any notice of change, because of the corrective influence, that were brought to bear, on the administrative structure, by the enlightened political leadership. However, as the years passed by, there was a qualitative change, in the style of politics. The fervour of freedom struggle, and the concept of sacrifice, that it implied, faded out quickly, yielding place to new styles and norms of behaviour by politicians to whom politics, became a career by itself... Vested interests grew on both sides, what started as a normal interaction, between the politician and the services, for the avowed objective of better administration, with better awareness, of public feelings and expectations, soon degenerated, into different forms of intercession, intervention and interference with malefide objectives unconnected with public interest. The interaction of the political party, in power with the civil services, in general and the police, in particular has also been considerably influenced, by the tactics adopted by some political parties in opposition, who believe in establishing their political presence, only by continuously, keeping up, agitational posture. The manners, in which different political parties, have functioned, particularly on the eve of periodic election, involve the free use of musclemen and Dadas to influence the attitude and conduct of sizeable sections of the electorate."

Criminalisation of Administration

The correspondent of *Hindu* reported as below on the 5th of August, 1978 on the elections in Bihar:

"The Panchayat elections, like other elections, in the recent past, have demonstrated once again, that there can be no sanity in Bihar, as long as politics, continues to be based on caste and gangsterism. A significant pointer, to this, was the frank confession, in the Assembly the other day by the Minister of Agriculture, Mr Kapildeo Singh that he patronised and would continue to patronise, gangsters and criminals, to fight and win elections, as long as the existing system of fighting is not changed. Speaking in the Assembly, Shri Singh declared: 'It is well known that each one of us, irrespective of all party affiliations, who is serious about fighting elections, patronises anti-social elements and elicits their support. It is another matter, that we do not admit this.' " The involvement of such people in political activity brings in its wake anti-social elements, who exploit their proximity to politicians, to gain protection, from possible police action under the law. The nexus between unscrupulous elements among the politicians and such anti-social elements particularly affect the enforcement of social and economic enactments such as those against prostitution, gambling, smuggling, black-marketing, hoarding, adulteration, prohibition, etc, whenever they involve politically influential accused.

Arrest and enlargement of bail of persons involved in such offences and their subsequent prosecution in the court attract political attention. This also results in a kind of link, being established, between the elected representatives and the Station House Officer, in the day to day affairs, of the police station, in which the local Dadas frequently gets involved. This link facilitates the practice of corruption and other malpractices, by the police and politician, acting in collusion, with each other. Consequent to the agitational posture, taken by some political parties, in opposition to protest demonstrations, public meetings, processions, politically motivated strikes in the industrial sector, *dharnas, gheraoes* for political, and social ends, etc, have become a recurrent feature of political activity in the country. Police have been increasingly drawn, into the resultant law and order situations. The entry of the criminals facing prosecution in the State and Central Legislatures makes the job of the police more difficult. The ruling party, expects the police to deal, with all such situations, with a political eye. Putting down dissent, has become a tacitly accepted objective, of the police system.

More and more time of the police is taken up with law and order work, which really means dealing with the street situations, in a manner, that would cause maximum satisfaction, to the ruling party. In the process, individual crimes, affecting the interests, of individual citizens, by way of loss of their property, or threat to their physical security, get progressively neglected. The police postings, are determined, on the basis of proximity, of the incumbent to the political bosses. Such officials and there is a vast majority of them, get progressively nearer, to the political party in power and correspondingly farther, from the uncommitted general public of the country. Since most of the law and order situations, have political overtones, the political party in power get habituated, to taking direct hand in directing and influencing police action, in such situations. This leads to a considerable misuse, of the police machinery, at the behest of individuals and groups in political circles. Police performance under the compulsions, of such an environment, naturally falls short of the requirements of law and impartial performance of duties on several occasions.

Interference in Punjab

The Punjab Police Commission (1961-62) said: "The evidence led before the Commission, has disclosed, that members of political parties, particularly of the ruling party, whether in the legislature or outside, interfere considerably, in the working of the police, for unlawful ends. We have been told, that politicians accompany, the complainants to the Police Stations, and try to influence the Station House Officer, to take down the reports, implicating innocent persons, against whom the complainant has enmity... no objection can be taken to politicians accompanying their constituents for lawful purposes, but the objection is, that they approach the SHO, for ulterior purposes, and use their position to influence him. He is threatened that if he does not support them, they will bring orders, from above for his transfer, or will otherwise harm him in his career... The result of this political interference is disastrous and it has considerably and very seriously affected the police work in the State. The police are demoralised."

Interference in Kerala

Kerala Police Reorganisation Committee observed: "The greatest obstacle, to the efficient police administration, flows, from the domination, of party politics, under the State Administration. Pressure is applied in varying degree, and so often affects, different branches of administration. The result of partisan interference is, often reflected in lawless enforcement of laws, inferior service and in the general decline of police prestige followed by irresponsible criticism and consequent widening of the cleavage between the police and the public in the integrity and the objective of the police force."

Interference in Tamil Nadu

The Tamil Nadu Police Commission (1971) said: "The problem of political interference, is not a new one. It cannot be dated, from February 1967. It has grown over the years, during the term of office, of a number of different Ministers. And it has grown, in spite of the most explicit public declarations, made by successive Chief Ministers (including the present one); that there should be, no political interference, and they expect the officers, to do their duty, without fear or favour, in the confident expectation of the Government support... The problem is by no means peculiar to Tamil Nadu. The position in this State, is no worse, than in the best among other States, and much better than in many."

Interference in West Bengal

The West Bengal Police Commission (1960-61) found that there were frequent allegations, that investigation of the offence is sometimes sought to be interfered with by influential persons highly placed in the society or office... and concluded: "We have little doubt that such interference takes place, although it is difficult to say, to what extent they are prevalent." The Committee on Police Training set up by the Government of India reported: "There have been instances, where Governments have been accused of, using the police machinery, for political ends. There are also instances, of individual politicians, interfering with the administration, and the work of the police. The Committee had found a great deal of political interference, in the administration. as well as the operation of the police force, particularly at the lower level.

Interference in Delhi

The Delhi Police Commission (1966-68) observed: "We have been informed that political interference is another rich source of corruption. Allegations have been made before us that some politicians resort to the device of securing the assistance of goondas and bad characters who are given protection by the police. This protection is the result, of influence exercised by the politicians, upon the policeman. We are not in a position to say, to what extent this allegation is true, and if there is a large semblance of truth in it, but the evil undoubtedly exists... and the only way to do away with it, is to take a strong stand, against political interference. This can come only, from within the police force and the higher officers, of the department should make it a code of their conduct to resist, all kinds of unlawful interference, and to see that their subordinates, also do not permit themselves to be influenced by this kind of pressure."

Some Observation of Other Studies

A study conducted by the Indian Institute of Public Opinion in 1978, at the instance of the Home Ministry regarding "The Image of the Police in India", showed the following conclusions:

1. Political interference, is seen by the public, as a major factor, contributing to the poor image of the police, and manifests itself, in the misuse and abuse of police powers and disregard of the law by the police.

2. People consider political interference, with police work as a greater evil than corruption.

3. Political interference appears, more pronounced, in rural areas, than in urban areas.

Types of Political Interference

Some typical situations or matters, where pressure is inflicted, on the police by political executive or other extraneous sources are listed below -

1. Arrest or non-arrest of a person, against whom a case is taken up for investigating by the police.

2. Deliberate handcuffing, of a person, in police custody, merely to humiliate him.

3. Release or non-release on bail after arrest.

4. Suppression of material evidence, that becomes available, during searches by the police.

5. Inclusion or non-inclusion, in the chargesheet, placed in the court, on conclusion of investigation.

6. Posting or non-posting, of police force, in an area where trouble is apprehended, to create an effect, to the advantage of one party or the other.

7. Registering of false criminal cases, against political functionaries, for achieving political ends.

8. Discretionary enforcement of law, while dealing with Public order situations, with emphasis on severity and ruthless dealings in regard to persons, opposed to the ruling party.

9. Taking persons, into preventive custody, to immobilise them, from legitimate political activity in opposition to the party in power.

10. Manoeuvring police intervention, by exaggerating a non-cognisable offence, or engineering a false complaint, to gain advantage, over any other party, in a situation, which will lie outside the domain of police action in the normal course.

11. Preparation of malicious and tendentious intelligence reports to facilitate action against an opponent.

Transfer or suspension, are used, as weapons to make the officials, toe the line of the political masters. Almost all political parties, have done it, some with finesse, and some crudely. Most of the time, the first casualties on the assumption of new Government, in the State, are the Chief of Police and the Chief Secretary. They are shifted, to make room, for more pliable officials. Pressure on the police, takes a variety of forms, ranging from a promise, of career advancement and preferential treatment, in service matters if the demand is yielded to, and a humiliating treatment in service matters, if the pressure is resisted. While it is not possible, to punish a police officer, with a statutory punishment, under the Discipline and Appeal Rules, without adequate grounds and following a prescribed procedure, it is very easy to subject him, to administrative action by way of transfer, or suspension, on the basis of an alleged complaint taken up for enquiry. While suspension acts as a humiliating factor, a transfer is a severe economic blow and disruption of the police officer's family, children's education, etc. The threat of transfer/suspension is the most potent weapon in the hands of the politician, to bend down the police, to his will. There have been frequent transfers of police personnel on the order of the political leadership, even when such transfers are not justified on normal administrative grounds. Hardships and loss of morale, are factors of least concern. Many obliging subordinates and officials, develop such a clout with the political leadership, that their seniors lean on them to retain their jobs. Their influence with the political leadership is so high, that if any senior official tries to control them, they get such an official shifted. The politically directed transfers seriously damage the discipline, morale, and chain of command.

A study conducted by the National Council of Applied Research on, the working conditions of the Constabulary in Delhi and Uttar Pradesh revealed "that about 53% to 43% of Constables in Uttar Pradesh and Delhi respectively were transferred from one District to another, or from one place to another in less than a year and they had mentioned it as a sore point of grievance. In their view, the transfers were too frequent, ad-hoc and arbitrary in nature, and were mostly ordered as a means of punishment and harassment, sometimes due to the influence of local politicians". During tours of the National

Police Commission, in the States, several officers brought to its notice, this phenomenon of frequent and indiscriminate transfers, ordered on political considerations. In one state, a Sub-Inspector broke down while narrating the history of 96 transfers in 28 years of his service."

The National Police Commission analysed, the frequency of transfers, and came to the conclusion, on the basis of data of 1937 to 1977, that the average period of stay in the same post/ same station in the case of an Inspector General of Police was 1 year and 8 months, SP was 1 year and 2 months and Sub-Inspectors was 1 year and 2 months. In one state the period of posting of the SPs was as low as 7 months and in three other states was 10 months. It felt that "the frequent changes of officers, particularly at the operational level, of sub-inspectors, in police stations and superintendents of Police in a district, coupled with frequent changes at the apex, namely, Inspector-General of Police, have no doubt largely contributed to the sharp decline in the quality (Now called DGP Director General of Police) of police service down the line. The Inspectors-General of some States have been changed as often as the Chief Ministers or Home Ministers changed. The interest of real professional service to the public have been sacrificed at the altar of political expediency."

Source of Pressure

Commenting on the source of pressure, the National Police Commission observed, that Political pressure emanates not only from political functionaries, in Government but also from outside the Government, who are connected, in any manner, with different political parties, including the ruling party. Further, an individual's capacity, to generate political pressure, on the police is not necessarily linked, with his formal association with a political party. He can operate through several links that are forged by considerations of money, caste, community, regional affinity, etc. Unhealthy influence and pressures, that are brought to bear on the police, do not always originate from political source alone. Capitalists, industrialists, businessmen, landlords and such others who form the richer and more influential sections of society have immense capacity to generate such pressures, operate at different levels in the police, either directly or indirectly through political sources, and influence the course of police action. Any corrective measure, to deal with this malady, has therefore, to cover that pressure group also.

Repercussions of Interference

Interference with any police system, by extraneous sources, especially the politicians encourages the police personnel, to believe that their career advancement, does not, at all depend, on the merits of their professional performance. It can only be secured, by currying favour with politicians, who count. Politicking and hobnobbing with functionaries, outside the police system appear, very worthwhile in the estimate of an average police officer. Deliberate and sustained cultivation of a few individuals, on the political plane, takes up all the time of a number of police personnel, to the detriment of the performance, of their normal professional jobs. This process sets, the system, on the downward slope, to decay and total ineffectiveness. Apart from the deterioration, in the quality of police performance, viewed from the public point of view, the exercise of such pressure on the police system from political and other extraneous sources, immediately damages the control system and weakens the normal chain of command, that has to operate efficiently if the discipline and health of the system are to be maintained. Interference in the operational level of the police stations, police circles, etc, results in the total by-passing of the supervisory officers in the hierarchy.

Subordinate officers see it, in every day of their official life, that their superior officers count little, in the ultimate disposal of a matter which lies in the normal course within their official cognisance only. Decisions taken at a far higher level— political level in the Government— are implemented without question at the operational level. The frequent, by-passing of the normal chain of command, results, in the atrophy of the supervisory structure. It therefore, fails to operate effectively, even in matters, which do not attract, any such extraneous interference. In this connection, the Home Ministry in a note submitted to the Conference of the Chief Ministers and Home Ministers convened by the Union Home Minister had observed that "There is a feeling in all States, that interference, not only in the matter of posting and transfers, but also in the matter of arrests, investigations and filing of chargesheets, is widespread. The principle grievance of the policeman is, that if there is any unwillingness, to comply with unlawful or improper suggestions, the persons concerned are harassed or humiliated.

The note went on to observe, that Government of India would like to impress upon the Chief Ministers, that efforts should be made, to ensure, that there is no unlawful interference, in the exercise of statutory powers. Secondly, in the matter of posting and transfers, states should seek to restore leadership and effectiveness, of the official hierarchy, with a view to ensure, that the requisite rapport, between the officers and men, is not eroded. At the end of the deliberations, of this conference, the participants agreed that the problem arising out of interference will bear effective solutions at the political level. The suggestion was noted, that Chief Ministers might discuss, with leaders of political parties, the basis for some consensus on the issue. It was also agreed, that a similar effort at the national level would also be explored and the Home Minister will request the Prime Minister to initiate appropriate steps in this behalf."

Issue of Illegal/Irregular Orders by State Governments

The National Police Commission also noted that "In their anxiety to ensure police performance in accordance with the appreciation of the situation by the political party in power, some State Governments are, known to have issued executive instructions, restricting the scope for police action even in situations, where a specific line of action, by the police is enjoined on them, by law itself." The Commission referred to the executive instructions, issued by the Government of West Bengal on 27th March, 1967, laying it down that in cases of Gherao of Industrial Establishments, by their workers, resulting in the confinement of managerial and other staff, the matter should be referred to the Labour Minister and his directions obtained before deciding upon the police intervention. When the affected party obtained an injunction from Calcutta High Court against the implementation of this order, the West Bengal issued a further order stating that "the police must not intervene in legitimate labour movement, and that in case of any complaint of unlawful detention in connection with such movements, the police must first investigate carefully, whether the complaint has any basis in fact, before proceeding to take any action provided under the law." Calcutta High Court struck down these instructions also as contrary to the law, without jurisdiction and invalid.

Another instance wherein the UP Government issued executive instructions on 1st March, 1977 governing police action in law and order situations, is as under:-

"Whenever situation, likely to have a bearing, on the general law and order situation, arises in the districts, the Superintendent of Police will immediately inform the District Magistrate, by the quickest means available and seek his instructions, in regard to the steps to be taken, to meet the situation, unless circumstances make it unpracticable to do so. Further action, to meet the situation, will be taken, according to the instructions of and in close and continuous consultation with and guidance from the District Magistrate." (UP Government Order No 7850/7-I-51-A/76 dated 21st March, 1977). This insistence on prior consultation with the executive functionary, who has direct contact, with Government before taking action, to deal with a law and order situation, would definitely inhibit the police, from taking even such steps, as are enjoined on them, directly by law, in a given situation. To that extent, we feel, that these executive instructions must be deemed to be illegal.

Several States have issued executive instructions, a kind of a supervisory and inspecting role, on the subordinate executive magistrate, vis-à-vis the police. Section 3 of the Police Act, 1861, runs as under:- Superintendence in the State Government — The superintendence of the police throughout a general police district shall vest in and be exercised by the State Government, to which such district is subordinate, and except as authorised under the provisions of this act, no person, officer, or court shall be empowered, by the State Government, to supersede or control any police functionary. The Act itself, does not confer any supervisory, or inspecting role on the subordinate, ranks of executive Magistrates, in a district and, therefore, any executive instructions, issued by the Government, empowering them, to control the police, in any manner would be illegal.

A former Commissioner of London Police, Sir Robert Mark, observed :

"Our authority, under the law, is strictly defined, and we are personally liable, for the consequence, whenever we invoke it. We play no part in determining guilt, or punishment, and our accountability to the courts, both criminal and civil, to local police authorities, to Parliament and to public opinion, is unsurpassed, anywhere else in the world. In the legal and constitutional framework, in which society requires us, to enforce the laws enacted by its elected representatives, the most essential weapons, in our armoury are not firearms, water cannon, tear gas or rubber bullets, but the confidence and support of the people, on whose behalf we act. The confidence and support, depends not only on the factors I have already mentioned, but on our personal and collective integrity, and in particular, on our long tradition of constitutional, freedom, from political interference, in our operational side. Notwithstanding the heavy responsibilities for the policing of England and Wales, given to the Home Secretary by the 1964 Police Act, it is important for you to understand, that the police are not the servants of the Government, at any level. We do not act, at the behest of a Minister or any political party, not even the party in Government. We act on behalf of the people, as a whole, and the power we exercise, cannot be restricted or widened, by anyone else, save Parliament alone. It is this, which above all else, determines our relationship, with the public, especially in relation to the maintenance of public order, and allows us to operate, reasonably effectively, with minimal numbers, limited powers and by the avoidance of force, or atleast with the use only of such force as will be approved, by the courts and by public opinion. To sum the position up, for you, in easily understandable and practicable terms, a chief officer of police, will always give the most careful consideration, to any views or representation, he may receive from the police authority, be it the Home Secretary or police committee, on any issue affecting enforcement of the law, whether public order or anything else, but in England and Wales, it is generally for him and him alone to decide, what operational action to take and to answer for the consequences.

In the case of Commissioner of Police of the Metropolis, his exercise of those responsibilities, will no doubt be, all the more scrupulous, in that he alone, of all chief police officers, enjoys no security of tenure and that subject to parliamentary approval, he may be removed by the Home Secretary. I emphasize this because while the police place great importance on their constitutional freedom the significance of their accountability should not be overlooked, as a counter balance to any improper use of it."

What applies to the police applies in equal measure to the public. The politician who uses a public servant for purely political purposes and the public servant who allows himself, to be so used, are doing, a disservice to the country.

National Police Commission felt that "The phenomenon of political interference appears, to have assumed larger dimensions, particularly after 1967, when the continued stability of the elected Governments in some States got disturbed and a period of political instability started. Increased political interference, in such a context, meant the increased division, of the police personnel, into different cliques and groups, with different political leanings. A police force which does not remain outside politics, but is constantly subjected, to influences and pressures, emanating within the system, from the politicised police personnel themselves, will in turn, seriously disturb, the stability of the duly elected political leadership, in the state itself and thereby cause serious damage, to the fabric of our democracy. This danger has to be realised, with equal seriousness and concern, by the politician, as well as by the police... The increasing scope for mala-fide interaction, between the politician and the police, has also encouraged unscrupulous policemen, at different levels, to forge a working relationship, with the politician, for gaining undue career advancement and advantage, besides pecuniary advantage resulting from corruption. The phenomenon of political interference has thus grown to enormous proportion, assiduously fed by vested interests, among the police, as well as the politician. We are conscious, that any remedial measures, we might think of, in this context will have to contend with resistance, from such vested interests on both sides."

Political Interference: The International Scene

It will be of interest here to quote the experience of other countries also. A study was made of the evolution of American police reforms, in the United States, by Robert M Fogelson, Professor of Urban Studies and History, at the Massachusetts Institute of Technology, and Consultant for President's Crime Commission. The following extract, from the report, which reflects the scene around 1900 is of interest to Indian situation:

"Whoever dominated the police, could assign to the police, hundreds of tough, well armed, if not necessarily, well disciplined men, whose jobs, the politicians reminded them, depended on the outcome. Empowered to maintain order, in the streets, the police decided, whether or not to permit, agitators, to speak, protesters to march, and labourers to picket, and if so, judged whether or not, the protests remained orderly. They also determined, whether or not to intervene, in racial or ethnic and religious clashes, and if so, at that point, on whose side, with how many men, and with how much force. Whoever controlled the police, possessed an enviable flexibility, to respond to confrontation and crises, in ways, consistent with their own political objectives, which was a tremendous advantage, in a society, so prone to group conflict.

"The Captain's war man, a patrolman, who collected the payoffs, in the precinct, had more influence, than many sergeants and round men; and so did veteran patrolmen, who were well regarded by local politicians. As every recruit, who survived for long, learned, most officers derived their prerogatives and influence, as much from their political connections, as from their official positions. Formal organisation also corresponded poorly, if at all, with actual operation. The Chiefs, could not possibly know, what went on outside headquarters; and their assistants, who owed their position to the political organisation, would rarely tell them. The Captains, who got their jobs through the ward bosses, felt no compunction, about ignoring departmental instructions inconsistent with the injunctions, of the local machines. But as the investigative Committees discovered, the police manuals were deceptive. Most politicians, including the Democrat, who paid lip service, to the concept of an apolitical police, and the Republicans who criticised their opponents, for interfering with the department, viewed control of the force, a prerogative of the party in power.

"To secure an appointment, most candidates went not to the Police Commissioners or the Police Chiefs but straight to the New York district leaders, the Philadelphia ward leaders, the Chicago Alderman and other influential politicians. Some politicians demanded a pay off; in the 1890s, the going rate for a patrolman, was dollars 300 in New York, and 400 dollars in San Francisco, according to the investigating Committee. But most politicians, preferred evidence, that the candidate and his friends or relatives, had been helpful, to the party in the past and could be counted on, by the organisation in the future. As most patrolmen, soon learned, the sympathetic concern of an influential politician, was far better protection, than the procedural safeguards of a departmental hearing."

It is obvious, that the phenomenon of transfers, at the dictates of political bosses was a noticeable feature in the American police system. A study report refers to an intransigent New York City Police Officer, who told a State Investigative Committee: "I have been transferred so continuously, that I keep my goods packed ready, to go at a minute's notice." The direction of subsequent police reforms in the United States, was towards strengthening the position, of the police chief, by giving him a reasonable tenure of office, and reducing the scope for political interference. Policing was developed, as a profession, with emphasis, on high admission standards, extensive training, and acquisition of a wide range of special skills. Policemen were made to subscribe, to a code of ethics, devoting themselves to the public interest. The position has been fully entrenched and misuse of office meets with severe retribution. President Nixon was impeached for watergate scandal and in recent times, President Bill Clinton while still in office was investigated and impeached.

In the United Kingdom, the need to prevent political patronage, from affecting the performance of civil service was recognised by the creation of a Civil Services Commission in 1855, which established independent civil services, recruited through open competitive examination. It however took nearly 15 years more for the political parties, to relinquish the patronage, they had till then enjoyed and agreed to the new arrangement. The experience of several other democracies, has also shown, the need, for evolving healthy norms, in the interaction between the political leadership in Government and the executive services to ensure, that each section performs its duly recognised role and benefits, by the corrective influence from the other, in constantly serving the cause of public interest.

In the early years after independence, the political leadership, provided by well-motivated administrators, and statesmen, had enabled the police service, to function effectively. The existing situation can be remedied, corrected and practical remedial measures can be evolved. Some of the views and remedies suggested by National Police Commission are as under:-

"The phenomenon of 'interference' with the police is, in popular estimate and belief linked, with the existing system of control, over the police by the political executive in Government. It has been argued before us, by functionaries, in the political executive in some States, that the Minister in charge of police, has to account for and defend police performance, in the States Legislature and in order to fulfil this responsibility properly he must have full control over the police. According to them, the police cannot be conceived as an agency independent of the Government control.

"Everyone will readily agree that while attempting to insulate the police from political and other extraneous sources, we should not confer a totally independent status, on the police which would make it function as a 'State within a State'. Our object, however, is to devise a system, in which police, will have professional and operational independence, particularly in matters, in which their duties and responsibilities, are categorically specified in law, with little or no room for discretion, and at the same time their overall performance can be effectively monitored and kept within the framework of law by an agency which will involve the Government also. In the existing set up the Government seeks to have full control over the police by virtue of Section 3 of the Police Act, 1861, according to which the Superintendence of the police throughout a general police district shall vest in and shall be exercised by the State Government to which such district is subordinate."

Supreme Court Rulings

While studying the nature of relationship that would be desirable in public interest in a democracy, we have examined the scope of supervision and control that can be deemed to flow from the word 'superintendence' occurring in the above section of law. In this context we have seen some rulings of the Supreme Court relating to Article 227 of the Constitution according to which:

"Every High Court shall have superintendence over all courts subject to its appellate jurisdiction. The purpose of some relevant observations of the Supreme Court is furnished below:

1. The general superintendence, which the High Court has over all courts and tribunals, is a duty to keep them within.

2. Conflict of jurisdiction (interference only when there is no other remedy.

3. Refusal or failure to proceed with a case.

4. Proceeding contrary to principles of natural justice.

5. Personal interest of judge in the issue to be decided.

6. Illegal orders of the Court.

7. Patently erroneous decision on facts.

Having regard, to the general principles enunciated above, in regard to the judiciary, it was, that the power of superintendence of the State Government over the police should be limited, for the purpose of ensuring, that police performance is in strict accordance with law. The measures suggested, included complete professional independence of the police, in the investigative tasks, assigned to it by law. It was also essential to review, all existing instructions issued by the Government, having a bearing on the investigation. They could either be cancelled or modified, depending upon legal parameters. If during the pendency of investigation, any person including a political functionary gets information, which he feels should be passed on, to the police for appropriate follow-up action, during the course of investigation itself, he should merely pass on such information, to the police without, in any way attempting to interfere with, the investigation... In the performance of preventing tasks and service oriented functions, the police will need to interact with other Government agencies and service organisations. For example, in planning preventive measures, in a near strike situation, in an educational situation or in an industrial unit, police will have to keep in touch, with the educational authorities, or the labour departmental authorities, to have a proper perception, of the developing situation. In the performance of such preventive tasks, there is considerable scope for exercise of discretion, having in view the overall public interests, involved, in any particular situation. Every police officer, should normally be left free to exercise this discretion, on his own judgement, but there may be situations, the disposal of which, may have repercussions beyond the jurisdiction of one police officer and it will become necessary in such cases, for the supervisory ranks, to step in, and exercise discretion at their level.

"Extending this analogy, one can visualise a State wide situation, in which the exercise of discretion, in regard to preventive tasks, may have to take into account, several factors of state-wide significance. It would be appropriate in public interest, that the exercise of discretion, in such situations conforms, to some policy approach, that may be evolved, at the highest political level in the Government. The ultimate responsibility, for the proper governance of the State, lies with the political executive. In the performance of, preventive tasks and service oriented functions, police should be subject, to overall guidance, from the Government which should lay down, broad policies, for adoption, in different situations, from time to time. There should, however, be no instructions, from time to time, as well as, in regard, to the actual operations in the fields."

A caution is necessary, against the political infiltration, into the police: It observed: "It is conceivable, that some political parties, adopt a deliberate strategy, of injecting into the police system, through channels of recruitment at different levels, young men who are strongly committed, to the ideologies of the political party, and could be expected, to influence from within. While we do not hold any brief for or against, any political party, to say, that the membership thereof or association, therewith should or should not act as a bar for recruitment, to the police at any level, we would state emphatically, that the continued involvement, in political activity, of any kind either directly or indirectly, by any personnel, after joining the police at any level, should not be tolerated in any circumstances. The weeding out of such persons should receive special attention of the Chief of Police from time to time. Here again, recourse may be had, to the provisions of Articles 311 (2) (b) or (c) of the Constitution, if need be in appropriate cases.

"Regarding transfers and suspensions, a trend has been noticed, indicating interference from higher levels, to bring about the suspensions, of officers, when the normally competent authority, may not consider it, necessary to do so.... The police officers should be, effectively protected, from such whimsical and malafide transfers/suspension orders. One such step for securing this protection, could be to incorporate a provision, in the Police Act itself, specifying the authorities, competent to issue transfer/suspension orders, regarding different ranks. Such a statutory provision, would render null and void any transfer/suspension order, passed by any authority, other than those specified in the Act. This would be an improvement over the present position where the powers of transfer/suspension are merely spelt out in rules or executive instructions, which can always be overruled by the Government as and when it feels like doing so, for reasons of its own.

"Another step could be, to lay down, as a rule, that every transfer/suspension order should also contain a brief paragraph, indicating the reasons for the issue of the order, and making it a further rule that any transfer/suspension order, which does not contain this explanatory paragraph, shall not be a valid order. The advantage of this arrangement, would be, that the recipient of the transfer/suspension order, will have some material with him, which he can agitate, before the authorised available forums, if he feels, that the reasons are malafide or otherwise, not sustainable. However, a rule like this would strike, at the very base of the sickness, the National Police Commission strives to cure. It would virtually not be possible, to shift even the most undesirable personnel, from their posts, once they are entrenched. Somewhere, we have to learn, to trust, that all politicians are not crooks nor all officials are saints. Situations arising from oral orders, issued by the superior officers including the political executive, while on tour or otherwise, are known to cause considerable embarrassment to the field officers, when the orders happen to require the commission of illegal, irregular, improper or unjust acts....However, administration would get badly cramped and become ineffective, in day to day service to the public, if it is rigidly insisted, that no functionary need take action, under orders, from higher ranking functionary, in the normal line of supervision unless the order is in writing. Several situations may occur, in daily life, in which a supervisory functionary, on the spot, may give an order, for immediate execution by the subordinates. Several such situations, can be easily imagined in law and order matters. There cannot and should not be, any rigid or inflexible rule, that every order, that flows from one level to the lower level, in administrative hierarchy, should be in writing, before the intended action is taken. Oral orders cannot be shut out, totally from the administrative system. However they can be avoided, in situations, which do not involve any element of urgency and can wait, for the oral orders to be confirmed in writing before the intended action is initiated. The final recommendations on the issue by the National Police was that:-

"1. Oral orders should be avoided, as far as possible and may be resorted to, only in situations, which call for immediate executive action and cannot wait for issue of written orders in confirmation of the oral orders.

2. A record of every oral, order be kept, both by the issuing officer, and the recipient officer, in the relevant file.

3. A subordinate officer, receiving oral orders, from a higher ranking officers, shall be entitled, to ask for, and get confirmatory orders, in writing from the higher functionary for record."

In a democracy it is essential to have facility for interaction between the executive and the elected representatives of the people so that corrective action, wherever called for, can be taken, in the public interest. It observed: "Persons subjected to flagrant injustice, by executive action, will be inclined, to share their grief and disappointment, with several others, including the elected representatives and will expect them to do something to set the matters right. While conceding the need, for interaction between elected representatives and the executive, in each situation, we are anxious to ensure, that this does not lead to unauthorised interference, as such with the performance of the executive. We, therefore, feel, that if a code of conduct, is laid down that elected representatives, will interact with the police at the level of the Deputy Superintendent of Police or above only, it would avoid situations, in which the executive at the operational level, in police stations and circles, may be overawed by the stature of the political functionary, and may be inclined to accept and act upon, whenever information is passed on to them, without making the necessary check and verification, which they might make normally". The National Police Commission also felt Rule (3) of the All India Services (Conduct) Rules, 1968 should be made applicable to the police personnel also. This Rule reads as under:-

"No member of the Service shall, in the performance of his official duties, or in exercise of the powers conferred on him, in the performance of his official duties or in exercise of powers conferred on him:

1. Act otherwise, than in his best judgement, except when he is acting, under the direction of his official superior, and he shall obtain such direction in writing,

wherever practicable and where it is not practicable, he shall obtain written confirmation, as soon thereafter as possible, and

2. Evade the responsibility, devolving on him, and seek instructions from or approval of, a superior authority when such instruction, or approval is not necessary, in the scheme of distribution of powers and responsibilities.

It also suggested, a code of conduct, for legislatures. It observed that "The conduct of the Government servants, (including the police) can be controlled, and guided by the issue of rules and instructions and enforcing their strict compliance, in actual practice. If, however, the political functionaries, whose conduct is not subject to such rules and regulations, do not change their present attitudes and approach to this matter, their inclination to interfere with the executive including the police will continue in some form or the other. While on one side, we may be thinking of, several remedial measures, to enable the executive, to resist the interference, our objective can be achieved, in a substantial measure, only when the political functionaries, also change their style of functioning. ... Our enquiries reveal, that this code of conduct, for legislatures, has not yet taken any shape. We recommend, that the Ministry of Home Affairs, complete their exercise expeditiously and have the code issued very soon, so that the elected representatives, as also the general public, at large, may know and appreciate the requirements, of ethics and propriety, in this important and sensitive matter. We also trust, that the contemplated exercise on the political plane, as decided at the Chief Minister's Conference on 6th June, 1979 will be taken up in right earnest and completed soon."

"It also suggested following special declaration, to be given by the policemen at the time of enrolment. It could be either sworn or affirmed. "I, A.B. do swear/solemnly affirm that I will be faithful and bear true allegiance to India and to the Constitution of India as by law established; that as member of the police in the State of —— I will honestly, impartially and truly serve the people without favour or affection, malice or ill-will, that I will to the best of my ability, skill and knowledge discharge according to the law, such functions and duties as may be entrusted to me as police officer, and in such a manner as to uphold and protect the dignity and rights of the citizen as proclaimed in the Constitution. ... Apart from the initial declaration, at the time of joining the police, it would further serve the purpose and embed the principle firmly, in the minds of all the police officers if this declaration is remembered and repeated by them, in groups and assemblies of police personnel, drawn up on an annual ceremonial occasion, like the 'Police Commemoration Day' which is observed on 21st October every year."

Obviously, sustained capacity of the police system, to function efficiently and impartially, would largely depend upon the attitudes and response, developed by the personnel at different levels, to different situations. This would depend on their training and guidance, after their entry into the system and inservice training later on. The structuring of the initial training courses, and inservice training courses, for all police personnel, should be targetted, to facilitate the growth of proper attitudes and sense of values, on the part of every police officer. " This is the only way, for dealing with interference, in the police work or its misuse, of police by pressures from political, executive or other extraneous sources.

11

TREATMENT OF JUVENILE DELINQUENTS

Juveniles, if not prevented from commiting crimes, only graduate to serious crimes, and to that extent, it is essential that the Juvenile Justice Act 1986, should be enforced effectively. This is an Act, to provide for the care, protection treatment, development and rehabilitation of neglected and delinquents and for the adjudication of matters, relating to juveniles. It was enacted by the Parliament in 1986 and replaced Acts like Childrens Act of 1960 and similar Acts of Madras, Bombay and Calcutta promulgated in 1920s. As a result of the review, of the working of various Childrens Acts, it was observed, that there is more scope for greater attention, to be given to children, found in situations of maladjustment, delinquency or neglect. The justice system as available for adults, was unsuitable, for being applied to juveniles. It was also felt, that it was necessary that a uniform juvenile justice system should be available throughout the country, which should make adequate provision, for dealing with all aspects, in the changing social, cultural and economic situation, in the country.

The Juvenile Justice Act

There is always need for larger involvement of informal systems and community based welfare agencies, in the care, protection, treatment development and rehabilitation of such juveniles. The result is the Juvenile

Justice Act, 1986, which aims, at achieving the following objectives:

1. To lay down, uniform legal framework for juvenile justice, in the country, to ensure that no child under any circumstances, is lodged in jail or police lock up. This is being ensured by establishing Juvenile Welfare Boards and Juvenile courts.

2. To provide for a specialised approach, towards the prevention and treatment of juvenile delinquency, in its full range, in keeping with the developmental, needs of the child, found in any situation of social maladjustment.

3. To spell out the machinery and infrastructure, required for care, protection, treatment and development and rehabilitation of various categories of children systems by establishing: (i) Observation Homes; (ii) Juvenile Homes for Delinquent juveniles;

4. To establish norms and standards, for the administration of juvenile justice, in terms of investigation, and prosecution, adjudication and disposition and care, treatment and rehabilitation;

5. to deploy appropriate linkages and co-ordination, between the formal system, of juvenile justice and voluntary agencies, engaged in the welfare of neglected or socially maladjusted children, and to specifically define, areas of their responsibility and roles;

6. to constitute special offences, in relation to juveniles and provide for punishments;

7. to bring the operation, of the juvenile justice system, in the country, in conformity with the United Nations Standards Minimum Rule for the Administration of Juvenile Justice.

The emphasis of this Act is to reform the juveniles, and not to punish them in conformity with modern theories of criminology.

8. This act has seven Chapters and 63 sections:

Chapter I deals with definition of various terms used.

Chapter II deals with (I) Authorities competent to deal with juveniles and (II) the various institutions meant for juveniles.

Chapter (III) deals with neglected juvenile delinquents.

Chapter (IV) deals with Juveniles.

Chapter (V) deals with procedures of competent authorities, and on the appeals and revision that can be made against the orders of these competent authorities.

Chapter (VI) deals with special offences in respect to juveniles.

Chapter (VII) deals with various miscellany pertaining to this Act.

9. This act categorizes the juveniles into two groups:

(i) Neglected Juveniles; and

(ii) Delinquent Juveniles

A neglected juvenile means a juvenile who:

(a) is found begging; or

(b) is found without having any home, or settled place of abode, and without any ostensible means of subsistence and is a destitute; or

(c) has a parent or a guardian who is unfit or incapacitated, to exercise control over juvenile or lives in a brothel, or with a prostitute, or frequently goes to any place, used for prostitution or any other person who leads an informal, drunken or deprived life;

(d) who is being or is likely to be abused, or exploited for immoral or illegal purposes or unconscious gain.

A delinquent juvenile means a juvenile who has been found to have committed an offence.

A juvenile is a boy, who has not attained the age of sixteen years, or a girl who has not attained the age of eighteen years.

10. This act allows juvenile welfare boards, for exercising the powers and discharging the duties conferred, on such boards, regarding neglected juveniles. These boards, may be as many, as the State Governments desire, and should consist of Chairman and as many other members as the Government would desire, of which one should be a woman member. These boards are vested with the powers of first class Magistrate.

11. To exercise powers and discharge duties of delinquent juveniles, the State Govt are empowered to constitute any member of juvenile courts. The Magistrates of these courts, should be assisted by a panel of two honorary social workers, one of which will be a woman. In case of difference of opinion, on anything concerning a juvenile, between, the Boards and Courts, the opinions of the majority and of the Chairman or the principal magistrate, will prevail on the members and the magistrate. The members must have special knowledge of child psychology and child welfare. These boards and courts, have to deal exclusively with all proceedings under the Act.

12. Wherever such boards and courts are not constituted:

(a) the District Magistrate; (b) the Sub-Divisional Magistrate; or (c) any Metropolitan Magistrate or Judicial Magistrate of Ist class may exercise powers that are to be exercised by courts and boards.

13. The Act contemplates establishment and maintenance of Juvenile Homes for the reception of neglected juveniles where the juveniles should be provided with:

a) Accommodation, b) maintenance and facilities for education, c) Vocational training and rehabilitation, d) facilities for the development of character and abilities. e) Training for reformation.

14. The Act also contemplates, establishment of Observation Homes, for the temporary reception of juveniles, during pendency of enquiry.

15. The Act also contemplates constitution of:

I) After care organisations

II) After care schemes and programmes

16. Under this Act any police officer, organisation or any other person, may take charge of a neglected child, and produce him before the board, or if information is placed before the police, about the neglected child, the SHO will enter it in a register, and if he does not propose to take charge, he shall forward the copy of the entry, to the board. If there are parents or guardian, of the neglected child, the police officer may report to the board, which will issue notice to the parents, why the child should not be dealt with as a neglected child, who has been neglected. The board may make orders, directing the juveniles, to be sent to juvenile homes, or they may make an order, to keep the child under the care of a parent, or a guardian or a fit person after demanding a bond.

17. If the juvenile, is accused of bailable or non bailable offence, he should be released, on bail, with or without surety but, he shall not be so released, if there appears reasonable ground, for believing that he is likely to be associated with any known criminal, or be exposed to moral danger, or that his release would defeat ends of justice.

18. The police officer, on arresting a juvenile shall, as soon as after the arrest inform: i) the parent or guardian and direct him to appear in the court where the juvenile is to be produced; ii) the probation officer, of such arrest will collect information, history background on the juvenile, so as to help the court.

19. The juvenile court constituted under this Act:

(a) may admonish the juvenile;

(b) may release the juvenile, on probation of good conduct, and place him under charge of parent / guardian or a fit person, or under a fit institution, for a period not exceeding 3 years;

(c) may direct the juvenile, to be sent to a special home, in the case of a boy of 14 years of age, or a girl of 16 years of age;

(d) may impose a fine, if the juvenile is over 14 years of age, and earns money. The Act emphasises, that no delinquent juvenile, should be convicted, to death or imprisonment, or committed to prison, in default of payment of fine, etc.

20. The Act looks upon, with severity all those, who employ any juvenile for begging, for drug peddling, prostitution, with a punishment upto 3 years and fine.

21. The State Government may create a fund, for the welfare and rehabilitation of juveniles, by raising it from voluntary donation, contribution or subscription. It may also constitute an Advisory Board, to advise it, on matters, relating to establishment of maintenance, of the mobilisation of resources, provision of facility for education, training and rehabilitation of neglected and delinquent juveniles and co-ordination among various non-official and official organisations. The Advisory Board shall consist of such number of officers and other persons and may include experts and representatives of voluntary organisations. The State Government may appoint three visitors for each of the homes. It empowers Probation Officer, for the inspection of homes, juveniles homes, special homes and observation homes.

Difficulties Faced in Implementing the Act

22. The implementation of this Act shows the following difficulties:

The policemen, who are supposed to take charge, of these neglected children, do not have time, to look after these offences, as seriously as the Act would warrant. The Policeman is more worried, about terrorism, VIP Security, airport, railway security and order duties rather than implementing this Act. Nor is he mentally equipped, to treat the children, in a soft manner given the present training methods, in the country. Perhaps women police would suit the job, but even they are reported to be tough and aggressive, and hence, not suitable for the job of handling the children with compassion, and softness they deserve. Further they are in meagre number.

The number of destitute and neglected children, in our country, is so large that, it is impossible to effectively bring them, to juvenile homes. Even if some of them, undergo training and discipline of training institutions, it would be well nigh impossible, for probation officers to move around, and keep track of these youngsters. The value of probation officers is generally not appreciated by the District Magistrates and Superintendents of Police, for whom this is a low priority work. The result is that nobody in practice, takes the work done by them, seriously. It is performed very ineffectively, as nobody is there to supervise and show interest in their job.

The higher ups in the State Administration, viz. the Political Executives, Administrative Executives and Police Executives, need to be conscientised about this Act. Otherwise, the power that is vested in them, to form juvenile courts, special homes, will remain a dream for a long time to come. Without this conscientisation, top executives of the State, are likely to brush aside, the importance of this social legislation. It is seen, that even where a few institutions are established by the State, they are being run, perfunctorily and shabbily.

The Act contemplates, that members of the board and magistrates, of the juvenile court should have special knowledge, of child psychology and child welfare. Such qualified persons, are not so easily available, and so to that extent it may not be possible for the government, to form the courts and boards, as fully expected in the Act. The Act is self defeating in this aspect. There is possibility for circumventing of the scheme demanding establishment of juvenile board or court by sheltering under the provision Section 7 (2) where Divisional Magistrates, Sub-Divisional Magistrates and J F C M S are permitted to exercise powers of court and board. Even where such boards have been formed, there is no evidence to show, that they have complied with, the expectations anywhere in the country.

At times, due to lack of guarding these juveniles, lodged in various homes, the juveniles tend to run away, from the homes. It is very difficult to get these juveniles back once again and placed in the homes by the police. Further, the authorities in various homes, do not report the desertion of children, from homes.

Heartless Homes: The Deplorable Condition

Whereas the Act contemplates, such institutions as special homes, juvenile courts, juvenile homes, observation homes and after care organisations, to be constituted by the State Government, what in practice, is found, is given in an article in the *Indian Express* dated 12th July, 1987, Sunday under the heading 'Heartless Homes'. It is mentioned, that the State of orphanages and destitute homes in Uttar Pradesh would shock the most hardened of humans. Destitute and orphaned children, are kept in government, semi-government and non governments homes. In UP there are six Bal Sadans (Children's homes), seven Shishu Sadans (infant homes) and four Balika Niketans (institutions for girls), run by the government. They have 558,201 and 264 children respectively. A sum of Rs 125 per month is granted for expenditure on each child. According to government sources, in the year 1985-86, a grant of Rs 16.95 lakh was given to Bal Sadan, Rs 11.78 lakh to Shishu Sadan in 1994-95 and Rs 1.77 lakh to Balika Niketan. It is apparent, that none of this money has been used for the welfare of the children.

There are 85 children in a Bal Sadan in Kanpur. Fifty children, sleep in three small rooms, while the others, rough it out on the veranda. A small child told me, that they manage during the summer but suffer in winter. In 1982 a boy named Harishankar Saxena died of cold. There are three wooden cots in one room, the children sleep on the floor in the other two rooms. According to the children, reptiles crawl out of deep holes, in the ground. The rooms are badly lit and the students cannot study in them. The authorities claimed that Rs 529 had just been spent on provisions, but the provisions could not be seen anywhere. Children receive no medical treatment, when they are ill. The superintendent of the home, Shamin Javed Farooqi was amazed, that the children had spoken their minds on the matter. He showed me his muscles, and said that he would have set each one of them right, if he had been there. He displayed his broken thumbs and said that they were in that condition, because he often beat the children. During the years 1982 to 85, three children died, due to negligence in Shishu Sadan, Almorah. The authorities produce, fake figures to show their 'achievements'. Bal Sadan at Ajamgarh reported that 94 children, were admitted to the home, but in fact not a single child was visible. This home has an annual yearly budget of Rs 1.15 lakh and a staff of 13 people.

Navchetana Bal Griha, Lucknow supposedly has 90 children but there are actually only 29. Vidya Niketan, Kanpur, had enrolled 40 children but I saw only 15. Ideal children home, Ajamgarh, was reported to have 66 children but not a single was visible. Vinay Shiksha Niketan, Gorakhpur, too, had no children, when I conducted the survey. There is a ban on the adoption, of these children, especially girls, by foreigners. On September 30, 1984, the Supreme Court decided, on the writ petition of Laxmikant, that if an Indian Parent did not adopt a child, a foreigner could be considered. But in 1985, Leelawati Munshi Destitute Home, Lucknow, gave away two grown up girls, 18 year old Shanti and 20 year old Shikha to S J Jibermin of France and J M Smeli of the Netherland for adoption. The foster care scheme, of the government, is in shambles. A destitute child, is meant to be brought up, by a family, instead of being kept, in a home. The family is given Rs 75 per month, for bringing up the child. In the whole of Uttar Pradesh, 12 institutions reported, that they had adopted the scheme. I visited some of these: Shahid Memorial Society, Lucknow, Azad Memorial Public Shiksha Samiti, Kanpur, Bala Sewa Sadan, Kanpur, Vidya Niketan Society, Kanpur, Kasturba Bal Vidhyalayha, Kanpur, Lal Bal Sadan, Agra and Satya Bal Sadan, Agra. None of the Supreintendents, divulged the names and addresses of the families, who were meant to have taken a child, in foster care. The State Minister for Social Welfare admitted, that the scheme is never implemented properly.

India has 46 orphanages. According to government sources, they have 1,105 children and get an annual grant of Rs 50,000 from the state government (Rs 10 to 15 per child per month). At times, this aid is denied to them. Every year the orphanages send requests for aid, but the grant is given entirely at the discretion of the Uttar Pradesh Administration Board. Eight inspectors in each region send regular reports, to the head office at Lucknow. The Social Welfare Head Office gives grants, based on these reports.

Destitute homes, however, are better off. Ninety percent of their expenditure, is met by the Central Government, and one unit (consisting of 25 children) is given a yearly grant of Rs 28,215. In 1980-81, 30 organisations applied for a grant, out of which the applications of only 10, were approved. In 1981-82, 16 organisations applied, but not a single, received a grant.

There is evidence of corruption and red tapism in the allotment of grants. Despite the fact, that these orphanages are granted a large sum of money, there is a great deal of mismanagement and the children are exploited and ill treated. Sriram Audyogik Anathalaya, Lucknow had un-hygeinic and dirty rooms; the store of food provisions is kept uncovered and unattended, resulting in the spread of diseases. Anjuman Islahul Musalman Mumtaz Orphanage, Lucknow, is a dilapidated building which has not been repaired since 1908. The rooms are in a state of ruin, the mattresses are dirty and thread-bare, and the walls and ceilings are covered with cobwebs. There are no fans, electric bulbs or games and toys for the children. When I went to the Hindu Anathalaya, Kanpur, at 12.30 p.m. one day, I noticed, that no food was being cooked. When I questioned the matron of the home, she said nonchalantly, 'Today is a day of fasting.' She later said, that somebody had called the children for lunch.

Doshar Viashya Bal Sadan, Kanpur, is in a state of ruin and has no bathroom. Gandhi Mandir, Takula, Naintal, is equally dilapidated. Haleem Muslim Islahul, Itfal Orphange, Modaha, has mud walls and no provisions for electricity, bathrooms, lavatories or a dispensary. Kashi Anathalaya, Varanasi, is in a building which is falling to pieces. The rooms are not cleaned for weeks and the bathrooms have no doors. If the children contract a minor disease, they die of it. Last year in October, a girl called Nitu received a minor injury on her head. She died after a few days. Hjamidiya Yatimkhana, Gorakhpur has no latrine and bathrooms. The authorities of Dayanand Anathalaya, Agra refuse to have anything to do with its children. On December 25, 1983, a 16 year old boy named Sukhdev, died under mysterious circumstances. A day earlier, he had climbed the terrace of the girls section, to retrieve a ball. The authorities thrashed him, and he was reported dead after 24 hours. Even after a decade and a half, the position has not improved. It is doubtful, if it will improve, unless some accountability is insisted upon, to improve the plight of the childrens' institutions, and trained and motivated staff is provided under effective supervision alongwith requisite funds and structure. Otherwise this Act will remain only on paper, as a kind of mental belief, to comfort the National Conscience, that whatever was legally possible, has been done.

12

THE CENTRAL ENFORCEMENT AGENCIES

The Police Structure and Setup

The police force in the country is entrusted with the responsibility of maintenance of public order and prevention and detection of crimes. Public order and police are State subjects, under the Constitution. As such, the police is maintained and controlled by States.

The police force in a state, is headed by the Director General of Police/Inspector General of Police. A State is divided into convenient territorial divisions called ranges and each police range is under the administrative control of an Inspector General/Deputy Inspector General of Police. A number of districts constitute the range. District police is further subdivided into police divisions, circles and policestations. Besides the civil police, states also maintain their own armed police and have separate intelligence branches, justice and law, crime branches, etc. Police set-up in big cities like Delhi, Kolkata, Mumbai, Chennai, Bangalore, Hyderabad, Ahmedabad, Nagpur, Pune, etc., is directly under a Commissioner of Police who enjoys magisterial powers. All senior police posts, in the States are manned by the Indian Police Service (IPS) cadres, recruitment to which, is made on an all-India basis. Recruitment, promotion and cadre control in respect of lower posts from police constable to deputy superintendent of police are done by the State governments. Though police is a State subject, the Central Government has created and maintains some Central Police forces, for guarding its own interests, the country's border and for investigating cases, involving its money as well as its employees. The followings are the organisations maintained by the Central Government, apart from small police forces the Union Territoreis under its control.

Central Bureau of Investigation (CBI)

The Central Bureau of Investigation (CBI) was renamed in April 1963. Earlier the organisation was known as Special Police Establishment. It is functioning under the Delhi Special Police Establishment Act, 1946. In 1963, after the creation of the Central Bureau of Investigation, the functions of this organisation were enlarged covering besides investigation, the role of National Central Bureau for India under the International Criminal Police Organisation (INTERPOL). National Central Bureau is the co-ordinating agency on behalf of all the police forces of the country, with Interpol and other countries. It is the CBI, which takes up cases, on behalf of several States, with other countries of the world. CBI maintains, indexed records of criminals, involved in International crimes and verifies fingerprints from various foreign national crime bureaus. It also disseminates, INTERPOL notices and notices, received from other police forces, from other countries to various enforcement agencies in the country.

The CBI, through its Special Police Establishment Division, is the principal investigating agency of the Central government. It is concerned with the investigation of cases, of misconduct by public servants in the employment of Central government and its corporate undertakings. It also deals with cases, in which the interest of the Central government or any corporation or body set up and financed by the Central government are involved. It investigates cases, relating to breaches of

Central laws, in the enforcement of which the Central government is interested. It also looks into big cases of fraud, cheating and embezzlement and other cases when committed by organised gangs of professional criminals having inter-state or international ramifications, on the requests of the Central Government or the orders of the Constitutional Courts, that is, High Courts and the Supreme Court. CBI derives its power to investigate offences mentioned above from the Delhi Special Police Establishment Act, 1946.

Indo-Tibetan Border Police (ITBP)

The Indo-Tibetan Border Police was raised in October 1962 in the wake of the Chinese aggression. The role of the ITBP is to: (i) safeguard the security of borders of India, with China and promote a sense of security, among the people living in border areas; (ii) prevent trans-border crimes, smuggling, unauthorised entry into or exit from the territory of India and any other illegal activity; (iii) provide security to sensitive installations, banks, persons of security risk; and (iv) restore and preserve order in any area in the event of disturbance therein.

The ITBP has 29 battalions including four specialist battalions, three training institutions and six sector headquarters each headed by a DIG. The ITBP personnel are deployed at high altitudes to guard the Indo-Tibetan Border, extending from Karakoram Pass in Ladakh (J&K) to Lipulekh Pass at the Tri Junction of Indo-Tibet-Nepal Border. ITBP also escorts pilgrims to the holy Kailash-Mansarover and provides them with medical and communication cover. Apart from its defined role, ITBP has specialised in the field of unconventional warfare, counter insurgency, anti-terrorist operations and mountain warfare. It also has been performing various other duties like VVIPs/VIPs security, election duty, rescue and relief operations, conducting anti-naxalite operations, etc. ITBP is also recognised for mountaineering, skiing and river-rafting skills. Officers and men of ITBP have scaled the world's highest mountain, Mount Everest four times, making a tally, of more than hundred glorious climbs in the Himalayas. It also has been conducting, river-rafting expeditions.

Border Security Force (BSF)

The Border Security Force (BSF) raised in 1965, is entrusted, with the task of maintaining permanent vigilance, on India's international borders. BSF consists of 157 battalions at present, and it is guarding a total of 6,475.7 kms of international borders, including mountains, inhospitable deserts, riverine and marshy areas. BSF has been assigned, the role of promoting a sense of security amongst the people living in the border areas and preventing trans-border crimes, such as smuggling, infiltration/exfiltration and other illegal activities.

Assam Rifles

The Assam Rifles, now over 166 years old is the oldest paramilitary force in the country. Raised as Cachar Levy in 1835, the Force has grown in size to 31 battalions. The force is primarily responsible, for the security of Indo-Tibet and Indo-Myanmar border, conducting counter insurgency operations in the north-east and elsewhere in India. It also is called 'The Sentinels of the North – East' and 'Friends of the Hill People'.

National Security Guards (NSG)

The National Security Guards (NSG) has been set up for handling terrorists, kidnappers, saboteurs, VIP security, anti-hijacking operations and recovery of hostages, etc. It is a highly trained and motivated force, created specifically for effectively dealing with the above activities in the country. It also trains state police commandos to upgrade their capability to meet the terrorist threats and carry out bomb detection/ diffusion operations.

Central Reserve Police Force (CRPF)

The Central Reserve Police Force is an armed force of the Union of India for internal security management. This Force was raised in 1939 as the Crown Representatives Police and was renamed as Central Reserve Police Force in 1949. CRPF has a strength of 1,67,368 personnel comprising of 137 battalions, five signal battalions and one Special Duty Group. The CRPF, like other central forces, has no legal authority, to function independently. Whenever it is deployed in the States, at their request, it only assists the State police forces, in the maintenance of law and order, or other duties. The State Governments have to pay, for use of the Central Forces whether they are using it for a National cause, to fight anti-national elements like the terrorists, or for elections and dealing with law and order.

Civil Defence

Civil Defence aims at saving lives, minimising damage to property and maintaining continuity of industrial production, in the event of any hostile attack. Central financial assistance, to the states for civil defence, is confined, to categorised towns only. Civil Defence is organised, on voluntary basis, except for a minimal paid staff and establishment which is augmented during emergencies. At present, Civil Defence activities are restricted to 225 categorised towns spread over 32 States/ Union Territories. The present target of Civil Defence volunteers is 9.29 lakhs, out of which 4.66 lakhs have already been raised and trained.

National Civil Defence College, Nagpur, a training establishment of the Home Ministry, conducts various courses in Civil Defence and Disaster Relief Management.

Home Guards

Home Guards is a voluntary force, first raised in India in December 1946, to assist the police in controlling civil disturbances and communal riots. Subsequently, the concept of the voluntary citizens force, was adopted by several states. In the wake of the Chinese aggression in 1962, the Centre advised the states and Union Territories, to merge their existing voluntary organisations, into one uniform voluntary force, known a Home Guards. The role of the Home Guards, is to serve as an auxiliary, to the police to serve the community, in any emergency such as floods, fire, cyclone, earthquake, epidemic, etc. It also helps in the maintenance of essential services and Civil Defence duties. Home Guards are of two types - rural and urban. In border states, Border Wing Home Guards Battalions, have also been raised, which serve as an auxiliary, to the security forces. The total strength of Home Guards, in the country is 5,73,793 against which the raised strength is 4,40,994 Home Guards. The Organisation is spread over, all States and Union Territories, except in Kerala.

Home Guards are raised under the Home Guards Acts and Rules of the States/ Union Territories. They are recruited, from the various cross-sections, of the people such as doctors, engineers, lawyers, teachers, professionals, government servants, employees of public and private-sector organisations, senior students, agricultural and industrial workers, etc.

Fire Service

Fire is a State subject and fire services are administrated by the States/ Union Territories. The Ministry of Home Affairs renders technical advice to State/ Union Territories and Central Ministries on fire service in the States. As per the statistics available in early 1998, 2,029 fire stations manned by 66,152 professionals are operating in the country with a fleet of 6,457 appliances/ vehicles.

Central Industrial Security Force (CISF)

The Central Industrial Security Force (CISF) was established in 1969 to provide security to industrial undertakings of the Government. Starting from about 3,000 personnel the force now numbers over 94,715. This force has the responsibility to provide state-of-the-art security to both property and personnel deployed in industrial complexes of Central Government. The force is governed by the CISF Act of 1968 and a set of Rules called CISF Rules of 1969. The CISF is presently stationed 13,233 public sector undertakings. Recently, the responsibility of guarding airports and Central Government Ministries has been assigned to it.

Police Training Institutes

Sardar Vallabhbhai Patel National Police Academy

The Sardar Vallabhbhai Patel National Police Academy is the premier police training institution in the country. It imparts both basic and in-service training, to Indian Police Service (IPS) officers. Established in 1948 at Mount Abu, Rajasthan, the academy was shifted to Hyderabad in 1975. The training programmes, conducted at the Academy are the basic course for IPS probationers, in-service management courses for officers of the junior, middle and top levels of the Indian Police Service, Induction Training Course for State Police Service Officers, to the Indian Police Service, Training of Trainers and Training Administrators' Course, Vertical Interaction Course for IPS officers, and Vertically Integrated Training Programme for Indian Administrative Service officers, and short-duration specialised courses, seminars and workshops for senior officers from IAS, IPS and Judicial Services. The Academy also promotes study and research on police-related topics.

National Institute of Criminology and Forensic Science

The National Institute of Criminology and Forensic Science, New Delhi, was set up in 1972 to undertake research and training in criminology and forensic science.

It conducts integrated in-service training programmes for the functionaries of criminal system. Officers from Government departments and public sector undertakings within the country and also from neighbouring countries come to this Institute for short-term and long-term orientation/international/professional courses. The Institute is a reference centre in the field of criminology and forensic science.

APPENDIX 1

COMMUNIQUE REGARDING CONSTITUTION OF POLICE ESTABLISHMENTS IN INDIA

Communique

From

The Police Commission,

To

The Secretary to the Government of India,

Home Department

Sir,

1. We have the honour to report that immediately on receiving the Government Resolution of the 17th August, regarding the constitution of police establishments throughout India, we proceeded to consider the matters therein set forth, and also the various principles embodied in the Memorandum to which that resolution gave cover.

2. The objects of those instructions appeared to be two-fold, namely:-

(i) That we should collect and collate information regarding all the existing Police Establishments.

(ii) That we should suggest reforms and improvements in general accordance with certain principles laid down.

3. In reference to the first division of the subject, we have collected all the information available at the Presidency regarding the existing police establishments, and we have made such references to the several local governments as are necessary, in order to render the facts and figures correct in detail.

4. In reference to the second head, which appears to be one of major difficulty and importance, we deemed it very desirable, to arrive at such decision, as we are able to form, while two of our collegues, (Colonel Phayre and Mr. Robinson, who are about to leave Calcutta shortly) were still present at our deliberations.

5. After mature and careful consideration of the various matters involved in the question of police organisation; after a review of the English and Irish systems of police; and after comparing the circumstances and requirements of the various provinces, in which the experience of the several members of our Commission has lain; we have arrived at unanimous conclusions regarding the principles, system, and method, on which a good police for all India should be organised. These conclusions we have embodied in a series of propositions; we have also drafted an Act which, in the event of these propositions being approved by Government, we recommend for submission to the Legislature.

6. We have now the honor to enclose a number of copies of the propositions and of the Draft Act, signed by all the Members of the Commission. We take this early occasion of submitting these documents for the consideration of His Excellency the Governor-General in Council; because, as already stated, two of our colleagues are about to depart; and because having advanced our proceedings to the present stage, we desire, for reasons to be stated hereafter, to be favored with directions as to the future conduct of our inquiries.

7. In framing our propositions, we have had due regard to the various principles set forth in the memorandum

attached to the Government Resolution. We have noted the principles and system of the English and Irish Constabulary. We have derived great assistance from the experience of results obtained by the new Police of the Madras Presidency, and by the Calcutta Police. We have endeavored to devise a practical plan for a really effective Civil Constabulary for all India; beginning from its original constitution and formation, and dealing with every point of essential importance. The propositions will, we hope, speak for themselves, and we shall not trouble the Government with a recapitulation of them in this letter. It may suffice here to state that our object has been to form a Civil Constabulary, so organized as to preserve internal tranquillity, in the country, under all ordinary circumstances, to keep the power, to protect life and property; to prevent and detect crime, to furnish guards for public property, for jails, treasuries and the like, to escort treasure, public stores, and prisoners; and to perform a variety of civil duties connected with the watching of *military* buildings and military stores and property, both in the station and on the road. We have proposed independent and separate departmental organization for this Police, completely suited, to all the above purposes. We have suggested the substitution of this one force, for *all* the various Police Establishments, Civil and Military, now existing, as the only means of securing unity, of action and system, and a real control, both departmental and financial. We have arranged for this force, being in all respects subordinate to the Civil Executive Government, and for its being an efficient instrument in the hands of the Magistrate for the prevention and detection of crime, and under his control for the criminal administration of the District. We have aimed, at placing the relations, between the Magistrates and the Officers of the police force, on a satisfactory footing, and at preserving the responsibility now vested in the Magistrate for the conduct of the Criminal Administration; and on the other hand we have taken care to secure to the Police Officers, that position, which is necessary, to the discharge, of their responsibility, for the efficiency of the police.

8. We have endeavored, to mark the line of definition, between the duties of the Military Forces and of the organized Civil Constabulary respectively. And we have aimed at the separation of Judicial and Police functions, so far as that principle can be practically carried out under existing circumstances in India.

9. We have been careful, in determining in detail, the various duties, to be performed, by the organized Civil Constabulary. We have consulted the Military Finance Commission on this subject, and we append a copy of their reply, in the whole of which we concur: and which we venture to commend to the consideration of Government.

10. The Draft Act, we have drawn up, on the basis of the British and Irish Constabulary Acts, so far as they are capable of adaptation to India. We have also consulted the Madras Police Act, and the Calcutta Police Act.

11. On the whole, we may state that the principles of the Propositions and of the Act are provided, on the English system, of which the success is becoming more and more apparent; and of which the operation, is being more and more extended. We believe that they are applicable to all parts of the British Territories in India, and especially to all the various Provinces, of which our several members have cognizance. And we are the more confident in the correctness of this conclusion, because this system has been actually tried, in the Madras Presidency, with results the most beneficial.

12. We have also paid due consideration, to the Despatch from Her Majesty's Government, of the 6th July, on the constitution of the police. We have endeavored to test our propositions by the principles therein laid down, and

in respect to this consideration we desire to offer the following observations.

13. From paras, 4 to 7, inclusive, of Her Majesty's Government Despatch, we clearly gather that the Civil element, in the Police, should at least predominate. It is evident indeed that this condition, is regarded by Her Majesty's Government, as essential. In respect to this point then, we trust that our propositions, will be found fully to provide, for the fulfilment of that condition. We propose to form, a purely civil though well organized constabulary, quite distinct from the military force, subordinate to the civil government, and at the disposal of the magistrates, capable of discharging *all* civil duties whatever, as described in the preceeding para. 9, with vigour and effect, and requiring no aid, whatever from any Military or semi-Military body, in the performance of the ordinary police work of the country.

14. It is obvious that a Police Force, which is to do all this work really well, must be thoroughly organized. We have therefore provided a complete civil organization, for the whole body, from the Inspector General to the common Constable. Further, we have been careful, to provide a complete system, of *supervision by European Officers*. The want of this, has, we believe, been one of the greatest disadvantages, of the civil police system, heretofore existing in India. We fully anticipate that, with this organization, and this supervision, the proposed organized constabulary will prove in a fair degree, competent for the discharge, of the important duties, to be entrusted, to it, as already described. It is certain, that the proper performance of all these duties, must be of daily importance, to the welfare of the country, and the happiness of the people; it is equally certain that these duties have not been, are not, and cannot be, efficiently performed by the existing civil and military police. And we are confident, that nothing short of such organization

and supervision, as that which we propose, will suffice, for the attainment, of this most desirable object.

15. Regarding the matter, then in a purely civil light,—looking solely to the due performance of civil work, irrespective of all other considerations, we submit that we organized civil constabulary, such as that proposed, is absolutely necessary. Whether a Military Police be employed, in addition to the Civil Police, or not; whether Native Troops, are to be engaged, during peace in Civil duties, or not; still, under *any* circumstances, an organized civil police will be required.

16. If then, such a police be organized, as we believe it must be, then the question arises, as to whether an additional military police, will be necessary or desirable.

17. That such a military police, will not by *necessary,* we can feel no doubt, whatever. It is not found necessary in the Madras Presidency, and has not been employed, since the formation of the organized police. In the North-Western Provinces, grave objections have been felt, by many of the Civil Authorities, against the military police.* In those Provinces, their duties have been much restricted. In the Punjab, we believe that the amalgamation, of the Military Police, with an organized Civil Constabulary, has been contemplated. We have proposed that the organised police should be properly drilled and disciplined; that their training should be continuously kept up, so that, they shall be equal, to all the duties of guarding treasuries and jails, and military stores, performing what are called escort duties, and of quelling all ordinary disturbance, which, indeed, are the only duties for which military police is entertained.

18. That the retention of the military police, after the organization of the civil constabulary, shall have been completed, will not be desirable, we feel equally confident.

* Vide Report by Agra Comittee and Appendices.

It is obviously very expensive. It would cause, a large number of men, who are virtually soldiers, to be maintained, and would add to the political objections, which must always, in future be felt, to attend the maintenance, of a numerically large native force. The financial objection too, which we have ventured to indicate, will apply with particular force, to this case. For if the civil police constabulary, shall (as we fully believe it must) be efficiently organized, then a considerable expense, must be incurred, for the pay and the equipment of the men and, above all, for providing of European Officers, to supervise and control them. Then the question presents itself, how is this expense to be met? If the military police can be reduced, or gradually abolished, then the great saving, hereby effected, will be available, as an offset, to the expense of organizing, the civil constabulary. But if an organized civil constabulary, and a military police, are to be maintained, then the cost of both together would, we fear, be found excessive.

19. If, therefore, the organized civil constabulary can do the work of the military police, then there is every financial reason, independent of other reasons, for abolishing the Military Police or amalgamating it with the civil constabulary. Now we believe, that an organized Constabulary, *will* be able, to do the work, relating to guards and escorts, and the suppression of ordinary disturbance now done by military police. And in respect to civil services required for the military departments, we believe that competent authorities, are agreed, that the organized Constabulary will fully suffice, and it certainly does so suffice, in the Madras Presidency. Obviously it is economical, to substitute an organized civil policeman, for a military policeman, who is a Native soldier, if the former can do the work required to be done; in as much even as a highly organized civil constabulary cost much less than a military police. Then it must ever be remembered that an organized policeman, though

trained to arms, does not, generally carry or possess arms. Politically therefore, while he is more useful, he is less dangerous, than a military policeman, who is really a native soldier. If it be said, that military police, may be required, for military service, we would submit, that this kind of service, ought always to be rendered, by the military forces, which we presume, are and will be kept up, in sufficient strength for the military requirements of the country. Indeed, the effectual separation of military from civil duties, is a matter which the authorities, both civil and military, concur in, considering as one of primary importance; and which we have laid down, as the basis of our propositions. Here again we would beg attention to the letter of the Military Finance Commission already alluded to.

20. In *fine,* then we submit, that, as soon as the civil constabulary, shall have been organized, the military police will not be needed, either for civil or military purposes; that if retained, it would be a cause of heavy and needless expense; and in a certain degree a source of political danger: that it should be gradually abolished or absorbed into the organized constabulary, or else that, if required for Military purposes, it be incorporated with the native army. We trust then, that, if the organization we have proposed, for the constabulary, shall satisfy the Government, as *to all* requirements, as already enumerated, the military police, may hereafter be dispensed with.

21. We have particularly observed, a passage in the 7th para. of Her Majesty's Government Despatch to the following effect:- "They (the civil police) should be under the control of the magistrates of districts, subject to the supervision of the commissioner of the division, where such officer exists." We trust, that our propositions, will show the care, we have taken, to preserve the responsibility, of the magistrate, for the general success, of the criminal administration, of the District: and to afford

him prompt means of ensuring, the obedience, of the organized constabulary to his lawful orders.

22. Our attention has been given to the observation made in para 8 to 11 inclusive, of Her Majesty's Government Despatch regarding village police. We have borne in mind that (as stated in the despatch) "no police system can be really effective in "India which is not closely connected with the village system."

23. We have therefore provided, in our propositions, that the village police, shall be retained in their existing status, and shall be brought, into direct relation, with the organized constabulary, in respect to his public duties. The working of the village police, only to the extent heretofore, conducted by the magistrate, and *no more,* will devolve on the officer of the constabulary. That the constabulary, should exercise this much of authority, over the village police, is indispensable to unity and efficiency, of police action. But as the organized Constabulary obey, by the orders of the magistrate, so ultimately the village police, who are subordinate to the organized police, continue under the control of the magistrate. The village watchman will still be appointed by, and will still be under the influence of, the landholder, wherever these functions are already vested in them. Wherever the case may be otherwise, the local custom will be followed. He will obey the orders of the organized police, but will *not* be incorporated into the body.

24. And in respect of the appointment of the watchman, of his succession to office; of the manorial influence, exercised over him by landholders or others:- whatever local custom, may prevail, in any province will remain intact.

25. We note the passage in para 12 of Her Majesty's Government Despatch to the effect that, "for protective purpose generally, for a wing a multitude, or for quelling "disturbance, a small body of military police is equal to a

much larger number of "Ordinary Policemen." This passage refers to the ordinary men of the existing civil police: and we appreciate the correctness of the observation regarding them. But we apprehend, that the men of the organised constabulary, which we propose will be trained to arms, and, if necessary armed, and will therefore, be fully able to cope with, an ordinary emergency as above described.

26. Paras 13 and 14 of Her Majesty' Government Despatch, refer to the duties to be performed by the native troops, in time of peace. It is stated, that native troops may be employed, on civil duties, which may beneficially give them employment in ordinary times. But then it is enjoined "that, for the discharge of such duties, no addition 'whatever is to be made to the native army, which must be kept at the minimum, "required for strictly military purposes." Further, it is declared that "not a man should be "added to the army beyond the number with, *on military grounds,* may be determined "necessary for the wants of the Empire." From this, we clearly infer, that native troops are not to be employed on police duties, unless they can be spared, from their military duties, and unless the military authorities, after the native army shall have been reduced to the minimum necessary for military requirements, shall be able to detach native soldiers for police duties. Now we understand that the native army is, in the course of being reduced, to the minimum as prescribed in Her Majesty's Government Despatch. When it shall have reached that minimum, we are confident that it will be impossible, for the military authority to detach soldiers for police duties, the numbers of the troops would be insufficient, and discipline would be ruined. All Military authorities, insist on this that, if the native Army be reduced to the minimum as above described, the force should not be frittered away, in doing civil duties, but should be devoted, to the perfecting of military discipline, under the eye of its officers. There

will be absolutely no spare men for miscellaneous non-military works. If, on the other hand, the native troops were kept up at a strength, exceeding absolute Military requirements, *in order,* that there might be men available for police duties, then the Despatch of Her Majesty's Government, would be contravened.

27. We would specially refer the Governor-General in Council, to the letter of the Military Finance Commission, already alluded to in our preceding para. 9, as to the great reduction expected in the native army, when the troops shall be relieved of miscellaneous and police duties, whereby an enormous financial saving will be effected. And when this shall have been carried outk as we suppose it will be under the terms of Her Majesty's Governments Despatch, then we certainly conclude that there will be no soldiers available for police duties in time of peace.

28. We have therefore, been careful to provide, such an organized constabulary, as shall be able, to relieve the Native Army, now in the course of reduction, from the duties in question.

29. With these remarks we submit the propositions and the Draft Act, as the unanimous result of our anxious deliberations, and thus we have fulfilled, the primary part of our instruction.

30. But the Government Resolution of the 17th August, while directing us to prepare a statement of the strength, and cost of the police of all classes, enjoins us, under the second head, of our enquiry, to report any alterations in system, which we consider likely to increase efficiency or diminish expense. Now any alterations, which we could propose, would be based, on the principle, set forth in our Propositions, if we were permitted to follow our own judgment, or upon any modification in our proposed plan which the Government might be pleased to order. In fact, the alteration, which we really propose is this, that the present police, civil and military, be abolished, and an

organised constabulary substituted, in all the provinces of India, where such a system does not already exist. We are confident, that this arrangement, would increase efficiency and diminish expense. But what the exact saving would be, we cannot say, without endeavoring to allot to each District in every Province and in the aggregate to each Local Government, the strength of organized police, that would suffice, to do the work of the civil and military police, and the civil duties now devolving on the native soldiery. If Government should desire it, we will, of course, use our best exertions, to frame an estimate of this kind, on the best data we can collect. But when we consider the great number and variety of the duties, to be undertaken by the organised police; the local authorities, civil and military, to be consulted; the multifixious arrangements, to be made; we doubt our ability, to frame an estimate, that would be an accurate financial guide, or would be practically suited, to take effect in the various, Districts. We learn that, when the organised Police, was introduced into the Madras Presidency, these arrangements, so intricate in their detail, and so important in their aggregate, occupied a considerable time, and could only be managed by officers on the spot. It appears, then that really reliable information of this kind cannot well be acquired, unless the system be more or less commenced and carried into effect. If the Government should be pleased to approve our plan; and if its introduction were sanctioned, then the new police authorities, in concert with the local authorities, civil and military, would form the new organized constabulary; reduce existing establishment with a great saving to the State; would diminish the work now done; and would allot to the new establishment, whatever duties might be determined upon. Thus the work would progress gradually and surely; reduction of cost and numbers would advance month by mònth; the duties would be arranged on the spot; and accurate and really practical information would be placed at the disposal of Government from time to time. And such information, would meet the requirements, of Her Majesty's Government Despatch and of the Government Despatch of 17th August.

31. In this manner an actual commencement of reduction in numbers and expenditure might be made at once. Whereas it is to be apprehended that, if this be deferred, until the information we are now collecting, shall be complete, some time must elapse, during which the present heavy expenditure, would continue undiminished.

32. But if there be any delay in carrying out the improved system we recommend, then we would submit that the expensive establishment, of military police now kept up, should be brought immediately, under financial examination, with a view to effecting such reductions, in detail, as might be, at once effected, under any circumstances, and pending the result of the investigation, now going on. We believe that some reduction, be it more or less, might be now effected in the Bengal Presidency generally, whatever be the system ultimately decided on. This Financial examination might be conducted either by the Military Finance Commission, or by this Commission. The Military Commission has peculiar facilities and appliances, for such an examination, which they would conduct, in the same manner as that, in which their examination into the native army expenditure, is conducted, and doubtless, they would effect in the military police reductions similar to those, they are effecting elsewhere This duty they are, as we have ascertained, willing to undertake, if Government entrust it to them. Or else, the examination, as above described, might be conducted by this Commission. In this case we should desire to be favored with specific instructions as to placing ourselves in communication with the several local Governments.

33. But the Financial examination above described, however useful it might be, would not, in our opinion, be so efficacious on ensuring an early reduction of expenditure, and the actual introduction of the improved system itself. This latter method would be the purest and safest means of securing both economy and efficiency.

M.H. Court, President

A.P. Phayre, Member

S. Wauchope, Member

W. Robinson, Member

R. Temple, Member

H. Bruce, Lieutenant-Colonel and Member

Police Commission: Calcutta

September, 1860.

APPENDIX 2

POLICE REGULATION BILL: PROVISIONS

Bill for

the Regulation of police within the Province of.............. and other parts of the British territories in India, to which it may please the Governor-General in Council to extend its provisions.

Whereas it is expedient to make the police force throughout the province of............. an efficient instrument at the disposal of the Magistrate for the prevention and detection of crime; and to reorganize the police force. It is enacted as follows:-

1. The following words and expressions in this Act shall have the meaning hereby assigned to them; unless there be something in the subject or context repugnant to such construction, (that is to say).

The word District Officer shall mean the Chief Magisterial Officer in charge of a District, and exercising the full powers of a Magistrate under the regulations, or by whatever designation the officer in executive administration of a District is styled.

The word Magistrate shall include all persons, within their respective jurisdictions, exercising all or any of the powers of a Magistrate.

The word Subordinate as applied to Police Functionaries, shall mean District Superintendents and their Assistants.

The word Police shall include General and Village Police, and all other persons, by whatever name known, who exercise any police functions throughout the Province of......................

The expression General Police District shall embrace any Province, District, Tract or Territory to which the operation of this Act shall be extended.

The word Property shall include any chattel, money, or valuable security.

Words importing the singular number shall include the plural number; and words importing the plural number shall include the singular number.

Words importing the masculine gender shall include females.

The word person shall include Company or Corporation.

The word month shall mean calendar month.

The word cattle shall, besides horned cattle, include elephants, camels, horses, asses, mules, sheep, goats, and swine.

2. The several Regulations and Acts mentioned in the Schedule hereunto annexed are hereby repealed, and amended to the extent and in the manner therein set forth, within the limits of the General Police District; except so far as they repeal the whole or any part of any other Regulation or Act; and except as to any act or offence which shall have been done or committed, or any fine or penalty which shall have been incurred, or to any proceedings which shall have been commenced, before this Act shall come into operation: provided also that nothing in this Section shall be construed to affect any judicial function or Jurisdiction, original or appellate, which by any existing law may be exercised by any of the officers mentioned in the enactments above repealed or amended.

3. The superintendence of the police thoughout the General Police District shall vest in, and be exercised by the Local Government under the control of the Governor General in Council, and except as authorized by the Local Government under the provisions of this Act, no person, officer, or court shall be empowered to appoint, supersede, or control any police functionary, any Regulation; Act or usage to the contrary notwithstanding.

4. The administration of the police throughout the General Police District shall be vested in an officer to be styled the Inspector-General of Police, and in such subordinates, subject to the general control and direction of the District Officer as to the local government shall seem fit; who shall from time to time be appointed by the said local government and may be removed by the same authority; and who shall receive such salary as the Governor General of India in Council shall allow.

5. All powers not inconsistent with the provisions of this Act which up to the passing of this Act belonged by law to the existing police authorities shall be vested in the police authorities appointed under this Act. Provided always that no police functionary so appointed shall possess or exercise any judicial or revenue authority. And the duties and responsibilities of land-holders and others as defined by law shall apply to the Police appointed under this Act.

6. The Inspector-General of Police shall be appointed a Justice of the peace. He shall also have the full powers of a Magistrate throughout the General Police District; but shall exercise these powers subject to such orders as may from time to time be issued by the local Government. The Local Government may vest any District Superintendent of Police with all the powers of a Magistrate within such limits as he may deem proper; but such Superintendent shall exercise the powers with which he shall be so invested only so far as may be necessary for the preservation of the peace, the prevention

of crime and the detection, apprehension and detention of offenders, in order to their being brought before a Magistrate, and as far as may be necessary for the performance of the duties assigned to him by this Act.

7. The entire Police establishment under each local government shall for the purpose of this Act be deemed to be one police force; and shall be formally enrolled; and shall consist of such number of officers and men, and shall be otherwise constituted in such manner, as shall be from time to time ordered by the local government, subject to the sanction of the Governor General of India in Council.

8. The Inspector-General of Police may from time to time, subject to the approval of the Local Government, frame such orders and regulations as he shall deem expedient, relative to the general organization and distribution of the force, the places of residence, the pay and rank, the classification, distribution and particular service of the members thereof; their inspection, the description of arms, accoutrements and other necessaries to be furnished to them; to the collecting and communication intelligence and information; and all such other orders and regulations relative to the said police force as the said Inspector-General shall, from time to time, deem expedient for preventing abuse or neglect, and for rendering such Force efficient in the discharge of all its duties.

9. The appointment of all police officers shall, under such rules as the local government shall from time to time sanction, rest with the Inspector-General of Police and the District Superintendents; who may under such rules as aforesaid at any time dismiss, suspend, reduce or fine to any amount not exceeding one month's pay, any police officer whom they shall think remiss or negligent in the discharge of his duty or otherwise unfit for the same.

10. Every person so appointed shall receive on his enrolment a Certificate (A) under the seal of the Inspector

General, by virtue of which he shall be vested with the powers, functions, and privileges of a police officer. Such certificate shall cease to have effect whenever the person named in it is suspended or dismissed, or otherwise removed from employment in the police force, and shall thereupon be immediately surrendered to his superior officer or other person empowered to receive it.

11. There shall be deducted from the pay of every police officer, of a Class not entitled to the benefit of the uncovenanted service pension rules, a sum, after such rate as the local government shall direct, not being a greater rate than one Anna in the Rupee; which sum so deducted and also the money accruing from the stoppages from the pay of police officers during absence from sickness or other cause, from fines imposed on police officers for misconduct, and from fines imposed by Magistrates and others upon drunken persons or for assaults upon police officers, and all money arising from the sale of worn or cast-off clothing or other articles supplied for the use of the police, or from any other miscellaneous sources which shall be permitted by the local government, shall from time to time be invested in such manner and in such securities as the local government may direct, and the interest and dividends thereof, or so much of the same as shall not be required for the purposes herein mentioned, shall be likewise invested as aforesaid, and accumulate, so as to form a fund to be called, The Police Superannuation Fund; and shall be applied from time to time to the payment of superannuation or retiring allowances, or gratuities, under such rules as may be passed by the said local government: provided always that any police officer may be dismissed or removed without superannuation allowance; and that no police officer shall be entitled as of right to any allowance from the fund; or shall retain any right to a refund of any deduction made from his pay while he may have been a police officer.

12. It shall be lawful for the Inspector-General of Police or any District Superintendent, if they shall think fit, and subject to the general direction of the District Officer, on the application of any person showing the necessity thereof, to depute any additional number of police officers, to keep the peace at any place within the general police district, at the charge of the person making the application, to be exclusively under the orders of the District Superintendent, and for such time as they shall think fit; provided always that it shall be lawful for the person on whose application such deputation shall have been made, on giving one month's notice in writing to the Inspector General or District Superintendent, to require that the Officers so deputed shall be discontinued; and such person shall be relieved from the charge of such additional Force from the expiration of such notice.

13. Whenever any railway, canal, or other public work, or any Manufacturing or commercial concern shall be carried on, or be in operation in any part of the country, and it shall appear to the Inspector General, that the appointment of an additional police force in such neighbourhood is rendered necessary by the behaviour, or reasonable apprehension of the behaviour of the persons employed upon such work, it shall be lawful for the Inspector General, with the consent of the local government, to direct the employment of such additional Force; and to maintain the same so long as such necessity shall continue; and to make orders from time to time upon the treasurer or other officer having the control or custody of the funds of any company or person carrying on such works, for the payment of the extra force so rendered necessary as aforesaid.

14. It shall be lawful for the Inspector General of Police, under the sanction of the local government, to depute any part of the police force, in excess of the fixed complement, to be quartered in any part of the general police district which shall be found to be in a disturbed

or dangerous state, or in any part of the general police district in which, from the misconduct of the inhabitants, he may deem it expedient to strengthen the number of police; and the inhabitants of the offending tract or part shall be charged with the cost of such body of men so deputed: and the District Officer shall assess the proportion in which such sum is to be paid by the inhabitants according to his judgement of their respective means.

15. All the money paid or recovered in respect of any additional force deputed as is mentioned in the three last preceeding sections, shall be paid into a fund to be called, "The General Police Fund,"; and shall be applied to the maintenance of the police force, under such orders as the local government may pass. All sums of money payable under those Sections shall be recoverable by distress and sale of the goods of the defaulter under the warrant of a Magistrate or by suit in any competent court.

16. When it shall appear that any tumult, riot or outrage has taken place, or may be reasonably apprehended in any place, and that the ordinary officers appointed for preserving the peace are not sufficient for its preservation, and for the protection of the inhabitants, and the security of property in such place, it shall be lawful for any police officer not below the rank of Inspector to apply to the nearest Magistrate to appoint so many of the public or village servants, or residents of the neighbourhood, as such police officer may require, to act as special police officer for such time and in such manner as he shall deem necessary; and it shall be the duty of such Magistrate at once to comply with such applications.

17. Every special Police Officer so appointed shall have the same powers, privileges and protection, and be liable to all such duties and penalties, and be subordinate to the same authorities as the ordinary officers of police.

18. If any person being appointed a special Police Officer as aforesaid, shall without sufficient excuse neglect or

refuse to serve as such, or to obey such lawful order or direction as may be given him for the performance of his duties, he shall be liable upon conviction before a Magistrate to a fine not exceeding fifty rupees for each and every such neglect, refusal or disobedience.

19. No police officer shall be at liberty to resign his office, or withdraw himself from the duties thereof; unless expressly allowed to do so in writing by the District Superintendent; or unless he shall have given to his superior officer two months' notice in writing of his intention to do so. Nor shall any such police officer engage in any employment or office whatever, other than his duties under this Act; unless expressly permitted to do so in writing under the seal of the Inspector General.

20. From and after the passing of this Act, every person, not being, or having ceased to be, a duly enrolled Police Officer, who shall unlawfully assume any function or power belonging to the police; and who shall not forthwith deliver up his Certificate and all the clothing, accoutrements, and appointments, and other necessaries which may have been supplied to him for the execution of his duty; or who shall have in his possession any distinctive article of the dress or appointment directed to be worn exclusively by the police force, without being able to account satisfactory for his possession thereof; or who shall put on the dress of any police officer, or any dress designed to represent it, or to be taken for it; or who shall otherwise impersonate the character or act the part of any police officer for any purpose whatever; shall, in addition to any other punishment to which he may be liable for any offence committed under the assumed character, be liable on conviction before a Magistrate to a penalty not exceeding two hundred rupees, or to imprisonment, with or without hard labor, for a period not exceeding six months, or both.

21. Every police officer shall, for all purposes in this Act contained, be considered to be always on duty and shall

have the powers of a police officer in every part of the General Police District. It shall be his duty to use his best endeavours and ability to prevent all crimes, offences, and public nuisances; to preserve the peace; to apprehend disorderly and suspicious characters; to detect and bring offenders to justice; to collect and communicate intelligence affecting the public peace; and promptly to obey and execute all orders and warrants lawfully issued to him by any competent authority.

22. It shall be the duty of every police officer, and he is hereby authorized to arrest, without warrant:

i) Any person who is charged on credible information, or whom he has reasonable ground to suspect, of having been concerned in any grave or forcible crime or outrage.

ii) Any person who is charged with committing an aggravated assault, in every case in which he shall have good reason to believe that such assault has been committed, although not in his view, and that by reason of the recent commission of the offence a warrant could not have been issued.

iii) Any person committing, or attempting to commit, any breach of the peace, in his view, and who refuses to desist on being required thereto.

iv) Any person found injuring the public buildings, roads, tanks, and water channels; or committing any offence punishable by Law:- provided always that, where such offence is of a slight and petty nature, it shall not be necessary for the police officer to arrest, if from the circumstances of the case, there is no reason to apprehend that the party will abscond.

v) Any vagrant whom he shall find disturbing the public peace, or whom he shall have good cause to suspect of having committed or being about to commit a crime; all persons whose name and residence is unknown, or whom he may find by night laying or loitering in any highway, road or other place, and who, in either case, are unable to give a satisfactory account of themselves.

vi) Any person who assaults, resists or obstructs such Police Officer in the execution of his duty; or aids or excites others to do so.

vii) All persons who, having been in legal custody, shall have escaped therefrom.

viii) All persons who are charged with having done any injury or damage to the person or property of another, and who refuse to give their name and residence; or who give one which there is ground to believe to be false, may be detained, solely for the purpose of ascertaining such name and residence, with a view to future proceedings.

23. In every case in which any person shall be given in charge to a police officer, on a false or frivolous charge; or in which a false and frivolous charge shall be made to a police officer against any person; or in which any information or complaint shall be laid or made before a Magistrate or police officer, and shall not be further prosecuted; or in which, if further prosecuted, it shall appear to the Magistrate by whom the case is heard, that there were no sufficient grounds for making the charge, the Magistrate shall have the power to award a fine not exceeding fifty rupees, imprisonment for a period not exceeding one month, or both; or to award such amends not exceeding fifty rupees, to be paid by the informer or complainant to the party informed or complained against, for his loss of time and expenses in the matter, as to the Magistrate shall seem fit. And such amends shall be recoverable in the manner provided for the levy of fines.

24. Every person taken into custody by any Police Officer, without warrant, except persons detained for the mere purpose of ascertaining their name and residence, shall forthwith be delivered into the custody of the Police Officer in charge of a Station House, in order that such person may be secured until he can be brought before a

Magistrate to be dealt with according to Law, or may give bail for his appearance before a Magistrate, if the officer in charge shall deem it prudent to take bail as hereinafter mentioned; provided always that, where bail is not taken, the prisoner shall be brought before a Magistrate within twenty-four hours, unless circumstances render delay unavoidable.

25. Whenever any person shall be brought in custody, without a warrant, to any Station House, at a time when he cannot at once be sent before a Magistrate, and shall be charged with any bailable offence, or with any unbailable offence of which it shall appear to the officer in charge of the Station House or other Superior Officer of police that the prisoner is falsely accused it shall be lawful for such Police Officer to release the accused on bail or on his own recognizance to appear before the Magistrate when required.

26. It shall be lawful for every Police Officer in charge of a Station or other Superior Officer of Police, to bind by recognizance any person, to appeal as prosecutor, or as a witness, before the Magistrate, by whom any grave charge, is being or about to be investigated; and if any such prosecutor or witness shall refuse to execute such recognizance, it shall be competent to such officer to forward the person in custody to the Magistrate's Court.

27. Every recognizance, so taken, shall be without fee or reward; shall be conditioned for appearance of the person thereby bound before a Magistrate at such time and place as may required; and the time and place of appearance and the sum thereby acknowledged, not exceeding one thousand rupees, shall be specified in said recognizance, or in the condition thereof and the officer taking the recognizance shall return the same forthwith to the Magistrate present at the time and place when and where the party is bound to appear.

28. If from the absence of witnesses from any other reasonable cause, it shall become necessary or advisable

to defer the examination of any case, or the further examination of any witness it shall be lawful for any Magistrate from time to time by his warrant to remand the accused to the custody of any Police Officer, for such time as shall deem necessary and reasonable, not exceeding eight clear days, to be secured in any Station House or Jail or to be otherwise detained in custody as to the said Magistrate shall appear expedient: provided always that any such Magistrate may order such accused party to be bought before him at any time or place before the expiration of the time for which such accused party shall have been remanded; or may discharge such accused party on his recognizances, with or without sureties, conditioned for his appearance at the time and place appointed for such further examination.

29. It shall be lawful for any police officer without a warrant to enter and inspect all drinking shops, gaming houses and other resorts of loose and disorderly characters, all premises of persons suspected of receiving stolen property, any locality, vessel, boat or conveyance in any part of which places he shall have just cause to believe that crime has been, or is about to be committed; or which he reasonably suspects to contain stolen property; and then and there to take all necessary measures for the effectual prevention and detection of crime; and to take charge of all property reasonably suspected to have been stolen, and of ali articles or things which may serve as evidence of the crime supposed to have been committed; and to take charge of all unclaimed property.

30. Every police officer, not below the grade of Inspector, shall, under such orders as may from time to time be issued by the Inspector General of Police, be an Inspector of weights and measures, and may enter any shop or premises for the purpose of inspecting the weights and measures and instruments for weighting, kept or used therein, and may seize any weight, measure, or

instrument for weighing, which he may have reason to believe is false.

31. No police officer shall receive any complaint of any petty offence; or take into his custody any person brought to him accused of such petty offences, as trespass, assault, quarrelling, or the like; and it shall be lawful for any police officer to refuse to receive and act upon any charge of an offence of a grave character, if he shall on enquiry made of the complainant alone, see good grounds for doubting its truth; provided always that if the charge be not of such a nature as under ordinary circumstances would justify the police officer in refusing to receive it, the particular reasons for refusing it are to be recorded by such officer at the time.

32. It shall be lawful for any police officer to lay any Information before the Magistrate, and to apply for summons, warrant, search warrant, or such other legal process as may by law issue, and may be expedient under the circumstances, against any person committing an offence against any law or enactment, or against any regulation for the protection of the revenue, or against any person committing or failing to remove any public nuisance or unwarrantable obstructions, keeping disorderly houses, harbouring thieves, disturbing the peace, obstructing the due course of justice, and the like; and to prosecute such offenders up to final judgment: provided always that any rewards, forfeitures, and penalties, or shares of rewards, forfeitures, or penalties, which by law are payable to informers, and all costs of prosecution which may by any enactment be awarded to the prosecutor, shall be paid into the "General Police Fund."

33. From and after the passing of this Act all summons warrants, search warrants, warrants of commitment for trial or order for escort and conveyance of prisoners, and all other processes issued by any officer in any criminal proceeding, shall be directed and delivered to officers of

the police alone; and such process shall be served and executed by them and none others, provided always that in all cases of petty-offence it shall be lawful for the Magistrate or other officer issuing a summon to require the party applying for a summon for the appearance of either the defendant or witnesses to deposit and eventually to pay any fee or such summons and all costs incurred by the Police in serving such process, the same to be paid into the "General Police Fund" for the maintenance of the police.

34. Where any such warrant, order, or process shall be directed or delivered to any of the said officers, unless it be necessary for the due execution thereof that such warrant be executed without delay, the person receiving it shall deliver the same to any officer authorised for that purpose, who shall take charge of it, and appoint by endorsement thereon one or more police officers to execute the same or endorse it to any other officer for a like purpose; and every police officer whose name shall be so endorsed thereon shall have the same powers, privileges, and protection as if the same had originally been directed to him by name; provided also that every such process shall be executed with all secrecy and despatch; and shall have full force in any part of the General Police District except within the limits of the Supreme Court, without further formality or local endorsement; and that all police authorities shall every where be assisting in the execution of such process.

35. Every summon, notice, or other criminal process may be served on the party named personally, or be left with some adult male member of his family, or a copy therefore may be affixed on some conspicuous part of his usual place of abode: and any party failing or neglecting to obey such summons or notice duly served, shall be liable, at the discretion of the Magistrate or Court that issued the process, to a penalty not exceeding fifty rupees; unless such person shall be able to prove that he was prevented

by unavoidable accident or other satisfactory cause from obeying such summons, notice or the like.

36. A magistrate may, without issuing any summons, forthwith issue his warrant to bring before him any person charged with an offence cognizable by him, or whose attendance it may for any reason be necessary to enforce, whenever it shall appear probable that such person will not attend unless compelled so to do.

37. A police officer executing a warrant of arrest shall notify the substance of the warrant, and if required so to do shall show the warrant.

38. In making an arrest, the police officer executing the warrant shall actually touch or confine the body of the person to be arrested; unless there be submission to the custody by word or action.

39. After arrest the prisoner shall not be subjected to any more restraint than such as may be necessary to prevent his escape.

40. Any police officer authorised by a warrant to arrest a person accused of any offence for which a warrant may issue on complaint, may break open any outer or inner door or window of a dwelling house, whether that of the person accused or of any other person, in order to execute such warrant, if, after notification of his authority and purpose, and demand of admittance duly made, he cannot otherwise obtain admittance.

41. If information be received that a person accused of any offence for which a warrant may issue, has concealed himself in a Zenanah or female apartment in the actual occupancy of women, the officer employed to execute the warrant shall take such precautions as may be necessary to prevent the escape of the accused; and if such person shall not deliver himself up, the police officer authorized to execute the warrant, may break open the Zenanah, and execute the process entrusted to him, giving notice

at the same time to any woman in the Zenanah that she is at liberty to withdraw.

42. After arrest made, the police officer executing the warrant shall without necessary delay bring the person arrested before the Magistrate or other authority described in the warrant.

43. No police officer shall offer to the person arrested any inducement, by threat or promise or otherwise, to make any disclosure. But no police officer shall prevent the person arrested, by any caution or otherwise, from making any disclosure which he may be disposed to make of his own free will.

44. If any police officer shall at any time find himself unable to effect an arrest, it shall be lawful for him to require any and every person present to assist and aid him in making the arrest; and any person who shall refuse or neglect to comply whith such requisition, shall be liable on conviction before a Magistrate a fine not exceeding fifty rupees or to imprisonment for a period not exceeding three months, or both.

45. Every police officer who shall be guilty of any violation of duty or wilful breach or neglect of any regulations lawful orders of other competent authority and not punishable under Section X. of this Act; or who shall cease to perform the duties of his office without leave; or without having given two months, notice as provided by this enactment; or engage without authority in any employment other than his police duty; who shall be guilty of prevarication in any judicial trial; or who shall maliciously and without probable cause prefer any false, vexatious or frivolous charge or information against any individual; or who shall knowingly and wilfully and with evil intent exceed his powers; or shall be guilty of any wilful and culpable neglect of duty in not bringing any person, who shall be in his custody without a warrant, before a Magistrate as hereinbefore provided; or who shall allow any person in

his custody to escape; or who shall offer any unwarrantable personal violence to any person in his custody, shall be liable on conviction by a Magistrate to a penalty not exceeding three months' pay, or to imprisonment with or without hard labor not exceeding three months, or both.

46. Any police officer who shall on any pretext or under any circumstance, directly or indirectly, collect or receive any fee, gratuity, diet money, allowance, or recompense other than he may be duly authorized by the Inspector General or other Officer acting under his order to collect or receive, shall on conviction before a Magistrate be liable to a penalty not exceeding six months pay, or to imprisonment with or withour hard labor not exceeding six months, or both.

47. Any police officer who shall directly or indirectly extort, exact, seek, or obtain any bribe or unauthorized reward or consideration, by any illegal threat, or pretence, or for doing or omitting or delaying to do any act which it may be his duty to do or to cause to be done; or for withholding or delaying any information which he is bound to afford or to communicate; or who shall connive at the escape of any person in his custody; or who shall attempt to commit any of the offences above said; or shall be guilty of cowardice, shall be liable upon conviction before a Magistrate to a fine not exceeding twelve months pay, or to imprisonment with or without hard labor not exceeding twelve months, or both. Provided always that nothing in the three last preceding sections shall be deemed to preclude the Magistrate from committing for trial any cases of this nature too serious for his cognizance.

48. If any person shall assault or resist any police officer in the execution of his duty; or shall aid or incite any other person so to do; or shall maliciously and without probable cause prefer any false or frivolous charge against any police officer; such person shall, on conviction of such offence before any Magistrate be liable to a fine not

exceeding two hundred rupees, or to imprisonment with or without hard labor not exceeding six months, or both.

49. Any person who in any street, or road, thoroughfare, or passage, within the limits of any town, commits any of the following offences, to the obstruction, inconvenience, annoyance, risk, or damage of the residents and passengers, shall, on, conviction, before a Magistrate be liable to a fine not exceeding fifty rupees, or to imprisonment not exceeding eight days; and it shall be lawful for any police officer to take into custody without a warrant any person who within view commits any offence.

a) Any person who shall slaughter any cattle or clean any carcass in the streets; any person in the streets; any person riding for driving any cattle, recklessly and furiously, or training or breaking any horse or other cattle on or near any public road, to the danger of the passerby.

b) Any person who wants only or cruelly abuses or tortures any animal.

c) Any person who shall keep any cattle, or conveyance of any kind standing in any road or street longer than is required for loading or unloading, or for taking up or setting down passengers; or who shall leave any conveyance in such a manner as to cause inconvenience or danger to the public.

d) Any person exposing goods for sale on the road so as to obstruct passengers.

e) Any person who throws or lays down any dirt, filth, rubbish or any stones or building material; or who constructs any pail, cowshed, stable, or the like within the bounds of any thoroughfare; or who causes any offensive matter to run from any house, factory, or the like into the street.

f) Any person found in any thoroughfare drunk and riotous or incapable of taking care of himself.

g) Any person who wilfully and indecently exposes his person or any offensive deformity or disease, or commits nuisance by easing himself in or by the side of, or near any public street or thoroughfare; or by bathing or washing in any tank or reservoir not being a place set apart for that purpose.

h) Any person who neglects the fence built duly to protect any well, tank, or other dangerous place or structure.

50. The Superintendent and Superior Officers of Police may, as occasion requires, direct the conduct of all assemblies and processions in the public roads, streets, or thoroughfares; prescribe the routes by which, and the times at which such processions may pass; keep order in the public roads, streets, throughfares, ghats, and landing places, and all other places of public resort; and prevent obstructions on the occasions of such assemblies and processions and in the neighbourhood of places of worship during the time of public worship and in any case when the roads, streets, or thoroughfares, ghauts or landing places, may be liable to be obstructed. They may also regulate the use of music in the streets, on the occasion of native festivals and ceremonies; and may direct all crowds of twelve or more persons to disperse, when they have reason to apprehend any breach of the peace; and every person opposing, or not obeying the orders so issued as aforesaid, or violating the conditions of such license, shall be liable to a fine not exceeding two hundred rupees. Provided always that nothing in this Section contained shall be deemed to interfere with the general control of Magistrate over such matters.

51. In all cases of convictions under this Act, the Magistrate trying the case shall be restrained within the limits of his ordinary jurisdiction as to the amount of fine or imprisonment he may inflict: provided always that such charges against Police Officers above the rank of a

constable shall only be adjudicated on by European functionaries.

52. Nothing contained in this Act, shall be construed to prevent any person from being prosecuted for any offence made punishable on conviction by this Act; or to prevent any person from being liable under any other law, regulation, or Act, to any other or higher penalty or punishment than is provided for such offence by this Act. Provided always that no person shall be punished twice for the same offence.

53. All fines and penalties imposed and all sums of money recoverable under the authority of this Act, may, in case of non-payment thereof, be levied by distress and sale of the goods and chattles of the offender by warrant of the Magistrate, in any manner provided by Law.

54. All actions and prosecutions against any person, which may be lawfully brought for any thing done or intended to be done under the provisions of this Act, or under the general police powers hereby given, shall be commenced within three months after the Act complained of shall have been committed, and not otherwise; and notice in writing of such action and of the cause thereof, shall be given to the defendant, or to the Superintendent or other Superior Officer of the District in which the act was committed one month at least before the commencement of the action. And no plaintiff shall recover in any such action if tender of sufficient amends shall have been made before such action brought, or if a sufficient sum of money shall have been paid into Court after such action brought, by or on behalf of the defendant; and though a decree shall be given for the plaintiff in any such action, such plaintiff shall not have costs against the defendant; unless the Judge, before whom the trial shall be, shall certify his approbation of the action: provided always that no action shall in any case lie where such officers shall have been prosecuted criminally for the same act.

55. When any action, prosecution, or proceeding shall be brought against any police officer for any act done by him in such capacity, it shall be lawful for him to plead that such act was done by him under the authority of warrant issued by a Magistrate. And such plea shall be proved by the production of the warrant directing the act and purporting to be signed by a Magistrate. And the defendant shall thereupon be entitled to a decree in his favor, notwithstanding any defect of jurisdiction in such Magistrate. And no proof of the signature of such official shall be necessary, unless the court shall see reason to doubt its being genuine: provided always that any remedy which the party may have against the authority issuing such warrant shall remain entire.

56. This Act shall take effect in any and every such District as the Governor in Council shall appoint by notification published in the Official Gazette.

APPENDIX 3

THE POLICE SYSTEM: PROVISION IN THE POLICE ACT

Propositions, unanimously recorded by the Police Commission, as the basis of a Police System—and of an Organized Constabulary.

1. That, with a view to simplicity in general administration, the maintenance of military discipline, uniformity and consistency of Police regulation, and effective financial control in both departments, a broad line of distinction should at once be drawn between military and civil bodies, functions and expenditure. There should be only *two* departments charged with protective and repressive duties and responsibilities; the one of the Military Armed Force under the orders of the Military Commander; the other a Civil Constabulary subject to the Civil Executive Government.

2. That the Military arm should confine itself absolutely to the occupation of the country, for its proper function of preventing invasion and supporting the Civil power only in event of rebellion or extended insurrection. The Military arm should be relieved from all non-Military duties; and the peace and order of the country should be preserved, on every occasion of tumult and apprehended disturbance by the civil power and not by a Military Force.

3. That bodies of men properly termed *"Military,"*— having Military formation and organization, employed for Military purposes, and liable to Military requisitions,

cannot be usefully employed as Civil Police, or be associated in the operations of a Civil Constabulary in any of its duties. That such bodies should be transferred to the military department; or be dispensed with; or be absorbed into a civil constabulary formed on sound general principles; thus enabling consolidation and reduction of force in both departments. That the Military Authorities should withdraw and cease to maintain in future any post, detachment of Guard not required for military occupation or other military purpose *alone;* so enabling concentration of force, maintenance of discipline and efficiency in the army, and thorough revision and accurate estimate of the requirements of the country in a military point of view.

4. That a civil protective force can be constituted in any part of India, starting from a civil basis, after the model of the British and Irish Constabulary forces, and under the control of carefully selected European Officers, which may be adapted, by special attention to its departmental constitution, and physical composition, to the performance of every duty which can be required of such a body in regard to the prevention of crime, the suppression of *local* outrage, the maintenance of order, and prevention of aggression on frontiers where armed invasion is not to be anticipated; for the guarding and watching of jails, treasuries and stores, and performing any escort duties connected with them and public property of every description.

5. That the Executive Govt. should at once constitute a Civil Force of such organization as shall make it thoroughly useful for every Civil Police purpose. The force should be so trained and constituted that it may be thoroughly relied upon for the performance of all duties of a preventive and detective police, and for the protection of property, and maintenance of local peace and order, with reference to the locality in which it is to be employed.

That the formation of such a force is the key to economy and military efficiency.

6. That the first step towards effecting this object is to combine into the body, under a responsible superintending authority, and under an uniform organisation and undivided control and responsibility, all the numerous bodies now engaged more or less independently, on various duties connected with the proper civil police administration of the country, and the ordinary guard and watching of property of every kind in whatever department. For the proper performance of all the important services of a police force, there must be unity of action and identity of system throughout the body to which these duties are entrusted. Economy in regard to numbers and finance can only thus be secured; while all the minor duties of guarding public property can be best and most economically performed by watchmen deputed from an organised and disciplined force. That, therefore, notwithstanding any difficulties which may arise in changing existing usages, simplifying complicated systems, and arranging intricate details in the transfer of patronage and power from many departments to one, yet the paramount object of instituting one efficient system of Police, should be persistently carried out.

7. That under the above view all separate establishments maintained for the watch and guard of jails (exclusive of the establishment of warders), of general and Tahseel treasuries and escorts; and all river and road police, of whatever denomination now in the pay of Government should be gradually relieved and absorbed into the constabulary, as the organization proceeds.

8. That the creation of an organised, efficient police, and the establishment of a uniform and widely spread system of management will likewise supersede the necessity of such separate establishments as those of the *thuggee* and dacoitee departments, avowedly maintained because the general police is inefficient. These

departments should gradually be absorbed into the police, and the existing establishment of officers, officials, approvers, be distributed among the police of the several provinces, so soon as the organisation of the police shall be sufficiently advanced to admit of it.

9. The cantontment police at military stations should form no exception to this broad rule. Every duty now performed by the separate establishment maintained, should be undertaken by the regular constabulary, strengthened, if necessary, by a subordinate European agency. The police officers should stand in the same relation to the Officer Commanding the Station, or Cantonment Joint Magistrate (as the case may be), as to the District Officer beyond the Cantonment limits.

10. That the views of the Military Finance Commission in regard to the duties to be performed by the Constabulary in *watching* military stores, and C., either in store or in movement, on payment being made, should be adopted; that the lucid exposition of the principle which should govern such matters' for which this Commission is indebted to Colonel Balfour, be printed and appended to these propositions. And every facility should be afforded in military cantonments for giving effect to the views advocated by the Military Finance Commision; enabling Military Officers to avail themselves of the aid of the Constabulary in guarding or watching property of every description on payment.

11. That further, all establishment of *chaprassee,* personal guards and orderlies, not required as Revenue bailiffs and office attendants, should be incorporated with the constabulary. The requisite number of men to attend the various officers, for all public purposes, will be supplied from the organized disciplined and economized force; and will be under the immediate control of those officers for all business of their respective offices.

12. That besides the several bodies of police hitherto in the service and pay of the Government, all other bodies

of men employed as police watchers should be brought under the organized constabulary from whatever source paid.

13. That all the men composing City Police Forces, who are provided for towns of Bengal Presidency by Act XX of 1856; all men employed as policemen over ferries or on mainroads, who are paid from ferry collections or other sources; and every other police of whatever denomination who receive a paid salary; should be provided from the organized constabulary and placed under the District Superintendent of Police.

14. That whether the constitution of the village police and the connection now existing between the Landholder or the village community and the village watchman should be preserved or no—the duty of supervising the village police in all their public duties should devolve on the District Superintendent, with the view of securing a regular and punctual performance of these duties, and of making the village watch man useful supplement to the organized constabulary.

15. That mounted bodies are exceedingly expensive as a part of a police force. They are more lawless in character, and less amenable to control than a foot constabulary. That such a force is useful only where peculiar circumstances attach to the crime of a Province; for instance, to check large organized bodies of lawless marauders; but are not so useful for the ordinary preventive and detective function of the Police in orderly districts. That therefore a closely supervised patrolling foot constabulary, is the proper basis of the police force, and should be very sparingly supplemented by Horse *only* where the peculiar necessity for them can be clearly established. That existing establishments of Horse Police should be most carefully examined in each district, with a view to their being either dispensed with, or be placed on the lowest scale in regard to numbers. These should be designated "Mounted Constabulary".

16. That no separate detective branch of the service be formed, and that every part of the police be held responsible for every duty preventive and detective properly belonging to it.

17. That the police thus constituted, should form a separate department in each local government of local administration, and under the immediate authority and control of it's Chief. And, having an independent departmental organisation and subordination of its own, be made an efficient instrument at the disposal of the district officer.

18. That it is not desirable to have under the Supreme Government of India any Executive Department in connection with the police, or any officer in supersession of the functions and responsibilities of the local Governments; but it is desirable in order to secure "the control of the Government of India, which should be confined to general principles and such other general supervision as may enable that Government to preserve some uniformity of practice and due proportion in the amount of expenditure allowed." That all returns, reports, and references regarding Police administration be placed in one of the secretariat departments of the Supreme Government.

19. That the police under each local government or administration, should constitute one force; and be under an officer to be styled Inspector General of Police; in whom should be vested, in communication with the Government, the organisation of the establishment, and the responsibility of maintaining it in a state of efficiency by proper attention to its discipline and interior economy, and to the general management of the force through its own officers.

20. That the Inspector General of Police, under the orders of his Government, and in communication with the district officer, should estimate and arrange for the numbers and allocation of the Police of each District, and

for the periodical re-adjustment, as circumstances may require, of these important matters. And the fixed allocation, once made, should not be altered, except as a joint arrangement of the Inspector General of Police and the District Officer; but the District Officer or Superintendent of Police should be empowered to assemble any portion of the District Force at any given place upon the occurrence of any emergency.

21. That the Inspector General of Police should be, with a view to affording information to Government, the centre of an intimate and constant communication with the District Officers in relation to all matters respecting the organisation of the Police, and the internal preservation of the peace, and the state of crime in the country. But he should not be in any sense an authority, appellate, or otherwise, over them.

22. That, in consequence of the appointment of an Inspector General of Police to be the chief inspecting and controlling power over the police, the executive function of officers above the grade of Magistrate of district, namely, of Commissioners of Divisions as Superintendent of Police, where such offices exist, should cease, as provided for in certain provinces by Act XXIV of 1857. But it is not intended to limit in any way their general control over the criminal administration, or their authority over the Magistrate.

23. The Inspector General of Police should not hold any extraneous executive charge, nor be hampered with details; in order that he may be able to devote his whole time to personal supervision of the police in different districts.

24. That such returns, statistics and reports regarding the state of crime, and the criminal administration, as the Inspector General of Police may require, should be furnished to him by the District Officer, in such manner as may be prescribed by the orders of local government.

25. That in every district under the jurisdiction of one magistrate, there should be at least one European Officer of Police, to be styled District Superintendent of Police: who should be departmentally subordinate to the Inspector General of Police, in every matter relating to interior economy and good management of the force, and efficient performance of every Police duty; but bound also to obey the orders of the District Officer in all matters relating to the prevention and detection of crime, the preservation of the peace, and other executive police duties, and responsible to him likewise for the efficiency with which the force performs its duty.

26. That on him should devolve the economic and control of all the establishments of police every denomination within such district. He should be held answerable for all matters relating to the interior economy of the force, for the physical qualifications and the general conduct of the men, for the maintenance of discipline and the punctual execution of all orders of the Magistracy. On him, subject to the general administrative and judicial control of the District Officer, with whom he should be in constant and intimate communication, should likewise devolve the maintenance of the public peace and the prevention and detection of crime.

27. That in such District Superintendent the promotion, suspension, and dismissal of police officials should be vested, subject to the powers from time to time entrusted to him by the Inspector General.

28. That as a rule, there should be a complete severance of executive police from judicial authorities that the official who collects and traces out the links of evidence—in other words, virtually prosecutes the offender—should never be the same as the officer, whether high or inferior grade, who is to sit in judgement on the case; even with a view to commit for trial before a higher tribunal. As the detection and prosecution of

criminals properly devolve on the Police, no police officer should be permitted to have any judicial function.

29. That the same true principle, that the judge and detective officer should not be one and the same, applies to officials having by Law, judicial functions, and should as far as possible, be carefully observed in practice. But with the constitution of the official agency now existing in India, an exception must be made in favor of the District Officer. The Magistrates have long been, in the eye of the law, executive officers having a general supervising authority in matters of police—originally without extensive judicial powers. In some parts of India this original function of the Magistrate has not been widely departed from, in other parts, extensive judicial powers have been superadded to their original and proper function. This circumstance has imported difficulties in regard to maintaining the leading principle enunciated above; for it is impracticable to relieve the Magistrates of their judicial duties, and on the other hand it is at present inexpedient to deprive the Police and Public of the valuable aid and supervision of the District Officer in the general management of police matters.

30. That, therefore, it is necessary that the District Officer, shall be recognized as the principal controlling officer in the police administration of his district. And that the civil constabulary, under its own officers shall be responsible to him, and under his orders, for the executive police administration.

31. That this departure from principle will be less objectionable in practice, when the Executive Police, though bound to obey the Magistrate's orders *quoad* the criminal administration, is kept departmentally distinct and subordinate to its own officers, and constitutes a special agency having no judicial function. As the organization becomes perfected and the force effective for the performance of its detective duties, any necessity

for the Magistrate to take personal action in any case judicially before him ought to cease.

32. That the word District Officer, as used in these propositions, means the chief magisterial officer in charge of a district, and exercising the full powers of a Magistrate under the regulations; such as Magistrates of Bengal, of the Districts of the North West Provinces, and Deputy Commissioners of non-Regulation Provinces, or by whatever other designation the officer in executive administration of a district is styled.

33. That the District Officer is the lowest grade in whom police and judicial functions should unite; and that consequently, all officers below that grade who are now invested with police functions, should not hereafter exercise those functions, beyond issuing such orders as may be necessary in their judicial capacity in specific cases before them.

34. That the general responsibility for the well-being of the district should continue to be vested in the District Officer, as the chief conservator of the peace of the district; the police being made an efficient instrument placed at his disposal for the protection of life and property, for the suppression of crime and the repression of local disturbances, and for the purpose of undertaking all the duties properly belonging to a constabulary.

35. That in large districts where the duties devolving upon the District Superintendent are so heavy as to demand the services of a second officer; there should be appointed an "Assistant District Superintendent."

36. That all the officers hitherto named should be European.

37. That the subordinate force should be composed of men of following designations; with the duties hereunder concisely sketched.

Inspector of Police: of various Grades, one or more to be at the Head Quarter of the District Superintendent, to superintend drill and discipline, the others to be in charge of Divisions, towns, and to supervise the performance of executive duties, go rounds, inspect posts and prosecute criminals. *These should be either European, Eurasian or Native.*

Head Constables: to be in charge of police parties, located at Station Houses, and having jurisdiction over a Sub-division of a district.

Serjeant: to be in charge of a party or a sub-division subordinate to a head constable.

Constables: to do the general duty of police who should be divided into 3 grades of pay.

38. That wherever practicable, the men of the police force, should be enrolled from the province in which they serve.

39. That every man should be enrolled for general service within the limits of the local government under which they serve.

40. That he should be enrolled without any conditions as to period of service, except that he shall not withdraw from the service without giving two months notice.

41. That the force under each District Superintendent be called after the name of the district police force. All the constables in each district force should be numbered consecutively 1, 2, 3 and so on; The force in each District should be divided into appropriate police sub-divisions; each sub-division to be directed by letters A,B, and so on.

42. That under each local government a uniform rate of pay be established, and, though the rates of pay in different provinces must occasionally vary, they should be assimilated as nearly as possible.

43. That the lower rank of the constabulary force should be divided into three grades; the lowest of which

should receive pay equal at least to the average ordinary wages of unskilled labour of the province.

44. That the pay of the Inspectors of Police, who will be the Superior Officers of the force and practically the detective and prosecuting agency of the country, should be on such liberal scale, as will command the services of Europeans and East Indians of respectability and education, or of the higher class of natives who now enter the public service. The rate should be graduated, so as to afford promotion and retain permanently the services of eligible men.

45. The pay of the Head Constables and Sergeants should be sufficient to place them above temptation, and to make promotion to these appointments, an object of ambition, open to the inferior grades.

46. That horse allowance be allowed to all officers above the grade of Sergeant.

47. That quarters should be provided for the police at the cost of the State; and that the accommodation of the families of the police should be discretional with the local Government.

48. That prospect of a pension at the expiration of a long and faithful service is essential, in order to the establishment of a good spirit in the force—and to retain the service of men, who from lengthened period of service have acquired efficiency, and are most exposed to tempting offers of service in other departments of government.

49. That a Superannuation Fund should be established on the same principles as founded amongst the English and Irish Constabulary, by a rateable deduction from the pay of every member of the force, not entitled to pension, under the Uncovenanted Service Pension rules.

50. That a suitable and inexpensive uniform be prescribed for all grades of the police under each local

government, which should be worn on all occasions. The uniform should be furnished to all officers of police below the rank of Inspector at the cost of the State.

51. That if any article supplied by Government shall be improperly used or damaged by any policeman, a proportionable deduction, at the discretion of the District Superintendent, should be made from the pay due to him.

52. That every constable be in some portion of his uniform distinguished by his number in the District Force, and the letter of the Division in which he is serving.

53. That the Arms of the Police should be of the lightest and most handy description, namely a light smooth bore carbine with a sword bayonet and a sword to be used as a side arm.

54. That the police should be thoroughly trained in the use of their arms, as well as other branches of drill exercise; but the police should never carry their arms except in the performance of any duty in which the carrying of their arms is prescribed.

55. That the police should ordinarily carry a baton or truncheon only.

56. That a revolver, or pistol should, at the discretion of the District Superintendent, be allowed to officers above the grade of Serjeant.

57. That the firearms and side arms of each police party be kept at the Station House; generally in the proportion of two swords and one carbine to every two constables.

58. That all surplus arms be kept at the head quarters of the District Superintendent.

59. That the:

a. Police district shall form into Police Divisions;

b. Divisions into Sub-divisions and Sections;

c. Sections into rural *walks* or city *beats* as the case may be;

d. That walks and beats be defined and numbered: and that arrangements be made for extending the walks and beat as circumstances require.

60. That the police districts, with their Divisions and Sections be rendered corresponding to and co-terminus with the existing magisterial jurisdictions.

61. That the residence of the District Superintendent be called the *"Headquarter of District Police,"* and that the Station of a Head Constable be called a *"Station House"* and that all minor posts be called *"Outposts."*

62. That in the distribution of the force: 1st the men must be kept together in sufficiently large parties, to admit of well-paid and efficient control, and allow of sufficient numerical strength being readily at hand for any emergency, or being rapidly concentrated for extraordinary emergency. 2nd, each man of the force must have a certain known daily routine duty connected with the observation of the country which he has to perform, unless required for special duty. 3rd, that every part of the country, every village, palting place, highway and thorough fare, shall be visited and inspected by the constabulary, and the village police communicated with, if possible, once in 24 hours.

63. That it should be lawful for the Inspector General of Police under the sanction of the local government, to depute any part of the police force in excess of the fixed establishment to be quartered in any District or part of the Province in which from the misconduct of the inhabitants it may be deemed expedient to strengthen the police; that the offending tract should be charged with the cost of the force then deputed.

64. That it should be lawful for the magistrate or the District Superintendent in communication with him to depute any portion of the police force of the District to

any locality where disturbance may be anticipated and to charge those whose conduct may have rendered this measure necessary with the cost.

65. That no private person or company should be permitted to keep up any body of men for the protection of life and property, if such men be in the opinion of the Magistrate likely to commit any breach of the peace; that in the event of assistance being required, the Magistrate should be bound to depute a party of the police for this purpose, charging the expense to the individual or company requiring that aid.

66. That all the members of the police force should be bound to obey the lawful orders of the Magistrate, and that for neglect of duty or disobedience of orders, the magistrate should have the power of inflicting summary criminal penalties; such sentence to be appealable in the usual course of law.

67. That the police should send to the Magistrate all such reports as he may require regarding crime and criminal administration. But the Magistrate ought not to require more reports, than are absolutely necessary.

68. That no separate class of clerks, writers or ministerial officials shall be allowed in the police; and that all duties connected with writing and accounts be performed by enrolled men of the force.

69. That the police should not be used as an agency for the record of any evidence, confession, inquest or the like; but a system of keeping faithful, accurate, and minute diaries should be maintained. These diaries should specify, concisely, but in detail, all duties in which any police officer may have been engaged, and every occurrence and information that may have required the attention of the police within their respective ranges. All police officers engaged in specific detective duties should keep an accurate and minute diary of every step taken, and every information obtained in following up the clue

of evidence, such diaries should be police documents only, and be sent to the District Superintendent, but should be open to the inspection of the District Officer.

70. That the police be strictly forbidden by law to take cognizance of, or interfere with petty offences of any description, or otherwise interfere with the liberties or convenience of the people.

M.H. Court.

S. Wauchope.

H. P. Phayre.

W. Robinson.

R. Temple.

H. Bruce.

To,

Colonel Balfour,

President, Military Finance Commission.

Sir,

In forwarding to you a printed copy of certain resolutions of the Police Commission, I have the honor to request the favor of your placing us in possession of the information sought for, with as little delay as possible.

In the opinion of this Commission, there must be but two organized bodies maintained in this country—the one in armed military force under the Commander-in-Chief, the other a civil constabulary subject to the Civil Executive Government.

That under a strict observance of this principle, the one body would only perform the duties strictly applicable to its own shore, but upon it should devolve sphere every duty connected with it.

Amongst duties strictly attached to the military department, we consider the guarding and watching of all military buildings in military cantonments, such as medical store depots, hospitals, commissariat and army clothing godowns, pension paymasters' cash chests, and the escorting of all military stores, ordnance, commissariat, to be included. But although all these duties belong to the military department, we are informed by our colleague, Mr. Temple, that many of these duties can be as efficiently performed by a constabulary at a very great saving to the State, and we observe in the Official Reports of the Madras Government, that many are actually performed by the Civil Police in that Presidency.

Our object is to ascertain the opinion of your Commission on this question, and in the event of your considering, that in truth any of these duties can be performed with equal efficiency and greater economy by the constabulary, to learn from you the duties, in detail you would assign to us—the additional force that will be required for these military duties—and the sum which would be carried to the credit of the Civil Government to provide that force.

I have the honor to be,

Sir,

Your obedient servant,

M.H. Court,

President of the Police Committee.

Calcutta;

Office of the Commissioner of Police,
The 28th August 1860.

(Copy)

1. That in the opinion of this Commission, the proper duties of a police force are entirely civil, not military; that under this rule, besides their ordinary functions connected with crime and property, their duties would

be to guard and watch treasuries, jails, and prisoners, and other purely civil establishments, as also to guard those frontiers where invasion is not apprehended.

2. That this would not allow the Police being employed in escort of any stores or supplies required in the Army Department, *e.g.* commissariat stores.

3. But in the Report of the Military Finance Commission, dated 30th April 1860, it appears to be considered of importance, in Imperial Finance, to relieve a Native Army of many duties which can be as efficiently performed, at a much less cost by a constabulary; and in para. 102 of that Report, they strongly recommend that the performance of escort or other duties attached to Military may be undertaken by the Civil Constabulary, on their being furnished, by the Department requiring their aid, with the pecuniary cost.

4. That previous, therefore, to coming to any ultimate decision, it is resolved that a copy of the above resolutions be forwarded to the Military Finance Commission, with a request that they will favor this commission with a general expression of their opinion on the extent of the employment of a civil constabulary in guarding or escorting military stores or other duties attached to the administration of the army; and, as far as possible, an estimate of the saving that will be effected to the State,—of the increase that will be necessary in the Civil Constabulary for the performance of these *non-civil* duties,—and of the amount that would be provided for the purpose from the *Military Department.*

No. 2339

From

The Military Finance Department.

To

M.H. Court, Esquire,

President of the Police Committee,

Calcutta.

Calcutta, 29th August, 1860

Sir,

I have the honor to acknowledge the receipt of your letter dated 28th August, and in compliance with the request therein conveyed, I proceed to state the opinion of the Military Finance Commission, on the subject of the relative position of the Civil Constabulary and the Military Forces, and the duties to be performed by them respectively.

2. It appears to the Military Finance Commission, that the difficulties that have hitherto arisen in distinguishing the duties properly appertaining to the Military Forces from those that should devolve on a Civil Constabulary, are attributable solely to the non-recognition of the important principle now clearly laid down by you, that there should be but two descriptions of forces maintained for the protection of the country, the one an armed Military Force under the Military Commander, and the other a Civil Constabulary subject to the Civil Executive Government: the former being kept on the lowest scale compatible with the efficient performance of the strictly Military services of repelling external aggression, and putting down internal revolt, and the latter being of such a strength as to provide for the general tranquillity of the country under ordinary circumstances, and afford protection to life and property.

3. Your Commission have referred to para. 162 of Report No. 5 dated 30th April, 1860 of the Military Finance

Commission, which has relation to the bearing on the finances of the employment of Civil Constabulary in the performance of duties of a civil nature, such as guards for treasuries, jails & mints for which Military guards have hitherto been employed. the recommendation of the Commission, to substitute police constabulary as far as possible for the Native Troops, in the performance of these duties, was not however based solely on economical grounds; and if your Commission will refer to paras. 155, 156, 157 and 158 of the same report, quoting the remarks of His Excelleney the Commander-in-Chief regarding the necessity of giving relief to the Native Troops of the Madras Presidency, as also to part of para. 165, wherein His Excellency refers to the injury to discipline that is entailed by the employment of the military forces in miscellaneous duties not strictly military, it will be apparent that the Commission, in making their recommendation, had in view the maintenance of military efficiency at least equally with the relief of the finances.

4. At the same time however I may state, that the Military Finance Commission, have seen no reason to depart from the opinion recorded in that Report, as to the great saving to the State, that might, for the various reasons enumerated in para 166, be effected by an extentive substitution of civil constabulary for the native Troops in the performance of miscellaneous duties, as already to a great extent successfully accomplished throughout several districts of the Madras Presidency; and your Commission will observe that in a former Report dated Bombay 29th October, 1859, the importance of concentrating the military forces, and freeing from the performance of non-Military duties, was strongly urged by the Commission, vide paras. 10, 11, 12 and 13.

5. As regards the direct bearing of this system on the position of the military forces, I may refer to para. 164 of the Madras Report, wherein it was shown that on the 13th December, 1859 there were 91 detachments of less

than one Regiment, absent from the Headquarters of Regiments of the Native Infantry of Madras: whereas, from

Strength of Detachment	*On 13th December 1859*	*On 10th August 1860*
Less than one Regiment ..	2	0
Less than a Wing ..	7	3
Less than 3 Companies ..	21	2
Less than 2 Dite ..	30	17
Less than 1 Ditte ..	31	7
	91	20

Returns furnished by the Quarter-Master General, dated 10th August, 1860, it appears that there were then only 29 Detachments of less than one Regiment absent from Headquarters. The numbers detached on the former date were equal to fully 120 companies, but on the latter date, or within about six months, equal to only 35 Companies; the numerical strength of the former being about 12,000 men, and of the latter only about 2,500, or less than a fourth; and even these numbers are in course of further reduction, as the organization of the constabulary advances towards completion.

6. The one important point to be borne in mind as regards the employment of the military forces in any area except strictly military services, is, that so long as a Military Commander is liable to calls for guards for the performance of civil duties, he cannot exercise effective control over the discipline and conduct of his men; and though willingly rendering obedience to the requisitions of the Civil Executive, he will naturally, from anxiety regarding the maintenance of military efficiency under such circumstances, be led to advocate increase of the military services, he would, without anxiety, be enabled to allow of extensive reductions in the strength of the Army.

7. A remarkable illustration of this fact is to be found in the case of the present Commander-in-Chief of the Madras Army, His excellency Lieut.-General Sir Patrick

Grant, who, in 1856, shortly after assuming the command, found the Native Army so over-worked as to induce him to address Government on the subject; and although between that period and the close of 1859, upwards of 15,000 men were added to the Madras Native Infantry, still His Excellency found it necessary, at intervals, up to the latter date, to make the forcible representations quoted in paras. 155, 156, 157, and 158 of the Report of the Military Finance Commission; the severity of the duty entailed on the Native Troops having increased even in a higher ratio than the numerical strength, large as the augmentation appears to have been.

8. No less remarkable are the immediate results of the measure adopted in the Madras Presidency, of placing the Military Forces entirely at the command of the military authorities, by the formation of an efficient constabulary force, to relieve the military forces from all the miscellaneous duties enumerated by the military finance commission in para. 162 of their Report. The introduction of this measure led to His Excellency the Commander-in-Chief giving an immediate assent to a reduction of the strength of the Madras Native Infantry; and at the same meeting of the Madras Council (on the 2nd January, 1860), at which it was resolved that the Madras Constabulary, even in its then imperfectly organized state, should take up the miscellaneous duties hitherto performed by the regular troops, it was also resolved that an extensive reduction should be made in the native infantry.

9. Since that date four extra regiments and two veteran battalions have been broken up, and about 320 men struck off the strength of each of the fifty-two Native Infantry Regiments: making a total numerical reduction of about 20,000 men. A further reduction of 100 men per regiment is now in contemplation, which, if effected, would make a total reduction of 25,000 Madras Native Infantry of all grades, being an actual decrease of fully

10,000 men below the establishment as existing in 1856, before the increase was made.

10. The Military Finance Commission can give you no stronger illustration than the above, of the direct bearing of the formation of an efficient Civil Constabulary on the reduction of the Military Forces, and consequently, of Military Expenditure: and have no doubt that similar results might be attained throughout India, by the adoption of the same measure.

11. The saving to the State in military expenditure, by the reduction of 25,000 Native Infantry, would, calculating at Rupees 200 per head per annum, (which may be accepted as approximately correct, but is at any rate the lowest estimate) amount to about 50 lakhs of rupees annually. As regards the effects of so large a numerical reduction of the Madras Forces on military efficiency—which the Military Finance Commission see no reason to apprehend risk: for, looking to His Excellency the Commander-in-Chief's painful description of the harassed and over-worked state of the Native Army before this relief was afforded, they fully anticipate that the morale of the troops will be found to be so greatly raised, and their discipline so much improved by their being employed only for purely military services, that a far smaller number than hitherto will amply suffice for maintaining the security of the country.

12. I have thus shown the saving to be effected in the military expenditure of the Madras Presidency, by reductions of the Military Forces consequent on the formation of an efficient Constabulary; and I need only refer you to Mr Robinson, Inspector General of the Madras Mofussil Police, who is a Member of your Commission, for all particulars as to the additional expense likely to be entailed on the civil department by the substitution of the new constabulary force for the old police force; only remarking here, that according to the information of the Military Finance Commission, the increased outlay for

the constabulary will not amount to more than one-fifth of the saving in military expenditure (50 lakhs) as above shown. The commission are not at this moment able to state the exact military saving that might be effected in the Bengal and Bombay Presidencies, by the introduction of the constabulary; but they have every reason to believe that the saving in both Presidencies would be relatively as great as in Madras. If fifty lakhs per annum can be saved in Madras, your Commission can form some idea of what would be saved in Bengal, by the adoption of a similar system.

13. I must here however distinctly point out, that in the opinion of the Military Finance Commission, the success of this measure, as regards admitting of a large reduction of the Military Forces without risk to Military efficiency, depends entirely on its being carried out in its full integrity; and to the full extent stated by the Commission in para. 162 of the Report referred to by you. For, if the relief given to the military troops be only partial, necessitating the constant absence of considerable portions of a regiment from Headquarters, or from under the eye of the officers, the commission cannot hold out the expectation that the Military Commanders will find the reduced strength of the Madras Forces, as above detailed, sufficient for the efficient performance of military services: or that it will be found practicable to reduce the Military Forces throughout India in the same proportion.

14. Your Commission being necessarily bound to keep in view the efficiency and economy of the Constabulary Force, in the same way as the Military Finance Commission keep in view those points in relation to the military forces, you must therefore be naturally anxious to have the duties to be undertaken by the Constabulary definitely fixed and limited. The Military Finance Commission are equally anxious to have a clear line of demarcation laid down between military duties, and those of the constabulary force; and think that no difficulty will

be found in so doing, if it be recognised that a distinction exists between *"guarding"* and *"watching."*

15. As regards the protection of military buildings in Military cantonments, as instanced by you, it appears to the Military Finance Commission, that under the ordinary circumstances of the country, the services of the Constabulary Force, as watchmen, would be all-sufficient. This is no new idea, for I observe, by the army estimates of 1860-61, that provision is made for the payment of police, for watching the Royal Arsenal at Woolwich, the Tower of London, the Small Arms Factory, Enfield, and the Army Clothing Depot Pimlieo. The Dock-yards at the sea-ports, as also the Bank of England, are watched night and day by Police; but at night a company of the Regiment quartered in the tower, moves into guard the bank, against external attack, the police at the same time performing their duties as watchmen, and thus leaving the military guard to their proper duties, of repelling attack.

16. If, however, the civil authorities should declare, that the constabulary does not suffice, for the security of any locality, the military authority should, on due requisition being made, furnish a guard of soldiers; but this should be looked on, as only an exceptional case, and under no circumstances, should the soldiers be permitted, to act as watchmen, which is the special province, of the constabulary. If throughout the country, the simple rule were acted on, that the services of the military forces, although at the command of the civil authorities, whenever real occasion may arise, are nevertheless, only to be called for, in case of emergency; and further, that troops thus called out, should be employed only, in a strictly military way, as laid down by the military commander with a view to meet the object of the civil authorities would be very careful in making requisitions for military guards, which would in no way lighten the duties of the constabulary, and would be a

kind of admission of the inefficiency of the constabulary force at their disposal, for maintaining the internal peace and tranquillity of the country.

17. As regards the acceptation of the term "escort," it appears to the Commission, not to be generally rightly understood. The escorting of treasure or military stores, as performed by the Military Forces, should, in the opinion of the Commission, consist only, in the detachment moving along as a military body, sufficiently near to guard against any external attack, not allowing the soldiers to walk beside carts, acting as watchmen. The necessity for a military escort being employed, as also the strength of such escort, will obviously depend on the state of the country to be travelled over; but now that tranquillity is generally re-established, it appears to the Commission that these calls need not be numerous. And for the special duties of watchmen, in the transport of treasure, stores, a sufficient force of constabulary, should be provided, on requisition being made by the department concerned.

18. It should be borne in mind however, that the military authorities, although equally entitled, with the inhabitants of the country, to the ordinary kind of protection from the constabulary force, whether in cantonment or in moving about, from one station, to another, are not entitled to obtain, without payment, any greater degree of protection, than is afforded to the inhabitants generally. The proposition of the Military Finance Commission, made in para. 162 of the Report already referred to, that payment should be required by the Constabulary Department, whenever any other head of department calls for the special services of the Constabulary, as for watching buildings and stores, and whether in cantonment or on the road, would, if adopted, act as an effectual check, on any abuse of the privilege, of obtaining the special services of constabulary as watchmen. And this arrangement might with advantage equally be extended to all private individuals, on the same

terms; for it appears to the Military Finance Commission that it is a great object to extend the influence of the Constabulary Force as much as possible throughout the country.

19. The system of payment for special police services is extensively practised at home; for by the English Civil Estimates, for the year ending 31st March, 1861, the payments by Public Departments, on account of the services of the Metropolitan Police, were estimated at £ 25,429 those from public companies and private individuals at £ 4406, and those from theatres at £ 692. And the Commission fully understand, that the services of the Police are willingly given, on payment, to all parties applying for them.

20. If a similar system were adopted in India, no unnecessary burden, would be entailed on the Civil Administration; and as regards increase of military charges, on account of services, thus rendered by the constabulary, the Military Finance Commission entertain no fear, but that, with the close and efficient audit of Military Expenditure, which they hope shortly to establish, all charges of this nature, would come under such strict investigation, as would suffice to protect the State, against any unnecessary requisitions, being made by Military Departments, for the services of the Constabulary Force.

21. It must not be understood, however, that the Military Finance Commission advocate, the substitution of Constabulary watchmen, for military guards at arsenals, magazines, and other military buildings. As already explained, the commission consider, the duties of constabulary and military guards, as entirely distinct. The Military Commander must provide, for the security of arsenals, and other military stores, in a military point of view, by means of the forces, placed at his disposal; and the determination of the strength of guard requisite for that purpose rests entirely with him. No doubt the extent to which such military precautions are taken must

depend in a great measure on the state of tranquillity of the country, as maintained by the Civil Constabulary Force; but in no instance would an efficient Commanding Officer either entirely dispense with certain military precautions, however profound be the peace of the country, or employ the Military or Police duties which could be better performed by the Constabulary.

22. The Military Finance Commission only desire to establish, that if the Military Commander in any locality, whilst duly regarding the responsibility resting on him, to provide for, security in a Military point of view, should deem it advisable, to employ the constabulary force, in the duties of watchmen, either as a relief to the troops, or as tending to economy, the services of the Constabulary, should be available, at his desire, on condition of payment being made on the regular scale fixed.

23. The Military Finance Commission do not anticipate, that any difficulty would be experienced, by the Constabulary Department, in meeting demands of this nature, however extensive they may become. It would be only a question, of increasing the numbers of constabulary, and allowing a short time for training; indeed, so uniform are the requirements of the military service, that, after a little experience, it would be easy, for each head of department, to send in, at the beginning of the year, an estimate of the extent, to which he is likely to require, the services of the constabulary during the ensuring year.

24. The respective comparative cost to the State, per head, of constabulary and regular Native Infantry, the Military Finance Commission understand to be about Rs. 130 per annum for the former, against Rs. 250, (which is the maximum charge) for the latter; and this would make a considerable saving, if the agency of the former be extensively substituted for that of the latter. The calculation of the scale of payment for services rendered

by constabulary, both to Government Departments and the public in general, should be so made as entirely to cover the cost of maintaining any number of Constabulary that may be required, beyond the number necessary, for the general preservation, of tranquillity, and affording due protection to life and property.

25. In making the above observations, the Military Finance Commission conclude, that it is the intention of your commission, to provide an efficient constabulary force, in Military cantonments, equally as elsewhere; and the Commission attach great importance, to this proviso, as it appears, to them, that it has not hitherto received, due weight, in the consideration of police arrangements, which, as already shown, have a most important bearing both on the efficiency of the Military Forces and the economy with which they can be maintained.

26. Having regard to all these considerations, which relate partly to military efficiency and partly to financial economy, the Military Finance Commission strongly recommend to the consideration of your Commission the following propositions:-

i) That, the military forces should be employed solely on Military services, which, in general terms, may be designated as the repelling of armed aggression, whether proceeding from external or internal sources.

ii) That, the repelling of such aggression, whether from civil or military property, is a strictly military duty; but that the watching of military buildings and property, whether in cantonment or in movement, in tranquil times, is *not* military, but civil duty.

iii) That, such civil duty ought to be performed by the civil constabulary, and that their services should be allowed by the civil authority to any military authority, or head of department, in the same manner and on the same conditions as to other parties.

iv) That, any military authority or department requiring extra and special service of the above description, should pay for it at the same rates as charged to private individuals.

v) That, such military authority or department should specify to the civil authority the nature of the extra or special duty to be performed; the civil authority being held responsible, for its due performance, and therefore fixing the number of men to be employed thereon.

vi) That, on the other hand, should the civil authority apply to the military authority for military aid, in repelling, or guarding against armed aggression, such aid should be given; the military authority being in like manner responsible for the performance of the duty, and deciding as to the strength of force to be employed.

vii) That, in accordance with the above propositions, all stores of the ordnance, medical, commissariat, public works, clothing, and barrack departments, in cantonments or in transit, all stores in arsenals, magazines, and depots, all a munitions of war, all military buildings whatever, should if required, be watched by the civil constabulary, on payment for the special service.

viii) That, all the duties now performed by military guards and patrols in cantonments, relating to the general safety and peace of the locality, ought to be undertaken by the civil constabulary as an ordinary duty.

ix) That, on the other hand, all duties that are points of military honor or military precaution, such as guarding colors and light field pieces of battery, the posting of piequets, and regimental and general guards, should always be provided for by the military authority.

x) That, while a military guard may be kept up, over particular military property, as a military precaution, still the duty of watch, should be uniformly performed, by the constabulary; for instance, there might be a police watch, at a magazine inside a fort, while there might be also a military guard posted there to secure the military possession of the place.

xi) That, even in the above case, there are certain kinds of duty, which may be advantageously performed, by a constabulary, to the relief of the military force: and that although a military guard, may sometimes be employed simultaneously, with a police watch, yet in all ordinary cases, whether within or beyond military jurisdiction, the latter should, under the usual circumstances of the country, alone suffice, and should be employed, in order to relieve the military forces.

xii) That, as it would not be expedient, that the military authority, should be permitted, to make unlimited demands, on the Civil Authority, for the services of the constabulary force, a sufficient check will be found in the proviso, that the Head of the Constabulary, who is responsible, for the due performance of the duty, shall fix the number of men, to be employed.

27. The Military Finance Commission, have long had under consideration, the question of properly adjusting the respective duties of the constabulary and military forces; and they offer these suggestions, believing that duties wholly unsuited to soldiers, may without inconvenience, to the civil administration, be undertaken by the constabulary force, with equal or even greater efficiency, and at a far less cost, to the State, than as hitherto performed, by the military forces; at the same time that the system of requiring payment for all extra services, will lead to a great diminution of demands of this nature.

28. The native army, when thus relieved, might not only be greatly diminished in strength, but further, the reduced military force to be maintained might be concentrated, whereby a still further saving to the state would be effected: whilst in the military forces thus freed from all extraneous duties, the improvement of discipline

and organization might be carried on under the immediate eye of the officers.

29. The Military Finance Commission fully anticipate that very important objects in a military, financial, and Political point of view, would thus be attained.

I have the honor to be,
Sir,
Your most obedient servant,
G. Balfour, *Colonel,*
President
Military Finance Commission.

APPENDIX-4

REPORT OF THE MILITARY FINANCE COMMISSION—1859

EXTRACT FROM REPORT NO. 2 OF THE MILITARY FINANCE COMMISSIONERS, DATED BOMBAY, THE 29TH OCTOBER 1859.

10. The Commission lay great stress on the troops being massed together in suitable military centres, in due proportions of Europeans and natives, and reserved for strictly military duties, since the possibility of reductions of military establishments and expenditure, consistently with the maintenance of complete efficiency, depends mainly on the proper development, of the principle of military occupation; as also on the regular troops being entirely freed, from the performance of the multifarious, non-military duties hitherto imposed on them.

11. At present the military forces, are employed on so many duties of this nature, within and beyond cantonments, and scattered about in small detachments to such an extent, as virtually to reduce a great portion of the regular troops, to the position of a mere military police: whereby the efficiency of the soldiery, both European and Native, is impaired, the prestige of the European troops greatly weakened, and that perfect training of soldiers is prevented, for which so many facilities exist in India. Taking the Bombay Presidency, we find that there were, on the Ist September last, absent from the headquarters of 10 European regiments,

17 small detachments of European Infantry, comprising 75 officers and 2,449 non-commissioned rank and file,—total 2,524 of all ranks; also 55 detachments absent from 29 regiments of Regular Native Infantry, comprising 41 European officers, 117 Native Officers, and 6,156 non-commissioned rank and file,—total 6,314 of all ranks. Further, between the Ist September, 1858 and 31st August, 1859, 91 detachments were sent on escort duty from 26 regiments of the Regular Native Infantry; of these regiments furnishing, respectively, as many as 11, 10, 7, and 6 escorts. These 91 escorts comprised altogether 46 European Officers, 129 Native Officers, and 4,518 non-commissioned rank and file,—being a total of 4,693 of all ranks, and giving an average for each escort of 51½ of all ranks. The average distance to which the escort duty extended was 80½ miles, making, with the return march, an average distance of 161 miles moved by each escort, and involving on the average an absence of at least twenty days from all proper military control. The whole distance would therefore have been for one escort (51½ men) 8,291½ miles marched: and for one single man of the 91 escorts 754,994 miles.

12. Some of these detachments and escorts, were no doubt indispensable for military reasons connected with the late exigencies; but even during the most peaceful times, the amount of detachments, guard, and escort duty has always been considerable, greatly unhinging military arrangements and destroying discipline; and the commission are convinced, that the time has now arrived when the practice of thus employing regular troops, must be entirely discontinued, in order to enable the Government of India, whilst placing definite limits to military expenditure, at the same time to maintain full military efficiency. Indeed, it cannot be too often repeated, that to this end the regular forces should be reserved for military purposes alone, so that every man borne upon the rolls of regiments may, at any moment, be available

for actual warfare; and this principle should equally be kept in mind as regards financial considerations, since all experience proves, that to employ soldiers of the regular army in the duties of policemen, watchmen, and messengers, is only to entail on Government the maintenance of a large numerical military force, with all the corresponding heavy charges for officers, equipments, and separate departmental establishments: the average charge throughout India (according to the present calculations of the Commission, which, however, require verification), being about a thousand rupees per annum, for each European soldier, and two hundred and fifty, for each Native soldier of the regular army.

13. It therefore appears, to the Commission, that it would be far preferable, in every point of view, to have the non-military duties, hitherto confided to small guards, detachments, and escorts of the regular forces, in future performed by the Civil and Military Police, of which large bodies are already kept up, especially in the Bombay Presidency. The Commission considers, that the police, if properly organised, and efficiency ensured, as far as possible, by careful independent inspections, would discharge these duties as well or even better than can be done by the regular troops, and far more economically: the charge to Government for each individual of the Native Police, judging from the cost of the Selude Police Corps, being probably less than one-third of the average for the regular troops, European and Native. But the Commission may here observe, that the expenditure for the civil and military Police of the country, should, equally with the bona fide military expenses, be carefully scrutinised, and kept within definite limits, otherwise the outlay in the police branch may be found to outweigh the saving effected in the army, and the change, unless judiciously carried out might not in any way benefit the country.

EXTRACT FROM REPORT NO. 5 OF THE MILITARY FINANCE COMMISSIONERS, DATED CALCUTTA, THE 30TH APRIL 1860.

153. "We would in any case suggest, that the 13 regiments of Native Infantry serving in the Eastern Settlements and to the Eastward, including China, should, as soon as possible, be immediately reduced to the peace establishment of 700 privates, as recently ordered for the rest of the Native Army of the Madras Presidency. Considering also, the difficulty of marching troops, in Pegu during many months of the year, when the whole country is nearly impassable on account of the floods and rains, and seeing that the fine water communications by the Irrawaddi afford great facilities for transport in the event of operations against Ava being necessary—since the rapid movement up the river of a small force by the Flotilla, to the rear of an invading army approaching from Ava, would greatly paralyze an enemy advancing from that quarter, along the narrow valley of the Irrawaddi—we are of opinion that the large transport cattle establishment, as per margin, recently maintained in Pegu, (nearly equal in numbers to that maintained in Madras Proper, for the Madras Army on the Continent of India,) might, without detriment to military efficiency, be still further reduced. We have no doubt that by these measures, and the greater concentration of the troops in these provinces, a clear saving of about 16 lakhs per annum might be effected, including all contingent charges of freight, passage money, batta and rations.

Relief of Regular Troops by Police

154. "Having shown above that a great increase was made to the strength of all the Native regiments of the Madras Army subsequent to May 1857, on account of the mutiny in Bengal, we must not omit to point out the causes which prevented a diminution being made, when the emergency was over, as rapidly as would otherwise have been practicable. In March 1859, when reductions

of the Native Forces were first resolved upon by the Madras Government. His Excellency the Commander-in-Chief, after full deliberation, pronounced it unadvisable, pending the organization of the Madras Police Constabulary, to reduce the strength of Native regiments below 1,000 privates, on the ground of the men being greatly overworked, by reason of the scattered state of the Forces over the vast extent of territory occupied by them, the long and frequent marches that had become unavoidable, in order to provide for the variety of foreign service to be performed; the great amount of detachment duty, and the unceasing calls on the regular troops for escorts and guards. Indeed, his excellency set forth the evils and hardships thus entailed on the Native Army, in such earnest and forcible language, that we quote his own words, as conveying the soundest principles.

155. "As Commander-in-Chief, Sir P. Grant feels bound to submit to Government his fixed opinion, that it is utterly impossible, that discipline and efficiency can co-exist with the present condition of this army, broken up as it is into small detachments, and dispersed here and there, over the vast surface of this extensive Presidency, together with portions of Bombay and Bengal, and the recent acquisition of territory in Burma. Deeply feeling the evils of the existing system, Lieutenant-General Grant earnestly recommends to the Government to consent to concentrate the troops, as much as may be practicable, at the headquarters of divisions and brigades; reducing, as far as possible, all single regiment stations, and altogether withdrawing to their company or regimental headquarters the innumerable small details, of artillery and infantry, which at present abound in every part of the country, ruining the discipline and efficiency of the troops, and, in reality, affording no adequate protection in any respect.

156. "Employing detachments of troops, more especially artillery and guns, on outpost duty or field

service of even the most trivial description, under Native Commissioned or Non-Commissioned Officers, is highly objectionable; and never can be necessary if these suggestions are carried into effect. By concentrating the troops, as now proposed, very many of the inconveniences now experienced, in arranging for the periodical relief, will be obviated: an effective force ready for any service, will always be, in hand, to move upon, any point, where troops may be required; opportunities for exercising together, in considerable bodies, the troops of all arms, will be afforded, than which nothing can be more desirable. An impetus to discipline and efficiency, which cannot be over-estimated, will be given, and an emulation and military spirit, conducive in the highest degree, to the good of the public service, cannot fail to be created.

157. "I have submitted to the government, a project to concentrate the troops, as much as possible, in suitable positions, instead of having them, as they now are, eat up into petty detachments and scattered all over the face of the country, affording no real protection or assistance, and absolutely ruining all discipline and efficiency. Many Brigade stations, have not even one complete regiment quartered at them, just now, and except at Secunderabad (in the Nizam's territories), there is not a point in the Madras Presidency, where a force of 3,000 men of all arms could be assembled. The men feel, that they are grievously ove rworked; that duty is constant and unceasing, and that there is no prospect of relief; their strength and energies are overtasked, and that they are plunged in irretrievable debt by the long and frequent marches. One-third of the army is permanently on duty from year's end to year's end, and the men are disheartened and dispirited; this season (1857) fully one-half of the Native Army has been in movement, or will be so, to occupy Pegu, and effect the general relief, and to give to Corps in regular succession their proportion of foreign service.

158. "The circumstances of the Native Army, are becoming daily more trying, and I feel it to be my duty again, to solicit that the relief to which in common justice and humanity they are entitled, may be granted to the troops. The enclosed Return, prepared in the office of the Adjutant General of the army, shows that 23 regiments (nearly half the army) have only 1½ reliefs: 18 regiments have 3 reliefs; 8 regiments have 3½ reliefs: and 3 regiments have 7 reliefs, whereas all should have full 4 reliefs. It is my duty as Commander-in-Chief emphatically to state my firm conviction that this state of things cannot much longer endure. The troops must have relief, and I have already indicated, how, in my opinion, it can best be given."

159. At the same time His Excellency, in a letter to the Madras Government, dated 17th March, 1859, expressed the opinion, "that the first step to be taken, in order to admit of any real reduction, being made in the Military expenses of the Madras Presidency, is the formation of an efficient and well organised police, a point which was first pressed upon notice by Lord Harris, in August 1855." The Act of the Legislative Council, authorising the formation of the Madras Police Constabulary only received the assent of the Governor-General on the 6th September, 1859; but it was then pressed rapidly forward, and on our arrival at Madras, in November last, we found one district of the Presidency, (Arcot) almost entirely occupied by the Constabulary, the relief of the regular troops as regards detachment and guard duty being already to some extent carried out. The Inspector General of Mofussil Police, Mr. Robinson, informed us, in a letter dated 28th December, that "the Veterans at Chittoor (2 companies) have been relieved of all duty by the Constabulary undertaking the jail and treasury guards of that place. The Veteran Guard at Palliconda has likewise been relieved. There are veterans at Arnee; but they are not performing, so far as I am

aware, any civil duty. If they are doing so, however, these duties will cease, before the end of January next, as the Arnee Division will by that time be taken up by the Constabulary. All guards furnished by the regulars (the 18th Regiment Native Infantry), for civil duties at Vellore, have been relieved. They consisted of jail and police guards, I believe that there are hospital, arsenal, and commissariat guards also furnished by the regulars at Vellore; and probably at Arcot likewise. It is for the Military authorities to judge, whether it is desirable to relieve any of these guards by the constabulary. The civil duties which now press so severely on the military forces, consist chiefly of jail and treasure guards. To furnish these, detachments are necessarily kept up in different parts of the country, and their relief is of the first importance. I consider that any energetic superintendent of police should, in most districts, be able to organize and train a body of men sufficient to undertake all these duties, and relieve the detachment within 3 months of his commencing work in his district."

160. The organization of the police constabulary thus in process of formation for the Madras Presidency, is very different from that of the Military Police of Bengal and Bombay, who are in every way constituted, on the model of the Sepoy Army, and would require as many reliefs, for their guards, as the native regiments of the line, in order to maintain a similar discipline; and in reference to which the Commissioners appointed to enquire into the organization of the Indian army, recorded in their report, that "they see in this force, in its numerical strength, and military organization, differing, as it does, in no essential respect from the regular Sepoy Army, the elements of future danger; and would therefore recommend that great caution be used, in not giving to this force a stricter Military training, than may be required for the maintenance of discipline, lest a new Native Force be formed, which may hereafter become a source of

embarrassment to Government." His Excellency Sir Charies Trevelyan, Governor of Madras, makes very similar remarks, in one of his Minutes, wherein he points out the difference between the proposed Madras Constabulary, and the other police bodies of India. "It is not 'Police Corps' which it is proposed to establish, These are neither police nor regular army, and while they cause a heavy expenditure, are a source of disquietude both to Government and the people."

161. The Madras Police Force, however, are not to be soldiers but constables; as explained by Mr. Robinson, they are to go through a certain degree of drill to "secure discipline and proper spirit; all are to be taught the use of arms, which are light carbines and swords, in the proportion of one fire-arm and sword for every 2 men: but excepting, when employed on treasure escort, or jail duty, they are not to carry arms, the baton being the ordinary and sufficient instrument of defence." They will

Number				*Rupees*
600	*Inspectors*		...	*6,60,000*
21,400	*Inferior Grades*		...	*18,04,000*
22,000				*24,64,000*
20	*Superintendents*		...	
20	*Asst. Ditto (travelling allowance inclusive)*		...	*3,00,000*
1	*Inspector General (Office, Travelling, &c., inclusive)*		...	*50,000*
22,041		*Total Rupees*	...	*28,14,000*
	Clothing ...	*2,00,000*		
	Arms, &c, Annual ...	*20,000*		
	Stationery ...	*20,000*		*2,40,000*
	Total annual charge Rupees			*30,54,000*

not be required to observe the strict discipline essential in a military body, and fewer reliefs will therefore be required for the men on duty: daily reliefs can only be carried out at a very heavy cost to the State, and not less than 3 are necessary for health and discipline. The composition and probable outlay for this Police Force is stated by Mr. Robinson as follows:—"The rate usually taken in estimating County Constabulary in England, is one policeman to 1,000 inhabitants, and to 4 square miles of area (on this latter point differences of opinion exist); and so far as I have gone, I am inclined to think, that this rate of one to every thousand inhabitants, should suffice for the presidency; but the area will of course be much greater. Calculating from the above data, and taking the grades and rates of pay already stated to your Commission, I estimate the cost of Constabulary for 22 millions of inhabitants at Rs. 30,54,000, as per margin. Of this sum, 12 to 13 lakhs will be recovered from existing expenditure on civil establishments." The increase to the present outlay for the protection of the country would, in that case, not be more than about 18 lakhs, and it is moreover possible that this amount may be, to a great degree, or even entirely covered by the revenue exemptions and money allowances, previously assigned to certain parties, for performing police duties, being resumed, or the privileges at least greatly modified. But even if these anticipations be not realised, the additional outlay should not be allowed to stand in the way of endeavoring to secure the highest state of efficiency in the Constabulary Force; for, as observed by His Excellency, Sir Charles Trevelyan, in one of his Minutes, "The key to the organization of our Indian Military system is the reformation of the existing police, on the English and Irish Constabulary principle;" and His Excellency lays special stress on the formation of a *"real police,* well organised, well paid, well superintended by selected European Officers."

162. In reference to the expense of employing military guards for civil duties, Mr. Robinson very justly remarks,

"that the first step towards reform of military expenditure will be for the Adjutant General to debit the cost of every sentinel or detachment he supplies, to the districts or department employing them; for then only will the enormous cost, at which many purely civil duties are now being done by military forces, oblige the heads of departments to see how easily they can dispense with military aid in much of the general administration of the country." Mr. Robinson further declares himself ready to provide all escorts required, on condition of being furnished with the pecuniary means by the department requiring them: a proviso which will, in itself, be a most useful check on requisitions of this nature, and we strongly recommend its adoption not only as regards escorts, but also for all duties of a civil nature, such as guards for treasuries, jails, mints, banks, public workshops, and a variety of miscellaneous purposes, for which military guards have hitherto been employed, but which, as now universally admitted, may be performed by hired police, as efficiently and at a smaller outlay. The Government of Madras have indeed already made practical experience in one instance of the economy to the State that may thus be effected; for, consequent on the reduction of the Native Forces, and the strength of the garrisons of the Presidency, the Mount and Palaveram being insufficient to furnish the usual number of orderlies employed in the offices of the Adjutant General and Town Major, Government sanctioned the employment of peons in room of these orderlies, only allowing, however, about half the number of peons, who receive a much lower rate of pay than Sepoy orderlies, the charge being moreover borne by the office by whom they are employed.

163. Whilst at Madras, we had several interviews with the Governor. His Excellency Sir Charles Trevelyan, who favored us with copies of all the Minutes recorded by him in regard to the formation of the new police; wherein he points out how intimately this measure is connected with

the reduction of the Military Forces, and that its organization on a proper basis is a key to economy and Military efficiency. And, although careful not to hurry on the new arrangements before the police body were in a state of efficiency, we still, learn from Mr. Robinson, that His Excellency being anxious, as far as possible, to facilitate the reduction of the military forces, had desired him "to keep in view the early relief of all petty military detachments, by trained bodies of police; even although it should retard a little the general organization of the Rural Police throughout the different districts." Mr. Robinson added that officers would therefore "shortly be deputed into several of the districts of the Southern Division, with directions to form effective and well trained local bodies of constabulary, to take up all civil duties now performed by the military." Consequent on this arrangement, His Excellency the Governor a few days subsequently proposed, and Government resolved on the reductions already detailed, namely, that all the Native Infantry regiments within the Frontier should be reduced by 320 Non-Commissioned rank and file, the three extra regiments being also broken up, and two Veteran Battalions absorbed into the pension list. And as we observe, since our arrival at Calcutta, that His Excellency the Commander-in-Chief has issued a general order, authorizing officers commanding divisions and forces to call in all Military Detachments as soon as the Inspector General of Mofussil Police intimates his readiness to replace them by the Constabulary Force; we presume that measures are now in full operation for relieving the Madras Army from all the numerous detachment duties which have hitherto pressed so heavily on them.

164. As an illustration of the scattered state of the Madras Forces, we may mention that at the time we commenced our enquiries, the European Troops alone occupied forty different posts, and we learn by returns furnished by the Quarter Master General, that on the

13th December 1859 the Native Infantry furnished, in addition to all detachments from regiments in the field, in Bengal, 91 permanent detachments (as per margin), varying in strength from more than 1 wing, but less than a regiment, down to less than 1 company, but not less than a Native Officer's guard: one-third of the whole (31) being of this latter strength, and another third (30) less than 2 companies, but more than 1; 21 less than 3 companies, but more than 2; 7 less than 1 wing, but more than 3 companies, and only 2 more than 1 wing. The still smaller detachments would, if included, no doubt greatly swell the number; but we may calculate the total strength of these 91 detachments alone to be at least equal to 120 companies. By a Return from the Quarter Master General, dated 20th March, 1860, we find, however, that in consequence of the progress of the new police arrangements, 31 of these detachments have already been called in, amongst which are included the 2 largest, comprising more than 1 wing, and the total strength of the 31 detachments may therefore be calculated at about 50 companies. Out of the 60 detachments still remaining, two-thirds consist of less than 2 companies each, and their duties could therefore, with ease, be taken by the police: indeed, we have no doubt that, within a short time, all the rest of the detachments will be called in, regiments being but rarely divided.

	Detachment
Centre Division	*12*
Northern	*15*
Southern	*18*
Mysore	*6*
Malahur and Canara	*10*
Ceded Districts	*3*
Hyderabad Suby. Force	*6*
Nagpore Force	*4*
Pegu Division	*14*
Straits Settlements	*3*
Total	*91*

165. We find also that the numbers of all ranks detached in 1858 for escort duty from the regiments of Native Infantry and Veterans stationed within the

permanent garrisons of Madras, were as per margin, divided into 87 escorts: thus giving an average of 37 Non-Commissioned Officers, rank and file, for each. A great amount of harassing duty was thus

Officers		*Non-Commissioned Bank and file*
European	*Native*	
16	*94*	*3,229*

involved, without any corresponding beneficial results: for His Excellency, Lieutenant-General Sir Patrick Grant, states, that "the best informed and most experienced civil officers will allow, that small parties of soldiers under Native Commissioned and Non-commissioned Officers afford no adequate support to the authorities, nor any real protection of small treasuries in the interior of the country, and that employing the men on duties of that description, while it is ruinous to discipline, not only falls short of the object in view, but is absolutely mischievous." His Excellency adds, "I am well aware that circumstances occasionally render the employment of detachments absolutely necessary for a time, as in the instance of Malliapooram, in Malabar : but let this be the exception, not the rule, as at present is the case."

166. The employment of regular troops on duties of this nature is, moreover, a positive waste of public funds, since every guard employed requires 3 or 4 reliefs: whereas, if the duty were taken by the police, 1 relief for each guard would suffice. These escort and detachment duties, as also the furnishing of guards for treasuries and jails, will, however, soon be mainly, if not entirely, taken by the police constabulary, whereby the whole of the regular soldiers of the Madras Army will be relieved from extraneous non-military duties; and the Madras Army will then, even with the large reductions of the forces already ordered, be stronger by reason of the improved discipline that may thus be maintained, than the present larger force, with all its drawbacks to discipline. We confidently anticipate also, that the establishment of an

efficient police constabulary will not only enable government to effect larger reductions in the Military Forces than are at present contemplated, but further facilitate the judicious location of the troops so essential to economy and efficiency; for, with the forces scattered in small detachments, the cost of lodging, feeding and every other charge is greatly enhanced, at the same time that the control and supervision of the officers over their men is greatly weakened.

APPENDIX 5

COMMUNIQUE ON THE INTRODUCTION OF CIVIL POLICE FORCE IN THE NORTH-WEST PROVINCE AND BENGAL

JUDICIAL - OCT. 3, 1860.

No. 37. From W. Grey, Esquire, Secretary to the Government of India, to G. Couper, Esquire, Secretary to the Government of the North-West Province, No. 2218, dated the 3rd October, 1860.

I am directed to forward for submission to the Hon'ble Lieutenant Governor, a copy of the report which has been presented to the Government of India by the Police Commission now assembled in Calcutta.

2. The Governor General in Council desires to request the attentive consideration of the Lieutenant Governor to this report and the papers which accompany it. The Governor General in Council will be gratified to learn that His Honor is prepared, in pursuance of the intimation already conveyed in your letter No. 1706A, dated the 30th of June, to take early measures for the introduction into the North-Western Provinces of an organised Civil Police Force of the character described by the Commission, and in the hope that this will be the case, I am instructed to inquire whether the Lieutenant Governor sees any objection to commence at once organizing a police, on the plan proposed by the Commission, in the Allahabad Division, under the direction of Mr. Court, who from his

great practical experience as a District Officer, and his entire acquiesence in the principles on which the Commission have based their recommendations, is admirably fitted to give the plan a fairtrial, and to present it in a favorable light to others to whom, as an innovation, it may not at first recommend itself.

3. Should the Lieutenant Governor be willing to act upon this suggestion, it will obviously be essential that the existing police both civil and military, within the limits assigned to the experiment, should be placed unreservedly, in the hands of the officer, selected for the task, subject only to the direct instructions, of the Lieutenant Governor. It must be an indispensable condition of any increase of charge in the civil constabulary, that atleast a corresponding decrease shall be simultaneously made in the Military Police, leaving further reductions to follow, and therefore the officer entrusted with the organization of the new force must necessarily be vested with full authority to offer to the men, either of the civil or the military police, an option between transfer to the new police, or discharge, and again to discharge other men without such option - but with regard to these last the Governor General in Council will be prepared to authorize the grant of such moderate gratuities as the Lieutenant Governor may recommend, to all who have served beyond a given time.

4. As the Governor General in Council is aware that the report of the Police Commission has already been for some time in the Lieutenant Governor's hands, I am desired to express a hope that His Honor will feel able to give an early intimation of his views on this important question, so that the whole of the cold season may be available for the organisation of the new force, within such limits as His Honor may be disposed to assign for the trial.

5. In the event of these suggestions being adopted, the Governor General in Council will be prepared to

consider any plan which the Lieutenant Governor may propose for giving the officer so employed the status assigned in the Committee's plan to an Inspector General of police, as in Madras, with a suitable establishment and salary.

6. I am directed to beg the particular attention of His Honor to the letter from Colonal Balfour, President of the Military Finance Commission which will be found among the enclosures to the Committee's Report, and which places in a very clear light some of the principal financial bearings of the question. It appears to the Governor General in Council that it is only by some such plan as that proposed by the Committee that reductions to the extent contemplated in Mr. Beadon's letter of the 20th April last can be effected, and I am desired to add, that it is absolutely essential in a financial point of view that such reductions should be carried out at the earliest possible period. The reductions hitherto proposed in the North-Western Provinces fall far short of what must be required in accordance with the limits which were then laid down. The Governor General in Council trusts that His Honor will impress on all officers under him that those general limits must be vigorously observed, and that it is a matter of absolute necessity that reductions to the prescribed extent should be resolutely carried out without further loss of time, whether by either of the plans suggested in Mr. Beadon's letters, the first of which is very much in accordance with the plan now submitted or by any other plan which in His Honor's opinion may be better adapted to the purpose.

JUDICIAL—OCT. 3, 1860

No. 38. From W. Grey, Esquire, Secretary to the Government of India, to W.S. Seton-Karr, Esquire, officiating Secretary to the Government of Bengal No. 1920, dated the 3rd October, 1860.

I am directed to forward for submission to the Hon'ble the Lieutenant Governor a copy of the report which has been furnished to the Government of India by the Police Commission now assembled in Calcutta, together with copy of a communication which has been made on this date to the Lieutenant Governor of the North-Western Provinces.

2. I am directed to request that, after fully considering the recommendations of the Commission, the Lieutenant Governor will report whether he is prepared to assent to the substitution of a single body of organised and efficient constabulary for the mixed system of a Military and a Civil Police which at present obtains in Bengal, and, if so, whether he is disposed to commence the change at once by entrusting to some selected officer, with the powers of inspector General of Police, the duty of organizing in one or more districts during the approaching cold season a new police force of the character described by the Commission.

3. The Governor General in Council is aware that the instructions contained in the 3rd paragraph of the letter to the North-Western provinces are inapplicable to the circumstances of the provinces under the Lieutenant Governor of Bengal, the aggregate cost of the police, civil and military, in the latter provinces being very much less than the expenditure on the same account in the North-Western Provinces, and less indeed than will probably be found necessary for the establishment in every district of such a police force as that contemplated by the Commissioners. Nevertheless, as it will be a primary object of the projected measure to get rid, as soon as possible, of the separate body of so called Military Police now existing, it should, from the first, be part of the instructions given to the officer entrusted with the conduct of the experiment, that he is to look to the military police for officers and men to complete the strength of the new constabulary in each district. When he shall have selected

as many of the present civil police of the district in which he is working as he may judge to be eligible for the new force, he should then proceed to take men from the Military Police giving them the option of transfer to the constabulary, or of discharge.

4. The first task, however, which will develop upon the officer selected by His Honor for the duty of commencing the organization of a new police, will be to take a given district, and after careful inquiry to fix the strength of the force which he considers that district to require. He should then at once submit a report to the Lieutenant Governor, showing as accurately as possible the cost of the proposed constabulary, as contrasted with the cost of the present police of the District, including all the guards which it is intended to supersede by the new force. From this report, carefully prepared for one district, may be framed an approximate estimate of the probable cost of the new constabulary throughout the lower provinces, and such an estimate, if the Lieutenant Governor shall be satisfied of the general expediency of adopting the projected change, the Governor General in Council would wish to be prepared and furnished to the Government of India at the earliest practicable date.

Index

P

Q

R